NEW YORK

Gary Valentine is a founding member of Blondie and wrote some of the group's early hits. He has also worked with Iggy Pop, Laura Logic, and with his own groups the Know and Fire Escape. In 2006 he was inducted into the Rock and Roll Hall of Fame. His CD, *Tomorrow Belongs to You*, is available from Overground Records, www.overgroundrecords.co.uk.

As Gary Lachman he is the author of *The Dedalus Occult Reader: The Garden of Hermetic Dreams* (2005), *A Dark Muse* (2005), *In Search of P.D. Ouspensky* (2004), *A Secret History of Consciousness* (2003), and *Turn Off Your Mind: The Mystic Sixties and the Dark Side of the Age of Aquarius* (2001). He is a frequent contributor to the Guardian, Independent on Sunday, *Fortean Times,* and other journals in the U.S. and UK. He lives in London.

Also by Gary Valentine

(as Gary Valentine Lachman)

Turn Off Your Mind:

The Mystic Sixties and the Dark Side of the Age of Aquarius

GARY VALENTINE

NEW YORK ROCKER

MY LIFE IN THE BLANK GENERATION WITH
BOLODIE, IGGY POP, AND OTHERS
1974–1981

THUNDER'S MOUTH PRESS • NEW YORK

NEW YORK ROCKER:
My Life in the Blank Generation with Blondie, Iggy Pop, and Others, 1974–1981

Published in the United States by
Thunder's Mouth Press
An imprint of Avalon Publishing Group, Inc.
245 West 17th Street, 11th floor
New York, NY 10011
www.thundersmouth.com

AVALON
publishing group incorporated

Copyright © 2002, renewed © 2006 by Gary Valentine

Published in Great Britain in 2002 by Sidgwick & Jackson, an imprint
of Pan Macmillan Ltd

First Thunder's Mouth Press edition, October 2006

Library of Congress Cataloging-in-Publication Data is available.

ISBN-10: 1-56025-944-2
ISBN-13: 978-1-56025-944-2

9 8 7 6 5 4 3 2 1

Typeset by SetSystems Ltd, Saffron Walden, Essex

Printed in the United States of America
Distributed by Publishers Group West

For Lisa and Benton

Surely by now they have both learned to love it

Contents

Acknowledgements

This book couldn't have been written without the help of many people. Special thanks go to Lisa Jane Persky, whose photographs tell at least half the story; Ruth Vaughn, who first read the manuscript and made indispensable suggestions; and Brendan Mullen, who made his definitive scrapbook on punk LA available to me. I would also like to thank Rob DuPrey, guitarist extraordinaire, John Browner, punk *noirist*, and Richard D'Andrea, a terrific lead bassist, for going over old times. Incomparable help was also provided by Gary Stewart, M. L. Compton, Dennis Spedaliere, and the flaming star, Max Décharné. The British Library was, as always, a source of material and inspiration. My sons Joshua and Max helped in the preparation of the final draft. And lastly, my parents, too, deserve a big hand, if for nothing else than for setting me on the road to rock and roll in the first place.

List of Illustrations

All pictures are courtesy of and by Lisa Jane Persky unless otherwise specified.

I can't escape my love of fate, my *amor fati*.

1. NIGHT OF THE LIPSTICK KILLERS

I had heard the New York Dolls' first album and liked it. It sounded, I thought, like good Rolling Stones. But I didn't know what to make of the picture of them in drag on the cover. It looked dangerous, and that attracted me. But it was dangerous in more than a cool way. It didn't take much to provoke the greaser morons who spent their school days beating up hippies like me. Later, when I took to wearing makeup and glitter openly in New Jersey, I often had to fend off attacks and calls of 'faggot'. At one point it became a little like *A Clockwork Orange*, when a member of one gang pulled a knife and I found out how difficult it is to run in platform shoes.

But when I went to New York's Academy of Music on East 14th Street for the Dolls' legendary St Valentine's Day Massacre Show, on 15 February 1974, I wasn't yet a glitter kid. I remember wearing jeans, a sweater and an old army fatigue jacket, thinking I looked reasonably okay. When I got there it was as if Halloween had arrived eight months early. Or I had landed on Mars.

I hadn't seen that many people in drag, or even makeup. Once I was accosted by a very masculine black woman in front of the old Fillmore East on Second Avenue, when a friend and I tried to sneak in to see Felix Pappalardi's group, Mountain. This creature emerged from the shadows, flapping its hands and saying, 'Do you want to boogie with me, honey? Do you want to *boogie*?' It got close enough for me to realize it needed a shave. I heard somebody say 'drag queen' and realized it was a man dressed as a woman. For the rest of the night this was all we talked about.

But this was no preparation for the audience at the Academy of Music. As soon as I walked in I knew my late hippie casuals just wouldn't do and that I'd have to get some new threads pretty quick. Everyone was dressed up. Rogue, eyeliner, lipstick, platform shoes, mascara, skintight leopard leotards, bouffant shag haircuts that scraped the ceiling, Little Orphan Annie curls, fingerless gloves, miniskirts, black net stockings, nail polish, false eyelashes, satin trousers, form fitting red leather shirts, top hats and knee-high black leather boots hit me as soon as I walked through the door. And glitter. Glitter was everywhere. Girls with low-neck tops splashed it on their cleavages. The whole place throbbed with sex, much more than at any other rock concert I had been to. It was as if I had entered a fantastic masquerade ball – a hundred times more interesting than those tired old Grateful Dead concerts where scruffy people slurped wine from skins. The Academy of Music had been a burlesque house back in the 1920s, and that area on 14th Street enjoyed a brisk prostitution trade fueled by the local porno houses. This was in keeping with the Dolls' aesthetic. The whole idea seemed to be 'Take a chance, change your identity, pretend, be someone else.'

The opener that night was Elliot Murphy, a singer song-writer who at the time got a lot of press – comparisons to Dylan were frequent – and who was expected to be a Next Big Thing. I don't know what happened to him and I can't remember much of his act. Next on were Kiss. At that time they were unknown and had just signed to Casablanca, Neil Bogart's label. They wore makeup too, but were much more in the Alice Cooper, *ersatz* demonic league. Later I would hear of them playing joints like Kenny's Kastaways out on Long Island. I didn't think much of them. They later admitted they were heavily influenced by the Dolls and, sadly, they saw the kind of success and fame their inspiration never did. But the next thing on stage changed my life.

By the time I saw the Dolls they had already passed their peak, as far as their career was concerned, and were quickly becoming yesterday's news. The problem was they were too good at living the myth of the rock star before they had the record sales to support it. Their rise and fall was a classic flash in the pan.

In 1972, during a trip to England before they even had a record deal, their drummer, Billy Murcia, drowned in a bathtub after an overdose of barbiturates. The English rock press loved them. *Melody Maker* called them the 'Next Sensation'. Nick Kent in *NME* said they were the 'only band so far to fully define just exactly where 1970s rock should be coming from'.

Soon after Murcia's death, Marty Thau, their manager, who had worked at Buddha Records, a bubblegum factory in the sixties, signed them to Mercury Records. At this time the Dolls were playing to crowds of makeup-smeared teenagers in the Oscar Wilde Room at the legendary Mercer Arts Center on Mercer Street. This was the Mecca of the New York rock scene until the Broadway Central Hotel literally collapsed on it in August of 1973. There were precious few places to play in New York then. Max's Kansas City on Park Avenue, home of the Warhol crowd, would later rival CBGB as a punk palace, but at that time it was only booking established acts and would soon close. In 1972 the Mercer, an off-Broadway theater complex, decided to book rock bands to pay its bills. The first truly 'underground' music scene in New York since 1966, when the Velvet Undergound's *Exploding Plastic Inevitable* opened at the Dom on St Mark's Place, had begun.

But by the time the Dolls hit the stage at the Academy of Music, they had alienated the established rock world to no end. Murcia's death had ironically signaled their rapid rise and fall. They were signed almost immediately after Jerry Nolan took Murcia's place on drums, but Billy Doll's death made the Dolls notorious. The camp/glam/trash look didn't help either. It went down well in England, which had a history of glitter ranging from Marc Bolan to Bowie. But cross-dressing rock stars didn't turn on American record execs, nor did they excite DJs or critics who had grown fat on Emerson Lake and Palmer, Yes or the Doobie Brothers. And the drugs and booze were certainly no gold star. Bassist Arthur Kane was well into his cups, and lead singer David Johansen was pulling up a close second. Pretty soon lead guitarist Johnny Thunders would with Nolan start the heroin habit that would more or less destroy them. Although their first release, the eponymous *New York Dolls*, would sell 110,000 copies, Mercury expected more from a group that had garnered such extravagant press a year earlier. And a few months after the Academy show, when their second album, the aptly named *Too Much Too Soon* (a title taken from the ill-fated Diana Barrymore's autobiography) peaked at a less-than-impressive 167 in the Billboard charts, the writing was all too clearly on the wall.

But in New York they were still, as Johansen himself said, 'the greatest thing since Bosco.'* And to me at least, that Academy of Music show proved it.

Bob Gruen, a photographer who's shot everyone from the Stones to the Sex Pistols and who would later take shots of Blondie, had come up with an idea for the Valentine's Day show. Taking a cue from the original Valentine Day's Massacre, when Chicago gangster Al Capone wiped out a

---

* A chocolate syrup popular in the 1960s.

rival gang – and which drove the plot of Billy Wilder's classic 1959 drag comedy film, *Some Like It Hot* – the Dolls' show started with a 1930s style newsreel of them featured as the Lipstick Killers, a gang of notorious bank robbers who couldn't pull a heist unless they had their lipstick right. Mixed in with genuine old news footage – Hitler patting Nazi youths on the head, Babe Ruth having his face done by a Hollywood makeup artist, a prison riot – are the Dolls. The Lipstick Killers appear shooting into the camera, and a serious voice warns the public that there's no telling where they'll strike next. Then there's footage of the gang putting on their war paint. The film ends with the Dolls roaring up 14th Street, machine guns blazing, and bursting into the theatre. The next thing I knew, the Lipstick Killers were running up the aisle to the stage.

Bob Gruen later remarked that for some people this was the experience of a lifetime. For me at least, seeing the Dolls' set that night convinced me that you didn't have to be Eric Clapton to play guitar. You didn't even have to be George Harrison. All you had to do was play an A chord like Johnny Thunders did in 'Personality Crisis'. Right then and there I decided that this was something I wanted to do.

The Academy of Music show was my first taste of the Dolls live. Two months later I was living the part. As part of the build up to the release of *Too Much Too Soon*, Leber and Krebs, the Dolls' booking agents, came up with the idea of a 'world tour', with all the stops located on Manhattan Island. The Dolls couldn't get arrested west of the Hudson River – which isn't literally true, as Johansen was jailed for lewd conduct and inciting a riot in Memphis when the Dolls opened for Iggy Pop – and for a lead singer other than Iggy to get arrested, he had to be pretty wild. But in New York they were kings. Their record company was losing patience with them and with the bar and hotel tabs they were running up. One

member was drinking himself into a detox center and two
others were making the wrong kind of tracks. But in New
York, the Dolls could do no wrong. Part of their tour included
a seedy, run-down drag club at 82 East 4th Street in the East
Village called, perhaps not so imaginatively, Club 82.

In the 1950s and sixties, Club 82 had been one of the
premier venues for female impersonators. But by the seventies,
people were wearing drag openly in the streets, and the need
for its speakeasy atmosphere had dissipated. The club was on
its last legs when the Dolls decided to do a show there on 17
April 1974, their notorious drag act. For a brief period after
this Club 82 became one of the spots for underground music
in New York. In between the fall of the Mercer Arts Center
and the rise of CBGB, groups like the pre-Blondie Stilletoes,
Suicide and Wayne County, and glitter casualties like Teenage
Lust and The Harlots of 42nd Street hit its stage, while celebs
like Lou Reed and David Bowie headed there for a walk on
the slum side.

In that spring and summer of 1974, it was a kind of home
away from home for me, a new found 'family', and a couple
other friends.

▶▶

In the early months of 1974 Zelda, the sixteen-year-old I had
lost my virginity to, told me she was pregnant. Zelda was very
experienced for a teenager and one day took it into her head
to seduce me. I was eighteen and in my first year at university.
Zelda's parents were separated and she and her two older
sisters, Maggie and Roxanne, lived with their father. He
worked at night and this meant that the girls had the place to
themselves. Almost every night they threw a party, with a lot
of drugs, a lot of boys and a lot of sex. It was at one of these
that Zelda took me in hand.

After sleeping with Zelda that first time I dropped out of

the sisters' scene and it wasn't until a few months later that I ran into her again. That's when she gave me the news. She also told me that Maggie and Roxanne had got their own place in Jersey City. Zelda was living at home with her mother and was on her way to visit them. She knew they'd love to see me, and asked if I wanted to come.

I got home late that night, after sleeping with Zelda once again and trying to understand exactly what it meant that she was pregnant. It must have been later than I thought, because my mother woke up and we had a terrific row. Relations with my parents were terrible at best and that night something snapped and I just couldn't take it any longer. I threw my coat back on, threw a few things in a knapsack, said goodbye and headed out the door. At a payphone I called Maggie. An hour later I got off the bus, found the building again, rang the buzzer and headed up the stairs. Then I flopped down on the couch and crashed out.

In the morning when I woke up, my life would be very different.

►►

Although in the early days Maggie and the others were fond of acid, the drug of preference in that Jersey City pad was dope. Maggie had also found a way to pay some bills and bring in extra cash. I couldn't be sure, but after I was there a few days it seemed pretty clear that with a friend of hers she had started turning tricks, at least occasionally. I, it turned out, had left home and was now living with junkies and hookers.

For a while I continued with classes, but life at the pad soon overcame my motivation. In the middle of my second term I dropped out of college and sank into the sisters' routine. This consisted of partying as often as possible and scrounging around for money or food when necessary, panhandling with the occasional grocery shoplift thrown in. We could throw a lot of energy into this when we had to. On the morning after spending an acid-filled night in Central Park, we walked the length of Fifth Avenue, asking for spare change. By the time we hit Washington Square we had quite a haul. On another occasion, with my dark glasses I pretended to be blind. This was less successful.

The girls treated me like one of the family. In their eyes I was their brother-in-law; the little bundle growing inside Zelda saw to that. Although Zelda was in high school and still lived with her mother, she came up to the pad as often as she could. Her mother didn't yet know she was pregnant. But when she did, all hell would break loose.

One of the books I had thrown into my knapsack was Baudelaire's *The Flowers of Evil*. At the time I was very excited by the idea of decadence. I read Oscar Wilde, was crazy about Beardsley, and knew all the symbolist poets of the *fin de siècle*. Another favourite was Huysmans's *Against the Grain*. I was fascinated by the hero's 'revolt against nature'; the idea of locking myself in a dark mansion filled with curious bric-a-brac to explore unusual sensations and rare pleasures seemed appealing.

A one-bedroom crash pad reeking of cat litter, garbage and dirty laundry, filled with half a dozen people – some of them junkies – wasn't ideal. But beggars can't be choosers.

My interest in decadence wasn't fueled by literature alone. In the last year I had discovered glitter rock and had taken to it in a big way. The person responsible for introducing it to me was Clem Burke. Clem was something of a star in our home town. In 1969, at fifteen, he had performed at Carnegie Hall in New York City, in a garage band that included a cousin of mine. He had been in several high school dance bands, cover groups with names like the Sweet Willie Jam Band. I hadn't known him that well, but occasionally I got into dances by carrying in his drums or helping the guitarist with his amplifier. The hippie girl who had turned me on to Hermann Hesse and who I had a crush on was his girlfriend, and I had seen a lot of him by hanging out around her. At that time his hair was shoulder length, and he had an immense beard. He wore denim jackets, bandannas and, like a lot of people in those days, looked, more or less, like Jerry Garcia.

But by late 1973 Clem had dropped the hippie look and had discovered glam. He cut his hair into a Rod Stewart shag, lost the beard, dropped some weight, wore flashier clothes and started painting his eyelids red, a dangerous practise in New Jersey. He met Roxanne somewhere along the line and started showing up at the pad – what his hippie girlfriend thought about this I didn't know. And he brought records.

The Rise and Fall of Ziggy Stardust and the Spiders from Mars, *Aladdin Sane*, *Hunky Dory*, Lou Reed's *Transformer*, 'All The Young Dudes', by Mott the Hoople, as well as 'All the Way from Memphis', and their great cover of 'Sweet Jane'. Roxy Music, Steve Harley and Cockney Rebel. Clem was a walking rock encyclopedia, and he always had his eye on whatever band he thought would be the Next Big Thing. In the spring of 1974, that was the New York Dolls, and it was through Clem that I heard their first album.

Around the same time I started living with the sisters, I fell in with two other individuals who would have a profound impact on my life.

One, a maniac poet named Ronnie Toast, would later gain some cult notoriety for penning lyrics to two Blondie tunes, 'Rifle Range' and 'Cautious Lip', and for writing the liner notes to the *Blondie* album. 'Cautious Lip' I know nothing about. But a couple of years later, after I had joined Blondie, I would play 'Rifle Range' a hundred times – in CBGB, on tour and in Plaza Sound at Radio City Music Hall, where we recorded our first album.

The other was named Crash.

I can't remember exactly how I met Ronnie. But I do know how he got his name. We were at college together, and one stoned afternoon were killing time playing cards. Ronnie had no concept of rules, and kept throwing his hand down haphazardly. I said, 'You are burnt, Ronnie. A piece of burnt toast.' He thought about it for a moment, agreed, and the name stuck.

Ronnie was one of those poor drug casualties who live out other people's fantasies. He took an amazing amount of drugs, practically anything he could get his hands on. He really did write some fascinating poetry, but he had no conception of the world around him. One time his father smashed his copy of *Ziggy Stardust* because he was sick of hearing Ronnie blast it full volume at 4 a.m. Ronnie retaliated by taking a pair of his father's trousers and setting them on fire in the gutter. A police car happened to pass by and saw him, and soon after Ronnie spent a few weeks in a state mental asylum. It was not the only visit. A year later, when Crash and I were living together in New York, Ronnie's parents saw fit to commit him again. Crash and I devised a plan to help him escape. But when we arrived at the asylum a week or so later and got one look at him, we had second thoughts, decided he was better off inside, and handed him a few joints.

Crash was a different sort. He had a small dark basement apartment not far from the sisters' place. It reeked of cheap incense and grass and usually the Velvet Underground or Bowie was blaring. What struck me first about Crash was his look. He was tall and thin and wore a blue Mao cap and jacket, tinted Roger McGuinn 'granny glasses', a black sleeveless T-shirt, tight black jeans and army boots. He also wore rouge, lipstick, eyeliner and false eyelashes on one eye, like Alex in *A Clockwork Orange*. I had heard the story of he and Ronnie being on the television news, breaking into the Dolls'

Halloween show at the Waldorf Astoria Hotel, dressed as droogs. Crash was also into Nietzsche and talked about the *Übermensch* a lot, taking that line from Bowie's 'Oh You Pretty Things' about making way for the *'homo superior'*, very seriously. He had a reputation for nearly killing one guy who had called him a faggot. He also had a malicious sense of humor. One time he brought home a drag queen, and told Ronnie he had brought a hooker home for him. Crash and I sat smoking grass in the other room. A few minutes went by. Then Ronnie screamed. 'A dick! You've got a fucking dick!' To which the drag queen replied, 'Of course I do you idiot! Whadju expect?' 'You fucking faggot! I've been kissing a faggot!' 'What's your problem asshole? I thought that's what you wanted.' It was a mean trick, but I felt more sorry for the drag queen. She was hustled out the door by Crash, with only a few joints and the train fare back to New York for her troubles.

After that Dolls show at the Academy of Music I plunged into the world of the Lipstick Killers with a vengeance. I had already seen Clem's red eyelids and Crash's mascara. We listened to the Dolls constantly, and Bowie was a walking beauty parlor advertisement. The whole idea of sexual ambiguity and erotic in-between-ness saturated the pad. Bowie's 'Rebel Rebel' was one of our theme songs. I don't remember exactly when it started but, half in fun, I let the girls make me up. The result was dramatic.

It now seems incredible that with all the dope going around, with the drag queens and homosexual flirtation, I never once tried dope nor had a gay experience. But I took to makeup. There was, of course, something erotic about letting oneself go, that melting languid feeling of giving over control and becoming passive under someone's hands. Getting attention from all three sisters didn't hurt. But the real surprise

about wearing makeup was how the reaction I got from the
sisters made me feel. Suddenly, from thinking I was boring
and unattractive, often too shy to talk, I was the object of
compliments. It made me feel somehow special. It was a badge
of sorts, a sign that I belonged to a select group. I really was
'walking on the wild side'. None of my school friends back
home would have dared to do this, and many of them thought
I had gone off the deep end when they heard about what had
happened to me.

But I didn't wear makeup everyday. It was more or less
reserved for special occasions. Like the forays out to East 4th
Street and Club 82 that became a regular ritual with us.

►►

One day Clem came to the pad with a copy of Lisa and
Richard Robinson's *Rock Scene* magazine.

Before the rise of Alan Betroc's *New York Rocker* and,
later, *Punk* magazine, *Rock Scene*, along with *Hit Parader*,
was one of the few magazines where you could find out what
was happening in undergound music in New York.* We also
read a lot of other papers, like *Rolling Stone*, the *Village Voice*
and, occasionally, Al Goldstein's *Screw*, which we looked at
for the dirty pictures and hilarious personal ads.

Rock Scene reported that David Bowie and Lou Reed had
been seen hanging out at a drag club in the East Village. This
was the time when they both had transvestite girlfriends.
The England Bowie had come from was still pretty backward
and Lou Reed's stories of drag queens and the rest had
impressed him no end. So when word got out that Club 82

---

* Lisa Robinson's article, 'The New York Bands', in the June 1975 issue
of *Hit Parader*, was the first extended coverage of the scene, devoting four
pages to Blondie, Television, the Heartbreakers, Patti Smith, the Miamis,
the Mumps, the Ramones, Wayne County and Cherry Vanilla.

was a happening scene, David and Lou decided to legitimize the place with their presence.

Hearing this, Crash was determined to meet them. He decided the best way to do this was to go to Club 82 as often as possible.

Legend has it that back in the old days, the actor Errol Flynn used to come to Club 82, sit at the piano, open his flies, and bang out a roaring three-hander. It wouldn't surprise me. The place was run by two very old bull dykes, Tommy and Butch. Tommy worked the door and Butch handled the bar. When I first saw them, they looked as if they'd been there for twenty years – which, in fact, they had. It took me a while to figure out they weren't men. Tommy's hair was short and greased back. She wore men's glasses and bowling shirts. Butch had to speak through a voice box she held to her throat. The stage was behind the bar, so with the band playing or dance music blasting it was impossible to make out what she was saying. If she was asking you what you had ordered you had to nod and hope for the best.

The place had the effect that all good sleazy joints do, of making it seem that once you were inside, the world outside didn't exist. Going in you really entered an underworld. It was a basement club, and to get to it you had to walk down a steep stairway, lined with photographs of famous female impersonators, actresses and celebrities. It had an aura of sadness and tragedy, a Cinderella quality that was especially apparent at the end of the night, when the music stopped, the lights came up and the dark mysterious faces were suddenly revealed in all their stubble.

We started going to Club 82 pretty regularly, Crash, Ronnie, Maggie, Roxanne and I. We'd start the night by listening to the Dolls or Bowie, and putting on our makeup. The girls would do me at first until I got the hang of it, although I never did manage to get my false eyelashes on quite right. I also refused to have my ears pierced and settled for some clip-on earrings I picked up at a thrift store, the kind somebody's grandmother must have worn. Then we headed down to Journal Square to catch the Path train to the city, running a gauntlet of catcalls and whistles from the other teenagers at the station.

Zelda would come with us occasionally. She had to be in school the next morning and more times than not her mother wouldn't let her out. Even when she did come, Maggie had to sweet-talk Tommy into letting her in. Club 82 had seen some trouble in its day and wasn't keen on being shut down for letting in minors. I had a hard time getting in myself at first. I looked younger than I was, especially with the makeup, and Tommy wasn't convinced I was eighteen. But Maggie could be persuasive, and Tommy probably liked having this young sexy babe plead with her to let in her 'brother' and kid sister.

There was nothing very remarkable about Club 82. It was dark and smelled, as all nightclubs do, of cigarettes and stale beer. The walls were mirrored and the ceiling was decorated with those rotating, strobe-lighted globes that *Saturday Night Fever* would soon make very popular. There was a hallway or foyer that ran behind the stage from one side of the place to the other, and often this was used by people to make out. It was dark, and when you walked from one end to the other you'd see couples leaning into the wall and each other. Guys with girls, girls with girls and guys with guys. Half of the times you couldn't tell who was with who, and that, I guess, was part of the attraction. The dance floor was to one side of the bar and stage. A few tables bordered this, but most of the seats were on a raised section which reached back into even greater darkness. Here people engaged in more serious matters, like snorting coke and getting head, sometimes simultaneously. Sometimes there'd be no one in the place except for a handful of drag queens, some glam rockers looking for the scene, and us. Other times it would be packed with tourists, weekend voyeurs anxious to be hip, well heeled individuals trying to impress their dates with some downtown slumming, gold coke spoons and openness to transvestitism. One of the regular attractions was Wayne County, a transvestite singer who, after a sex change some years later, would become Jayne County. Wayne had been a mainstay at the Mercer Arts Center and was part of the Warhol crowd. If the Dolls brought trash to rock and roll, Wayne was a one man landfill.

Wayne's get-up included a skintight flesh colored bodysuit, fake vagina and pubic hair, false breasts with pasties and tassels, and a massive dildo which he sucked until it came over the audience. He topped this off with a helping of dog food. Occasionally a urinal graced the stage. Wayne wore a ridiculously curly blonde wig with little lettered cards stuck in it that spelled out 'The Dave Clark Five'. One of his songs was 'If you don't want to fuck me baby, fuck off'. It was that kind of place.

Although what got us there was glitter and glam, in terms of the music, disco was the rage. Occasionally the DJ would blast 'Rebel Rebel' or 'Suffragette City'. Once in a while you heard some Stones. But most of the time the PA was given over to 'Rock The Boat', 'Honey Bee', Barry White or some Donna Summer dreck. Crash and I hated disco, although the girls liked it; they liked anything they could dance to. I don't remember ever dancing there, although I must have. What I do remember mostly is sitting back in the rafters, nursing the single tequilla sunrise that had to last me the night, listening to Crash's ramblings about the *Übermensch*.

But occasionally I had some adventures.

One time I got a massive whiff of amyl nitrite, and felt that my head was about to burst onto East 4th Street.

Clem had tagged along that night. It may have been a night the Dolls played. Out of nowhere, he passed a vial under my nose, looked at me and said, 'Here. Take a sniff of this!' I hadn't had amyl nitrite before. I had done some crazy things to get high, like hyperventilating on a friend's roof, passing out, and thinking I was four years old and had just fallen off my tricycle when I woke up. But my drug experiments were mainly limited to grass. Clem was wearing his shades and I remember this immense grin spreading out across his face. Amyl nitrite is used to revive heart attack victims. It's also popular with gays as a sex stimulant and orgasm enhancer. I had never heard of it and it certainly wasn't on my list of things to do. But there was Clem, that grin and the vial in front of my nose. I inhaled. Immediately I looked at Clem. His grin had collapsed and his mouth was wide open. Then I felt it. Something was happening to my head. It was expanding. At the same time it was as if it were a balloon, rising up to the ceiling.

Then I heard Clem's voice. It came from far away.

'Fuck man! Not that much!'

Evidently I had sucked in the equivalent of several poppers. Something black rushed up from my feet and filled my eyesight and a couple seconds later I passed out and hit the crowded floor.

Another adventure was less damaging.

Although I was considered Zelda's boyfriend the relationship was loose, and in that atmosphere to occasionally have sex with someone else seemed natural. When she came around Zelda even asked me if I had seen any cute girls or boys the night before. I think she half expected me to wind up with some guy.

I rarely tried to hit on girls, but one night was different. For some reason, one girl in particular attracted me. I think I was only just realizing that I could do it, that girls might find me attractive, and was excited by the thrill of the hunt. In any case she was attractive and I was certain she was looking at me as well. I went over and started dancing next to her. When the last number stopped, we walked over to one side, leaned against the wall and started talking. After a while, when my intentions were clear and the possibility of going home with her arose, she asked me a question.

She said, 'Are you bi? Because, you know, I only go with guys who are bi.'

I lied. 'Oh yeah. Sure.'

She looked at me.

'Really?'

'Oh yeah. All the time.'

'Yeah?'

'Yeah.'

She looked across the room.

'Do you see that drag queen over there?' She nodded at someone sitting on a bar stool talking, I guess, to a friend.

'Yeah.'

'Well, if you're bi, go over there and kiss him.'

'Yeah?'

'Yeah. And really kiss him. Not a peck on the cheek.'

'Right.'

I walked across the room.

'Excuse me,' I said, 'but the girl across the room wants me to kiss you.'

She – he – turned from her friend and looked at me.

'Really?'

'Yeah. It's kind of a bet.'

She smiled.

'Oooh. A gambling man. Well darling, in that case I guess you better go ahead.'

Then she turned to me and puckered.

It wasn't bad. There was alcohol and cigarettes on his breath and he needed a shave, but as far as kisses go, it was memorable. Our tongues fenced for a few seconds and I gave it some thought. I think I even closed my eyes. Interesting, but not really my cup of tea. A lot was riding on this so I lingered a bit. Then I pulled away.

'Well, darling,' she said. 'That was nice!'

I went back to find my 'girlfriend', but she had disappeared. She must have left the club, because I spent the rest of the night looking for her. And when I think about it now, I'm not sure she was a girl at all.

▶▶

Crash had an old eight track cassette player and one of the tapes was Lou Reed's live album, *Rock & Roll Animal*. The trouble with eight tracks was that they would switch tracks in the middle of a song. When I started staying at Crash's more often than at the sisters, *Rock & Roll Animal* was a tape Crash liked to fall asleep to. For weeks on end I would drift off to Reed's extended hard rock version of 'Heroin'. In the middle of it the track would switch and I would sink into dreamland only to be jolted awake a few seconds later by the song coming back on.

My initiation into the world of rock and roll stardom was equally anticlimactic.

We had gone through the usual routine. There was no reason to think that anything out of the ordinary would happen. But maybe Crash had an intuition that something would. He had a Sobranie Black Russian tin that he kept his joints in, and that night I remember that he took a larger supply than usual. He even put a little cocaine into a couple joints, twisting the ends of these in a certain way, so he could tell them apart from the others. He didn't do this that often, usually reserving it for special occasions.

We were sitting, as we usually did, way up in the back. The usual disco dreck was on. The girls were on the dance floor. Ronnie, Crash and I had just got through a joint and we sat, feeling stoned, wondering how we could make way for the *homo superior*.

And then we saw them.

Bowie and Lou Reed were sitting at a table near the dance floor.

Crash was tone-deaf and one of the most unmusical people I've ever met. But he had dreams of becoming a rock star.* He wanted to meet David and Lou because he wanted to interest them in an idea he had for a band.

I've forgotten the name of Bowie's girlfriend, but Lou Reed's was called Rachel. Rachel was very protective of Lou, very territorial. She had a reputation for keeping everyone away from him. It worked most of the time, but somehow that night her defenses were down and Crash, Ronnie and I managed to get within talking distance of him and David.

It's amazing there was a free table next to them. Maybe nobody recognized them. Or maybe it was that New York cool thing, where to show any interest in anything like that is definitely not done. Such considerations didn't detain us. We got up, left the rafters and made our way to the dance floor.

We grabbed the seats and sat down.

And then Crash pulled out the Black Russian tin.

It was, I think, a special occasion.

He pulled out one of the cocained joints, checked it out, tightened the ends, twirled it in his fingers and looked across the table. David and Lou were sitting with their dates. A few other people filled out the party. The music was blaring, the dance floor was packed. Conversation at the next table was lively. Crash was patient, waiting for the right moment. Then I saw that he had pulled out his Zippo lighter and was about to light the joint. There was a break in the conversation. David, who was closest to us, looked around the room. He

---

* The two are not mutually exclusive.

was momentarily bored. Crash flicked open the Zippo. The pungent smell of lighter fluid leaked out. Crash lit the joint, took a puff, drew it in, then exhaled in Bowie's direction. David caught the scent and turned involuntarily. Crash pointed the joint at him.

'Here David,' he said, 'would you like some of this?'

David would. He took the joint and took a drag. Then he took another. Then he handed the joint to his date. She took a drag. Then she handed it to Lou. He took a drag. A big drag. Then he handed it to Rachel. She had some. Then she handed it back to Lou, who took another big drag. Then somebody else got it.

Maybe they hadn't smoked anything that night or maybe they were too stoned already to care, but that cocained joint disappeared pretty quickly. As did the next.

The attraction of anything else in the room weakened for a moment. By default, Crash had Bowie's attention. He started to tell him about his idea for a band.

'David, you might be interested in a project I'm working on, a band. We're really influenced by your music . . .'

A kind of film came over Bowie's eyes. The connection faltered. Then his date got his attention and that was it. We sank back into the periphery and became part of the white noise once again. Years later other encounters with Bowie would prove more intense, but that night at least we could say we turned on David Bowie and Lou Reed.

The most famous event at Club 82 was the Dolls' drag show. I had seen them at the Academy of Music, but that was from a distance. At Club 82 they were right in front of my face. Until I saw the Ramones they were the loudest thing I ever heard.

The Dolls had a reputation for dressing up – after all they

were the Lipstick Killers – but this was the only time they actually played in dresses. Jerry Nolan was in polka dots, with the trademark baby doll hanging from his kick drum. Johansen wore a low cut red and white sequined dress. Arthur Kane sported his famous tutu. Syl Sylvain was in chaps. Everyone dressed up except Thunders, who refused. The audience was in costume too. What I remember most is moving as close to the bar as I could and feeling that my eardrums had been pierced.

It was also at this show that Maggie somehow sidled up to Thunders. She wound up having her picture taken with him and it later turned up in *Rock Scene*, a small fuzzy snapshot at the bottom of the page. Thunders had developed his heroin habit by then and I think Maggie was still indulging. I don't know if this is how she worked her way to him, but for a while after that she was always talking about 'Johnny' and how she was going to see him and so on. Thunders at that time could pick and choose and I guess a chick from Jersey City probably had a lot of competition. I don't think she saw him much after that and pretty soon in fact the whole scene in Jersey was about to come crashing down.

For one thing the girls lost their apartment after Ronnie threw the cat litter box at the neighbor across the hall. The woman had complained about the noise, the number of people visiting the place, and the smell. Ronnie thought intimidation tactics were indicated. He grabbed the box and rang the bell, and when the woman opened the door he threw it at her. A few days later an eviction notice arrived.

We all slunk into Crash's hole after that. And it was around this time that the reality of Zelda's condition began to loom larger and larger. Although we both knew that in a couple months the shit would hit the fan we rarely spoke of the future and when we did it was in vague terms of living together and having the baby. This pipe dream would later lead to tragic consequences, but at the time I imagined that somehow things would work out all right.

Into two tiny rooms jammed Crash, Ronnie, Maggie, Roxanne, sometimes Zelda, assorted other individuals, frequent visitors like Clem, and myself. Rickety furniture, unwashed sheets, brimming ashtrays, a poster of Bob Dylan and dozens of melted candles sticking out of empty wine bottles made up the decor. Once we had a mescaline party that lasted three days. Part of this I spent in a nearby graveyard, expecting to encounter the devil. Although Crash had enjoyed Maggie a few times he was ambivalent about her, and over an Easter dinner of instant lobster bisque he informed me that she wasn't quite *homo superior* material. The living arrangement was supposed to be temporary, and when Maggie started bringing her hooker friend around relations were strained. But the last straw was the junkies.

The problem was they would turn up, turn on and drop out. Literally. They wound up crashing out on the floor and we'd have to step over them. This annoyed Crash. He had some kind of 'in' with the police. Rumor was he had informed once on some guy who had burned him. And there were times when we were picked up and he would have a word with the sergeant and then we'd be let go. He decided he had had enough of these lowlifes and so one afternoon when they adorned our floor he put in a call.

The idea was the cops would come, pick up the junkies and leave us behind.

The problem was that Zelda was there and she was underage.

The lot of us were hauled in for 'contributing to the deliquency of a minor' and for having dope on the premises. There was enough grass lying around to make it worth their while but for some reason the cops ignored it. None of them realized Zelda was pregnant. We went through the whole routine, fingerprints, mugshots. They checked us for tracks, put a flashlight up my nose to see if I had snorted anything. Then they threw us in a cell, all of us, except for Zelda.

The junkies were curled up on the floor, vegetating. Crash nodded at one body and said to Maggie, 'Go through his pockets.' One of the junkies had been flashing a wad earlier and Crash knew it was in there somewhere.

'What?' she whispered. 'Crash! What do you mean? And in any case he'll notice, and we're locked up in here.'

'They're out. They'll be that way for a while. If he tells the cops, do you think they'll care? There's probably a hundred bucks in there.'

The logic of the situation impressed itself on Maggie. I had read Burroughs's *Junkie* and remembered the scenes of him 'rolling drunks' in the subway. Adroitly, Maggie proceeded to work a variation of this.

'Got it.'

A half-hour or so later the junkie started to come around. First thing he felt for was the wad.

'Hey. Where's my money? I had some money here . . . Where's my money?'

Luckily the cops came soon after. Crash's luck was still with him. They let us go and kept the junkies. Crash and Maggie split the cash between them and we ate well that night.

Soon after this Crash gave up the pad. Maggie and he had a final falling-out. She and Roxanne found another apartment. Crash moved back to his parents for a while, and for lack of anywhere else to go, so did I.

2. VILLAGE OF THE DAMNED

I had been living at home only a short while when Zelda's mother finally twigged that her daughter was pregnant.

As you might expect, my relations with my parents were not good. When a police sergeant I knew from an earlier marijuana bust came to the door and told my mother he had to take me in, they certainly didn't get any better. To be busted again for grass would be bad enough. But that wasn't why he was there. Zelda's mother had called the cops and told them I had raped her underage daughter.

The scene deserves a little attention.

Earlier in the day my mother and I had one of our biggest rows yet, during which she threw a TV tray table at me. It hit me square in my face and cut a deep gash under my left eye. Only a short while ago we had returned from the emergency ward where they had patched me up.

I was sitting in my room, a bandage over one side of my face, with my headphones on, listening to music, probably Bowie or Mott the Hoople. This accounts for the fact that I didn't hear the doorbell ring.

I had a tiny bit of grass, lit it, and carefully blew the smoke out the window. I sat back, listened to the music, and tried as much as possible to forget everything.

And then the door opened. There was Sergeant So-and-so. The first thing I thought was that I hoped he couldn't smell the grass. Then I took the headphones off.

That's when I heard him.

'Gary, man! What have you done?'

'What do you mean?'

'Zelda, your girlfriend. Her mother . . . She called and said you raped her.'

Bang on cue my mother freaked.

'*He raped her?*'

'What? I didn't rape anybody, man.'

'That's what her mother said.'

'Oh, man!'

'You raped her?'

'No. I . . .'

'Listen, Gary. I know you. You're not a bad kid. There's probably some mistake. But I still gotta take you in.'

Sergeant So-and-so was young and black and had a reputation for being hip. Compared to the other cops I knew, he was all right. He told my mother where I'd be, told her not to worry and said we had to go.

I turned my stereo off. Then, slightly stoned, I stood up, put my dark glasses on over my bandaged eye and headed out the door.

I saw a few different police stations that day. For some reason, cops need to move you around, I don't know quite why. Something about jurisdiction. After a few brief stops I wound up in a holding cell in Jersey City. It was a nasty summer that year and there had been riots on Ocean Avenue, a predominantly black neighborhood. The police station was in that precinct. The police had picked up quite a haul and I was the only white guy in the place. The cops wouldn't let me have my dark glasses and I didn't have my regular specs. I sat on a bench, the bandage covering one eye, squinting with the other. One guy asked me what I was in there for. When I said 'rape' he 'ooohed'. No one else spoke with me.

Eventually my parents arrived. The rape arrest was a

mistake. I was really charged with statutory rape, my crime being that I was eighteen years old when sixteen-year-old Zelda seduced me. It was assumed without question that I was the cause of her pregnancy. The fact that she wasn't a virgin when she seduced me and had obviously slept with other guys wasn't discussed. I was released on probation until the case came to court. According to the conditions of my probation I was not allowed to leave the state of New Jersey unless I okayed it with my probation officer. In the meantime I had to make weekly visits to a psychiatrist. Friends had told me I was crazy to sleep with Zelda and evidently the police thought so too.

Everyone, from her sisters to my psychiatrist, impressed on me that I had to convince Zelda to have an abortion.

She refused.

As you can imagine, it was in my best interest not to associate with Zelda or the others. If Zelda wouldn't have an abortion, then her mother was determined that I would either marry her or go to jail. I knew I didn't want to marry Zelda. I also didn't want to go to jail. I didn't know if I was the father or not, but I had slept with her, and I did feel affectionate. I even scrounged up some money for her to go to a doctor, not realizing that her mother was already taking care of that. I later heard from her mother's lawyers that my noble efforts would be used against me in court.

Then the inevitable happened: time ran out and Zelda had the baby.

In the meantime Crash had got himself some new digs in the city.

We had stayed friends. For a while I had a job on the late shift at a warehouse, boxing clothes and other goods for the E. J. Korvettes company. My shift ended at midnight and Crash and Ronnie would meet me for a late-night smoke. The warehouse was on the edge of town, near the oil refineries, the city dump and the polluted New York Bay. We'd walk amidst the debris and contemplate the future. I wore my dark glasses. Crash said he had had it with Jersey and was going to find a crib in the city. A few weeks later he told us he had.

Pretty soon Ronnie and I started making journeys across the Hudson to visit Crash.

During my time at the E. J. Korvettes warehouse, President Nixon lost his job. I remember hearing the news on the radio and cheering. The foreman heard me and came over. He had already told me not to wear my dark glasses, and was suspicious of the fact that I used my lunch hour to read. Now he asked me if I was some kind of communist or something. The same day that President Nixon lost his job, I lost mine.

Not long after this I had another row with my mother.

I packed a bag and headed up to Journal Square for the Path train.

I didn't mention it to my probation officer.

►►

A few weeks later Crash told us he had a storefront on East 10th Street in the East Village.

Second Avenue, a block and a half away, was fine. At the corner of St Mark's Place and Second – a five minute walk from the storefront – was the Gem Spa, a soda fountain news-stand that was the home of the world's best egg cream, a New York drink made of chocolate syrup, seltzer water and milk. No egg. It had been a Beat mecca in the 1950s, a hippie hangout in the sixties and more recently was the scene of a famous photograph of the Dolls.

First Avenue was okay too. The coffee shops weren't as good as the B&H Dairy Restaurant up on Second Avenue, and the fruit stands were a little tattier, but you still felt you were 'home' and more or less within a sphere of relative safety.

But by the time you reached Avenue A the neighborhood definitely looked dicey. Hispanic street gangs prowled the blocks, anxious junkies filed up tenement steps, and last chance hookers flagged down economy class johns on their way home from work. Avenue B was a repeat of this, but even more so, and by the time you hit Avenue C, you had definitely reached the Negative Zone. On a stoned walk with Ronnie we once found ourselves inadvertently ambling down that way. It didn't take us long to realize we had drifted over the edge. If you were a white kid like me and wanted to get killed it was a good place to be.

The storefront Crash had found was a narrow space bordered on one side by a kind of Hispanic Baptist church, itself housed in a storefront, and on the other by a tenement building. Across the street was a Russian bath that William Burroughs mentions in one of his books. The sign said the place had been established in 1890-something, and I always enjoyed seeing this as I passed on the way to Crash's. I had a passion for the late nineteenth century and anything from that period excited my imagination.

Crash's friend told him he had converted the storefront into a loft. What this meant was that he built a sleeping space over what he called a kitchen. When you hear the word 'loft' you usually think of some vast open room, with lots of light and empty space. Crash's storefront had neither. The loft bed was so close to the ceiling that if you forgot this and sat up quickly, you would knock yourself unconscious. The place was dark, cramped and jammed with junk – not the drug but the disposable stuff. It was filthy and the only heating was a less than dependable gas oven. My bed was a ratty couch, more holes than couch. The windows wouldn't open, electricity was at a premium and I don't think we ever washed a dish. But for a few months in the winter and spring of 1975 it was home.

When I first arrived at Crash's new crib, I had a lot of time on my hands, my only obligation my weekly visit to the psychiatrist. Officially registered as a sex-offender – the term would play a large role in my fortunes later on – I had to endure a tedious fifty-minute hour during which a bespec-tacled thirty-ish shrink showed me dirty pictures and asked what I thought of them. This went on until the shrink figured out that there was nothing abnormal about my feelings for sex, reports of my earlier predilection for lipstick and mas-cara notwithstanding. Eventually he came to the conclusion that my visits were a waste of time and suggested they end.

Business went on as usual. We smoked a lot of grass and lived in squalor, the difference being that where before I was worried about Zelda's pregnancy, I now had a possible jail sentence hanging over my head. Zelda had had the baby, but there were complications. She was all right, but the baby wasn't. I don't know exactly what was wrong with the little boy – communication between Zelda and me was brief and infrequent – but for the span of his short life, he didn't leave the intensive care ward where eventually he died, a year later. At one point I visited the hospital. For a few minutes I saw a child that may have been my son obscured by an incubator. I don't know who he looked like, and to this day I don't know for certain whether he was mine or not. At the time it tore a hole in me and if I think about it too much now it just opens.

Crash had found a job working for Manhattan Transit. What exactly he did, I didn't know. He had a secretive nature, kept to himself a great deal and would often be gone from the place for days without notice. His fantasy about starting a band had grown and often we spent hours together, mapping out a plan of action. Increasingly, Crash's attention had turned to questions of religion. The Bible, especially the Book of Revelations, had ousted Nietzsche as his bedside reading. He wanted to name our group the Fallen Angels and, presciently, he had written some lyrics about the Antichrist.

I was not that crazy about the idea. Crash's fantasy may have grown, but not his talent. He had no voice, his lyrics sucked and he had absolutely no sense of rhythm. He may have had a vision, but he lacked the means of making it a reality.

That's where I came in.

I liked the thought of writing songs. All along I continued to write poetry, but it was becoming clear to me that my chances of getting anywhere that way were minimal. Seeing the Dolls convinced me that with a minimum of musical ability and a lot of attitude, one could get more across to an audience than a hundred bearded poets mumbling their verse in clichéd coffee houses. I had picked up the rudiments of the guitar from my muso high school friends, and had taught myself some drumming basics by whacking a pair of sticks on my knees while listening to Beatle tunes. I actually did own a guitar at one point, a cheap second-hand acoustic, a long-fought-for concession my parents made to my rock and roll fantasies. Early on I had broken the treble strings – high E to G – and had restrung it as a kind of three-string bass. This I used to pluck at in the cellar of my parents' house, working out riffs like the Stones' 'Satisfaction' and Cream's 'Sunshine of Your Love'.

I had also learned how to finger a few chords on the piano.

This was in the most basic way possible, but at that point was all I needed. At Crash's storefront there was a battered old piano. Practically every other key was broken, and what keys did work were ridiculously out of tune. But that didn't matter. What I could play sounded close enough to chords. Gradually I mastered my instrument. I stopped writing poetry, started writing lyrics and made my first attempts at writing songs.

In the meantime, there were other problems.

►►

My favorite writer at the time was Henry Miller. I read *Tropic of Cancer*, his account of his days starving in Paris, over and over. Miller would beg, steal and starve before he would give up his freedom and I decided early on that so would I. What pained the body was good for the soul, I thought. Yet I had to admit it was difficult to concentrate on poetry or my soul when I felt those squeezing pangs gnawing at my stomach. I had read somewhere that the French writer René Daumal used to drink warm water to ease his hunger pangs when he and his wife were on the run from the Nazis. I tried it, but it didn't really work, and in the long run it didn't help Daumal that much either – he died of tuberculosis at the age of thirty-six.

My few attempts at panhandling were odious. With the sisters it had almost been fun, but standing on my own on Sixth Avenue asking for spare change was no joke. I had found a copy of yippie Abbie Hoffman's *Steal This Book*, his late sixties DIY manual for giving the system the finger. In it he advised that one of the best places to ask for money was the Port Authority Building – Manhattan's main bus depot. The idea was to target motherly-looking women and say you were trying to get home to Boston or Philadelphia and that you only needed a few dollars more for the fare. I tried it a few times. But the pickings were lean and the hours long, so I gave it up.

Friends knew of my plight. Occasionally they brought food when they dropped by. But these care packages were few and far between and most of the time the problem of filling my stomach was left to my own devices.

Eventually I was led to a life of crime.

►►

It was a *coup* to have a place in the city and Clem often came to the storefront to hang out and listen to music. He was still in college, and occasionally he'd ask me to write a paper for him, or a poem for a creative writing class. Payment was usually some grass or, if I was lucky, some food. But on one visit he gave me a old pair of red Beatle boots. They were at least a size too big and I could barely walk in them, but I thought they looked cool. In any case, I liked them.

For a while I went to meetings of the followers of Sun Myung Moon, and sat through the lectures in order to get free coffee and doughnuts. I did this a few times and got to know quite a bit about their religion, which seemed to have a lot to do with the United States saving the world from communism. But when they noticed me stuffing my pockets with jelly doughnuts they figured I wasn't prime material and asked me not to come back.

Then one morning when there was absolutely nothing in the place and the warm water didn't work, I knew I just had to get something to eat.

I decided that I would steal something.

I threw on an old overcoat Crash had lying around and for some reason put on Clem's red Beatle boots. At a little grocery store I never went into I stopped and stood in the aisle, looking at the food. I decided I would take something small, just enough to take off the edge.

I picked up a packet of cheese and quickly stashed it away.

That was easy, I thought, and let out a deep breath.

Then I began to fill the pockets of the overcoat.

Soon I looked as if I was weighted down with bricks. I headed for the door. Five minutes hadn't passed. I was still in a trance and magic was possible.

Then the spell was broken.

The owner said, 'Are you gonna pay for those things?'

I wasn't.

So I ran.

But I had forgotten one thing.

The red Beatle boots.

My ankles twisted dangerously with each step. I was out the door but the owner was not far behind me and I couldn't get up much speed. I had about a minute's grace and had to make a quick decision.

I reached into a pocket and grabbed something.

The mayonnaise landed with a nasty plop.

Then came the pickles.

Next was the soap.

The tuna was a loss but it went flying.

I jettisoned the chocolate milk and with a last fling abandoned the Spaghettios.

The grocery store owner decided to collect what he could of his goods.

I headed across town and found a quiet spot. Then I pulled out what was left in my pocket, ripped open the package and started gnawing at the cheese.

My next adventure was a bit more premeditated.

The idea for it came again from Abbie Hoffman. In *Steal This Book* Hoffman had thought long and hard about one way to strike a blow against the oppressive imperialist regime: skipping out on meals at restaurants.

This was one subversive act I thought was really right on.

Hoffman's advice was simple. Armed with a splinter of glass one goes to a restaurant or coffee shop and orders a meal. Three quarters of the way through one shouts 'Ow!'

and rushes to the toilet. With a quick decisive thrust, one slices one's lip. One then gives the wound a squeeze to release the blood and with an air of shock and surprise, one goes out and tells the owner that there was glass in one's meal. One then tells the owner that he better be more careful because next time the customer might not be as understanding. Then one leaves.

There is, of course, no thought of paying for the meal.

I don't recall if Hoffman ever tried this or not. Anyway, I had nothing to lose.

First thing was the glass. I found a Coke bottle, sacrificed the two cents deposit I could have collected and brought it back to the storefront. There I wrapped it in an old T-shirt, found a hammer and smashed it. Then I unrolled the T-shirt and selected a particularly sharp sliver. This I put into a cup of boiling water mixed with soap. Satisfied that I had disinfected it, I wrapped the sliver in some toilet paper.

I headed for the West Village. On the west side of Sixth Avenue, behind the West 4th Street subway entrance, was a coffee shop called the Waverly. Waverly Place was nearby and there was a theater right next to it called the Waverly, too. I had walked by it many times on my rambles. I don't know why I picked it out. Maybe the smell of the coffee and burgers as I walked by was particularly appetizing. In any case I decided, this was the place.

I tried to look as if it wasn't too obvious that I was there to rip them off. The whole point was that you could obviously pay for your meal but would refuse because of the injury inflicted upon your person in their establishment. My wardrobe was limited to T-shirts, jeans and a fatigue jacket, and there was little I could do to spruce it up. But I decided for once not to wear my dark glasses and from past experience also passed on the Beatle boots.

I went in and sat down at a booth. The waiter came over and plopped down a menu and a glass of water. I nodded thanks, and opened the menu.

'You ready to order?' the waiter asked.

'Yeah,' I said. 'I'll have a cheese omelette.'

'Coffee?'

'Coffee.'

I waited. A few minutes later the waiter appeared with my destiny.

It looked ravishing.

I picked up a slice of toast – it was dripping in butter – grabbed the jam jar and sunk my knife in. The coffee was superb. I dipped some hash browns into the ketchup. Then I settled on the omelette.

Fifteen minutes went by during which I completely forgot what I was doing there. I got through a second cup of coffee and polished off the toast; a few potatoes were remaining and a corner of the omelette was left to go. Then I remembered. I had to leave something on the plate, otherwise it would be too obvious. I took a last sip of coffee, swirled it around in my mouth, then swallowed. Then, as casually as I could, I reached in my pocket for the glass and felt it.

I sliced off one last forkful of the omelette, put it in my mouth and chewed.

Then, as spontaneously as I could, I said 'Ow!' and got up and headed for the men's room.

You may think it's easy to slice your own lip. It's not. Either the flesh had a resilience I didn't expect or my thrusts lacked conviction, but I poked a few times and each time the wet skin bounced back unharmed. I concentrated, took aim and jabbed. The sliver went home. The next step was the blood. To be really convincing I needed some gore. I took the wound between my thumb and forefinger and squeezed.

It took a second but soon it came. I dabbed some on my fingers, let it drip down from my mouth, and dipped the glass in for good measure. Then I turned around and went outside.

'You all right?' the waiter asked.

'Glass,' I said. 'There was a piece of glass in my food.'

'What?'

'A piece of glass. I bit on it. In the omelette.'

'What?'

'This.'

I showed him the sliver.

He wasn't convinced.

'You found that in your food?'

'Yes.'

'Whaddayou, kiddin?'

'No.'

'You didn't find that in your food.'

'No, really. I bit down on it. Didn't you hear me?'

'Yeah, I heard ya.'

'Well, that's what happened. See? Blood.'

'You gotta be kiddin.'

'Look, lucky it was only my lip. If I swallowed it, well, who knows? You guys should be more careful.'

'Hey Tony.' He yelled to the cook. 'You break any glass back there today?'

'No.'

'Nobody broke any glass.'

'Look, I don't know how it got there but I nearly swallowed it. It could have killed me. Accidents happen, I know. So I'll forget about it. But maybe the next time it could be worse.'

I headed for the door.

'Hey. You gonna pay for this?'

I hurried.

'I just told you I almost killed myself swallowing that glass.'

He looked at me. 'Son of a bitch isn't gonna pay. Son of a bitch! You think you can just come in here and have a free meal? Get outta here, you punk. I know your face. You ever come back here you'll get more than that piece of glass in your lip.'

Hoffman never mentioned what happened when his revolutionary strategy didn't work. I hurried out, feeling a bit sheepish, my lip aching from its abuse, realizing I'd have to stay away from this neighborhood for a while.

▶▶

One day Crash came back from his job and explained that if I wanted to stay at the storefront I'd have to pay rent. He had let it go for a month but now I'd have to split the bills. Our relationship had soured a bit in recent days. The main reason was his increasing obsession with the end of the world. He was convinced it was on its way. I had my doubts.

In our late-night songwriting sessions, Crash ranted about how everything in the Book of Revelations was true. Why, if the end of the world was coming, he wanted to start a rock and roll band, I didn't know. But as our conversations veered more and more in that direction I began to have the distinct suspicion that Crash was losing his marbles.

He had made some friends. One, Buster, an old Jehovah's Witness, had an apartment in Jersey. Buster had had quite a life. He was a friend of Einstein's, had travelled around the world, and had his own radio program in the fifties. Then he met the Witnesses and everything changed. He gave up the program, gave away his money, and took to wearing a red carnation while standing on street corners, handing out the *Watchtower*. He was also an amateur historian. Crash

was impressed by Buster's theories and invited me to meet
him. His tiny apartment was wallpapered with news clip-
pings, magazine articles, photographs and pages xeroxed
from books. These were fixed along a time line that started
with the Big Bang somewhere in the bedroom and ended with
the anticipation of an equally big bang somewhere around
2000 which, I think, was in the kitchen. Buster's Biblical
exegesis had convinced him that come the millennium it was
lights out for everyone, except the Witnesses. One of the
signs of the coming end, Revelations said, was that there
would be 'blood on the moon'. Buster believed that with the
1969 Apollo moon landing, this criterion had been filled.
There was, after all, blood in Neil Armstrong.

Other friends of Crash included a group of Jesus freaks,
born-agains who also believed the end was nigh. As a friendly
gesture I came along to one of their meetings. It was in
another grimy storefront somewhere. It was okay at first, but
pretty soon I detected that unmistakable gleam in their eyes.
When the state of my soul became a topic of conversation I
got the creeps and left. This offended Crash. And when he
also said that the spirit of the Lord was better than drugs I
knew that yes, indeed, the end *was* nigh.

I got a job at a messenger service in mid-town. The pay
was minimal, but the hours were bearable and, given my lack
of training and limited attire, I couldn't have expected more.
I soon discovered that it was at times hard work. It was cold,
and I was pretty much on my feet most of the day, with a
quick bite snatched somewhere in the middle – when, that is,
I had a bite to snatch. Often I went hungry until I got home
and was even hungry there too. If I was lucky I'd smoke
one or two of the cigarette butts I had taken from some
secretary's ashtray. The dispatcher would give us a subway
token or, when he didn't have tokens thirty-five cents, to take
a train when the pickup and delivery were far apart. I was a

pretty fast walker and figured that if I ran a few blocks and kept a brisk step, I could pocket the thirty-five cents or the token and go on foot. If there were a few of these in a day I'd come home with a dollar maybe, and that could translate into food. Later I discovered that a grocery store nearby would accept the tokens in lieu of coins, and soon one ride on the New York subway would turn into a couple slices of cheese and some bread for me a few times a week. Sometimes I'd even splurge and scour the sidewalk stalls of the Strand bookstore on Broadway and 12th Street, famous for some of its employees, including Patti Smith, Richard Hell and Tom Verlaine.

I enjoyed the work, and got to see different parts of the city. But even with the job I was still coming up short. I just wasn't making rent. And my doubts about the second coming were making Crash think twice about my suitability for the Fallen Angels. Things were changing. There seemed to be less pot. Maybe he was smoking it on his own, not sharing with me. That was bad, but understandable. But maybe he had gone off it altogether, high now on the 'spirit of the Lord'.

That was worse and something I couldn't understand at all.

▶▶

Around this time Clem had started playing in a rock and roll band in New York. He had answered an ad in the *Village Voice* that read 'Wanted, power drummer.' He had been playing for a while in a glitter rock band in Jersey called Sweet Revenge. They were good and did originals. I came to some of their gigs and hung out at a few rehearsals. But it was impossible to get anywhere in Jersey. Bruce Springsteen did, but he was an exception. You could make a decent living playing bars in Jersey, but you had to do covers. And you had to be happy playing bonefuck who the hell knows where.

If you didn't mind cranking out Steely Dan in New Brunswick, then it was great.

But Clem did, and it wasn't.

I had become aware that *something* was happening on the music scene in the East Village. With the demise of glitter and Club 82, a hole opened up and a momentum that had carried us along died. We still listened to the Dolls, Bowie, the Velvets and the Stooges, but even they had changed course. After the Orwellian *Diamond Dogs*, Bowie came out with his soul gospel persona, embodied in *Young Americans*. I hated it. The worst moment was when Crash and I went to see Bowie at Radio City Music Hall. He had prepared the Sobranie tin for the special occasion. We wanted Ziggy Stardust; we got wimpy funk instead. We sat there, wondering what had happened to the *homo superior*. And the Dolls show at the Little Hippodrome in February proved equally disappointing. Trying to salvage what was left of the group after a failed second album and the loss of Marty Thau, fashion impresario Malcolm McLaren clad the Lipstick Killers in Chairman Mao red and unleashed the world's first Commie rock group.

Malcolm had encountered the Dolls when they invaded his shop Let it Rock during their London adventure; after one look at them, just the *idea* of New York was enough to get him excited. In late 1974, tired of London, he ditched the shop (and Vivienne Westwood) and headed for Gotham, arriving in Manhattan armed to the teeth with rubber dresses and platform shoes. By February he was managing Johansen and Co. But the revolution was a dud. McLaren would have to wait another year to successfully translate his situationist kitsch politics into a barely marketable product. For the Dolls, however, their late fling with *Das Kapital* was merely a sign of their own personality crisis. Arthur Kane was drinking himself into unconsciousness, and in a series of comeback shows in, of all places, Florida, their roadie Peter Jordan had to fill in on bass. And Thunders and Nolan had become much more intimate of late with another Chinese import, this one brown and administered via a syringe. It was in Florida that the inevitable happened and the Dolls broke up, rumour has it when Nolan and Thunders hightailed it back north for a pressing meeting with their pharmacist.

It's just possible that even at the Hippodrome McLaren knew that, as great as they were, the Dolls were yesterday's papers. During those shows McLaren had become friendly with the bass player from the opening band. He wasn't wearing red, or even makeup. He wore a torn shirt, rumpled suit, fly-eyed shades and his hair stood up like he had his finger in an electric socket. He could barely play, but then that never was important. His name was Richard Hell. His band's name was Television. And they were taking a break from their regular gig, playing a seedy little dive down on the Bowery.

3. IN THE FLESH

In March 1974, two disheveled young men carrying guitar cases and dressed in charity shop chic made their way south on Manhattan's boulevard of broken dreams, the Bowery, to a rehearsal studio in the depths of Chinatown. About half a block before Houston Street, the unofficial boundary line between the East Village and the Lower East Side, they passed a bar with the curious and unpromising name CBGB/OMFUG.* As legend has it, the owner was outside engaged in some much needed DIY.

The place had been around for a while, sharing the street with the incongruently named Palace Hotel, a flophouse that catered to the human wrecks that populated the area, and an empty lot strewn with broken bottles, rusted cans, shriveled condoms, used syringes and an assortment of other urban waste. It had a history as a biker bar, slaking the thirsts of the Hell's Angels who dominated nearby East 3rd Street, and for a brief while it had opened its doors to some of the overflow from the Mercer Arts Center, with the likes of Wayne County and Suicide entertaining the lost souls who inadvertently wandered in. But Hilly Kristal, the bar's owner, thought he had a nose for popular trends and was convinced that country and western music was going to be the ever

---

* Country, Blue Grass, Blues and Other Music for Uplifting Gourmandizers, henceforth known as CBGB or, to its initiates, CBs.

elusive Next Big Thing. He was trying to corral some plaintive cowboy minstrels and attract some aspiring poets from the nearby St Marks Poetry Project when, like fairy godmothers, the two guitarists crossed his path.

It was kismet. The guitarists, whose band had debuted earlier in the month at the unmemorable Townhouse Theatre, were on the lookout for a new place to play, and whether the Bowery was their regular route down to their rehearsal loft, or whether this was the first time they took its depressed and grimy gateway to the east, we do not know. But they found what they were looking for. As we've seen, after the Mercer Arts Center collapsed, a hole opened up in the New York underground, only partially filled by the disco and drag dominated Club 82. In fact, the group the two played in was resolutely anti-glitter, preferring their drab and torn second-hand threads in reaction to the voluptuous extravagance of glam. Their music was equally stripped down and minimal, which is basically a nice way of saying that they could barely play.

When they asked Mr Kristal if he would consider booking them, he told them of his vision. Can you play country? he asked them. Can you play western? Can you play the blues?

Oh yeah, they said, sure. Anything you like. We even do originals.

Perhaps an angel of intuition fluttered near Hilly's head. Why not? he thought. They're young. I'll give 'em a break. You never know.

He agreed and gave them a gig.

It was unquestionably the smartest move of his career.

The two guitarists were Tom Verlaine and Richard Lloyd, and on 31 March 1974, with Billy Ficca on drums and Richard Hell on bass, Television played their first show at CBGB.

Rock and roll, as the cliché goes, hasn't been the same since.

▶▶

Clem was a frequent visitor to the storefront, and along with oversized Beatle boots, cool records and occasional care packages, he brought news. Once again, *Rock Scene* proved an invaluable source. According to Lisa Robinson, a new venue for exciting rock and roll had appeared in the depths of downtown Manhattan. Other voices agreed. As early as late April 1974, the *Soho Weekly News* – a brief competitor of the *Village Voice* and, in the early days, as important an organ for the new music as *New York Rocker* and *Punk* – hailed the fledgling *artistes*, and provided perhaps the first media recognition of the burgeoning scene. The mention also inaugurated the cliché that would soon become a rallying cry for the punk and new wave movements to come: that while the group could barely play their way out of a paper bag, this wasn't half as important as the energy they put into their attempts, and the excitement their tiny (or elite, depending on how you looked at it) audience felt watching them. Television, as well as the other bands to emerge from CBGB, eventually mastered their instruments, but it was this 'dangerous' element to the music that first drew early fans in. Somehow, watching Hell plunk away with manic repetition at his limited choice on the bass, was more satisfying than the more musically accomplished ventures of any number of jazz fusion bands. Of course, the sunglasses, shocked hair and split suits helped.

By the time Clem told us about CBGB, I had already seen flyers for Television and another rising star, Patti Smith, jockeying for space on St Mark's Place, and had observed Richard Hell prowling the streets of the East Village with what seemed a perpetual sneer cut into his face. Outside the

Gem Spa, hundreds of notices for political rallies, avant-garde art events and assorted other pieces of samizdat self-advertising created a kind of graphic foliage. But with the demise of Club 82, we had hunkered down in the storefront, myself concentrating on songs and awaiting news of my rape case; Crash sinking deeper and deeper into his apocalyptic fantasies. With all this, lack of money and sheer inertia, it took a while before I twigged that CBGB was the place to be. Even my first visit didn't impress me that much, and I remember not being sure if who I was seeing was Richard Hell *or* Patti Smith – with their black hair, tight black jeans and white shirts, they looked remarkably similar.

When Clem first told us that he was playing in a band in the city, Crash was conspicuously uninterested. Not me. I wanted to know more about it and asked the usual questions. Who were they? What were they like? What kind of music did they play?

'Well, they're pretty campy,' Clem said. 'Debbie, the singer, is great. Really sexy, and her voice is terrific. The guitarist's kind of a nut though. He has really weird ideas about how to play. And Fred, the bass player's, good. The music's sorta like what the Shangri-Las would have been like if they were drag queens. Actually, you saw them once at Club 82, as the Stilletoes. You should come see us play. We're doing a show tomorrow.'

'Yeah? Where are you playing?'

'White's, a pub near Wall Street. Here's the address. Be there when I get there. I think Toast is coming too.'

'All right.'

Twenty-five years on the scene is not in hard focus, but I'm pretty sure this is the first time I met Chris Stein and Debbie Harry.

White's certainly wasn't on the rock and roll circuit back then, even if the circuit itself was an inch away from being non-existent. Its clientele was mostly alky business executives from the financial district, holed up for the afternoon with a three-Martini lunch. There wasn't a stage, and when I saw the group they were set up on the floor, a couple of empty tables pushed aside to make room. The band had done some afternoon shows recently, serenading the regulars during happy hour. But tonight was their big break. They had finally managed to score a slot for the supper club.

It was the winter of 1975. We have to keep this in mind when we try to picture the scene. Short hair was still unusual. If you wore ripped clothes that was because they were what you had. As far as Blondie was concerned, there wasn't a skinny tie in sight, the sixties retro look that would be our trademark was still in the future. No black suits, paisley or polka dots. Not even a leather jacket. Hell's well dressed corpse was pretty much his own thing, and Verlaine's non-descript casuals hadn't influenced either Debbie or Chris in their choice of attire. They were still holding on to the rags of camp. Sometimes Debbie's outfits included turquoise stretch leotards and red stockings, or a gold lamé dress with the occasional fish bowl accessory.

I had seen the Stilletoes once and I can muster a single image of Debbie, standing before a mic-stand on the stage at Club 82, surrounded by a halo of glitter. She had gone through a few different girl group incarnations before deciding to go it alone. There was Angel and the Snake, Blondie and the Banzai Babies and, I think, a couple others. Debbie's whole approach then was very heavily influenced by the gay camp scene that eddied around the Andy Warhol crowd and flowed into Club 82. As one commentator put it, the show was more pastiche than pop.* I think for a long time she just

* Clinton Heylin, *From The Velvets to the Voidoids*, (New York, Penguin, 1993) p. 158.

wasn't confident enough in herself and her singing to do without props, and for a while in the early days of Blondie, a lot of this *schtick* was still in her arsenal. For people of their generation, Warhol was the holy of holies. Debbie and Chris had always aspired to penetrate his circle. For a time in the late sixties, Debbie had worked as a waitress at Max's Kansas City, the exclusive watering hole of New York's hip intelligentsia, a stone's throw from Warhol's Factory on Union Square. Like my own early experience at CBGB, rubbing elbows with Factory workers like Taylor Mead, Ultra Violet, Candy Darling and Jackie Curtis had a powerful effect on Debbie. Later these old connections would come in handy, and when I started living with Chris and Debbie, I loved hearing stories about people like the mad Eric Emerson, famous for doing a striptease on the tables at Max's and for putting his hands through walls, who had died in a car accident only the year before. Hearing stories about him and Billy Murcia was, I thought, like getting the oral history of my tribe. I had never thought much of Warhol, except for his brief association with the Velvet Underground, but the sense that I was becoming part of an underground scene that reached back in time was exciting.

I arrived at White's the next night eager to hear what Clem was doing. I don't remember a great deal about the show, except that Ronnie and I sat in the back, huddled in a dark corner, rationing the one beer we could afford. I don't think I said much. The place was practically empty, and what I do remember of the audience is a handful of barflies occasionally letting out a frank appraisal of the singer. If they didn't always appreciate the material – made up mostly of oldies and disco numbers like 'Lady Marmalade' with occasional originals like 'Platinum Blonde' – at least they liked her looks. It was only later that I found out they got the gig because Debbie worked there as a waitress.

My memories of Debbie from that night are vague. But
I was impressed by Chris's voodoo attire. He was always
covered in skulls, pentagrams, crossbones and swastikas,
this last item a bit odd for a Jew, sort of like being black and
really into the Ku Klux Klan. He wore dark eyeliner, his
nails were long and black (he never used a plectrum and
played his guitar as if it were a banjo) and his hair fell around
his rouged face in gypsy ringlets. Chris was the last to
abandon the remnants of glitter, and when Blondie had its
first incarnation in sixties retro, I always thought he looked
out of place in 'Mod' suit, skinny tie and Beatle boots.

Also there that night was Fred Smith. Fred had been
working with Chris and Debbie for about a year, weathering
the turbulence that had nearly wrecked the band a half-
dozen times. The most recent catastrophe was when Billy
O'Connor, the drummer prior to Clem, came to his senses
and gave up rock and roll for a career in law. After Billy, it
was only Clem's insistence – and long-distance telephone
calls from New Jersey – that kept the group going. From the
original Stilletoes to the shedding of several backup singers –
among them Tish and Snooky, later members of the Sic
Fucks and proprietors of the punk boutique Manic Panic –
Fred had remained loyal. Even when Ivan Kral left the group
for apparently greener pastures, Fred stayed. But strangely,
Fred's path was linked to Ivan's. The Polish guitarist's
defection to the camp of Patti Smith inaugurated the legendary Debbie–Patti feud, and in the not so distant future the
machinations – imagined or otherwise – of Ms Smith would
again have repercussions that affected Blondie, Fred and,
oddly enough, myself.

►►

At the less-than-revolutionary New York Dolls appearance
at the Little Hippodrome, the bass player for the opening act

and the lead guitarist for the headliner had a conversation. While Malcolm McLaren tried unsuccessfully to secure a beachhead for his red leather comrades, Johnny Thunders listened as Richard Hell voiced his growing misgivings about the commissar of his own band. Television, he felt, was becoming more and more a vehicle for its lead guitarist and increasingly more vocal front man, Tom Verlaine. Their association went way back. But now it seemed that the telly was going to lose one of its most important parts.

Hell and Verlaine – aka Richard Meyers and Tom Miller – had a history that any romantic poet would die for. In a relationship not quite paralleled by that between the nineteenth century poet Paul Verlaine and his evil genius, Arthur Rimbaud, as teenagers Hell and Verlaine had run away together from an upmarket reform school in Virginia. Among other adventures on the road, while hitch-hiking to Florida they spent a night in an open field and started a fire to keep warm. Events are unclear, but in order to pass the time the two bored proto-punks killed a few hours by setting the field aflame. With the fire engines came police, and the runaways were jailed. One wonders if Verlaine's later choice of covering the Thirteenth Floor Elevators' garage-psychedelic classic, 'Fire Engine', was motivated by this event.

Verlaine eventually returned to school, and even made it briefly to college. But Hell had other plans. He scrambled together a hundred bucks and in 1967 hightailed it north to the bright lights of New York City, just in time for the last sunset of the summer of love. Hell was determined to be a poet, and like another CBGB shaman, Patti Smith, his influences were those nineteenth century French poets who can loosely be characterized as decadents and symbolists – Baudelaire, Gerard de Nerval, Lautremont, Huysmans, and the aforementioned Paul Verlaine and Arthur Rimbaud. Patti Smith's mantric chant of 'Go Rimbaud' would mark her as

New York City's resident punk Francophile, but Hell was
there too. And where Smith's near-hippie aesthetic led to
visionary indulgence and excess, Hell chose the darker path,
leading to a morbid preoccupation with death and a fondness for Edgar Allen Poe. He was also attracted to Poe's
dangerous stimulant, opium – easily accessible in its more
powerful derivative form, heroin, in a dozen dank staircases
in Alphabet City. Hell told one interviewer that on heroin he
could see Edgar Allen Poe's living room, although he failed
to make clear what the point of the visit would be.

Hell holed up in a tiny room in New York and, inspired
by a meager diet and a single copy of the Who's 'My
Generation' which he played over and over again, banged
away at a fairly unreadable first 'novel', *The Voidoid* – later
the name of his own group. Back home, Verlaine, dissatisfied
with academia, sank heavily into music. Although Verlaine
himself was no mean poet, writing some of the most memorable and sophisticated lyrics to emerge from the CBGB
scene, his deep passion was sound, his early love avant-garde
saxophonists like John Coltrane and Albert Ayer. This love
of complex improvisational jazz would later re-emerge in the
Verlaine-dominated, post-Hell Television. But when Tom's
interest first shifted from the sax to the guitar, it was the
rough, rhythm-oriented sound of mid sixties garage bands
that excited him. By the early seventies, the killer guitar
riffs produced by the Who, the Kinks, the Yardbirds, the
Standells, the Seeds and other 'hook'-oriented groups, had
been obscured by the predilection for interminable solos and
long Wagnerian opuses. When Hell finally talked Verlaine
into joining him, the two decided to combine symbolist
poetry and proto-punk and start a band.

Before that fateful meeting with Hilly Kristal outside
CBGB, Meyers and Miller – now Hell and Verlaine – had
gone through a few incarnations, along the way attracting a

couple other conspirators to the cause. Their first collaboration was as the fictitious Theresa Stern, a composite *nom de plume* the wild boys adopted for a joint poetry publication they released on Hell's own printing press. Theresa, however, failed to set the Hudson aflame, and receded into starving poet oblivion. Then came their musical debut as the Neon Boys, which included Verlaine's drumming friend, Billy Ficca. Like the Dolls and their handful of *cognoscenti*, Verlaine and Hell felt that rock and roll had grown fat and complacent and needed a good kick in the head. But admirable intentions and reactionary zeal, desirable as they are, do not necessarily make for a rocking act. Ficca was a pro and Verlaine had done his homework, but Hell was as innocent of musical knowledge and ability as the harvest of punk rockers that would sprout in the next few years. This being the case, he originally declined the bass position, deciding to remain a lyricist and 'ideas man'. But after two abortive auditions with Douglas Colvin – later Dee Dee Ramone* – and a Chris Stein just starting a working relationship with Debbie Harry, Hell relented, and was given the deceptively easy-looking task of supplying the bass line for the group. But even with a great name and a subsequent collector's item demo, the Neon Boys did not light up New York. In 1973 their bulbs went out.

For some time after that, Hell acted as Verlaine's manager while Tom tried the folk approach, twanging poignantly away at West Village spots like Gerdes Folk City. A town that had seen the likes of Dylan and the thousand lonesome minstrels he brought in his wake was not noticeably

---

* Dee Dee, apparently, was even less *au fait* with the bass than Hell. At his audition, Verlaine would say 'Let's play a C,' and watch as Dee Dee plunked each note in succession, throwing questioning looks at the Neon Boys. They shook their heads until he hit the right one.

impressed. But one show at Reno Sweeny, during which Verlaine subjected the minimal audience to a blast of loud solo electric guitar, met with approval by at least one listener. Richard Lloyd, a flash guitarist who had been a glitter kid in LA after hitching there from New Jersey at eighteen, thought he could add just the right leavening to Verlaine's raw rhythms. Terry Ork, who ran the bookstore Cinemabilia – like the Strand, another rest stop for fledgling New York rockers including Verlaine and Hell – had told Lloyd about Verlaine. They had met at the shop, and Ork suggested Lloyd go to the show. Lloyd had been living at Ork's Chinatown loft and knew good advice when he heard it. Verlaine and Lloyd hit it off, and with some friendly harassment Hell started working on his playing as well. All they needed was a new name. Hell, ever the image maker, hit a bullseye. Television was about to be turned on.

But even in their inception, the tensions that would tear them apart little more than a year later were clear. The choice of stage names by the two front men is evidence enough. Miller chose Verlaine as a nod to an influence, but Richard Hell was Meyers' own invention, a more creative work than either his poetry or his playing. While Verlaine worked steadily at developing an unmistakable guitar sound – joining, in his own way, the ranks of virtuosi like Jimi Hendrix and Robert Fripp – Hell worked on himself. Or rather, on the image of the self he wanted to project. Hell's calculated nihilistic dandyism was lost in the wash of safety pins and spit that followed in the wake of the Sex Pistols, but if anyone can claim the credit for inventing punk rock, it's him.*

Like some postcultural magpie, Hell gathered a collection

---

* As Hell himself has been keen to point out. See his article 'How I Invented Punk Rock', *New Musical Express*, 5 April 1981.

of personae and late romantic icons and with them feathered the nest of his self-image. Nietzsche – who, along with Rimbaud, deserves credit as one of the intellectual sources for the New York punk movement (although at the time his writings were inspiring people, they weren't called punks and there was no movement) – had written that, 'The great man is the play actor of his ideal.' Meaning that in order to become who you want to be, you have to look the part first. Hell took the syphilitic philospher seriously and set out to do just that. For Hell, rock and roll was about one thing: inventing yourself, DIY in the extreme. 'If you can just amass the courage that is necessary,' he told one interviewer, 'you can completely invent yourself.' In his little room, Hell took Rimbaud, Nietzsche, the opium-addicted playwright Antonin Artaud, some film *noir* atmosphere, Edgar Allen Poe's living room, Francois Truffaut's *The 400 Blows*, electric Bob Dylan, a frustration with establishment rock and roll, and an enervating obsession with death and threw them into the existential blender. Out popped a wild-haired, torn-bloused beatnik who looked like Frankenstein with anorexia. Unfortunately, like Moses, Hell wouldn't see the promised land, and that fateful night at the Little Hippodrome another less poetic magpie – this one from across the Atlantic – got one look at his ripped shirt and saw the light.

Reports of the early Television shows concur that there was a peculiar friction between the saintly Verlaine, scanning the clear light of a tortuous solo, and the manic Hell, perpetually bursting at the seams with an energy that, sadly, was never captured on tape. Like all good legends, they live in the memories of that handful of people who caught their performances between the springs of 1974 and 1975. And again like good legends, they were short lived. By the time I had seen Blondie busking in the depths of downtown Manhattan, Verlaine had lost whatever interest he had in Hell's

ideas on the poetics of rock and roll. When his namesake
Paul Verlaine broke with his lover/torturer Rimbaud, he
brought out his pistol and shot him in the hand, thereby
earning a prison sentence. Verlaine *à la* NYC circa 1975 took
an easier route. He just booted him out of the band.

Verlaine himself never cared about image, the scene, or if
his shirt was torn the right way. As his playing and songwriting proficiency grew, producing works like the haunting
'(I Fell Into the Arms of) Venus de Milo', he discovered he
was what Hell considered an endangered species: a serious
musician. Gradually he took more control of the band – in
today's parlance, grabbed the remote – and started dictating
what was on TV. One thing was for sure: a lot less Hell. In
the early days, the two shared singing and songwriting duties,
but increasingly Verlaine suggested they drop existing tunes
and work on new ones. Invariably the jettisoned numbers
were Hell's and the new arrivals were Verlaine's. Hell, perhaps cowed by his lack of musical ability, grudgingly went
along. Except, that is, when it came to the last tune. If
anything shows Verlaine's lack of empathy with or even
interest in what was undeniably beginning to gel into an
authentic underground scene against the Bowery's bleak
backdrop, it was his suggestion that they drop that tune, too.
Its title was 'Blank Generation'.

If the growing scene had anything like an anthem, this
was it. In later years, Verlaine's songs bear more listening,
simply because they *are* songs. (He was capable of anthemic
works too, as the success of 'Marquee Moon' showed.)
Hell's epileptic expressions are much more of their time and
place. Of none was this more true than 'Blank Generation'.
If you couldn't remember all the verses – which wouldn't be
surprising, given their density and resistance to melody – you
were sure to absorb the chorus. Set to a descending pattern
reminiscent of Peggy Lee's 'Fever', Hell coined a phrase that,

with a little help from Malcolm McLaren, would sprout British clones like the Sex Pistols' 'Pretty Vacant'. Who couldn't remember 'I belong to the blank generation?' And who couldn't share in Richard's *angst*, veering dizzyingly from post apocalyptic ennui to spoilt schoolboy *Weltschmerz*? Hell later complained that the message of the tune had been misconstrued, and that the whole point was to fill in the _____ with some positive content. But the reigning *Zeitgeist* lacked his Nietzschean drive to self-creation, and most of the punters saw fit to leave it empty.

All of which didn't mean diddly squat to Verlaine. He wanted a band, not an art project, and a bass player, not an archetype. The music just wasn't getting anywhere. When Verlaine heard the demo tapes, there just wasn't any bottom. Hell's voice bothered him too, and he was also getting anxious about the frequent visits to Edgar Allen Poe's living room, which were becoming something of a habit. When Verlaine suggested that they drop 'Blank Generation' too, Hell thought to go one better and leave a blank himself. After the last show at the Little Hippodrome, Verlaine finally got the Hell out of Television. Richard quit. Two days later, he got a call from Johnny Thunders. Fed up with Florida, McLaren and lack of dope, he and Nolan had quit the Dolls and returned to New York. Johnny had heard the news. You too, huh? Hey Richard, listen, you wanna make a band together? A month and a half later the Heartbreakers debuted with a trial run at Coventry's in Queens before really coming out along with a cartload of other bands in July and August at the CBGB Festival of Unrecorded Rock Talent.

Verlaine's decision wasn't spontaneous. He had been considering finding another bass player for a while, and had actually played with one a few times. A recent friend, Patti Smith, thought he might be the right guy. Before she nabbed Ivan Kral, Patti had seen Fred Smith play with Blondie once or twice. Now she started putting a little word into Fred's ear too. We may never know exactly what she said, but we can surmise. At that time, Blondie had a reputation as the band *least* likely to succeed. Even for the first few months I was playing with them, we were known as the band who would open for *anybody*. Not so Television, who, along with Ms Smith, were quickly becoming the critics' choice in the New York rock revival. At Clem's first gig at CBGB, in March 1975, Blondie suffered yet another discouraging setback, when in between sets Fred dropped the bombshell that he was taking Richard Hell's place in Television.

►►

In 1967 the twenty-year-old Patti Smith, self-styled avatar of Arthur Rimbaud, arrived in Manhattan, exiled from Woodbury Gardens, New Jersey. From early on she had been privy to visionary worlds; a childhood case of scarlet fever left her with a tendency to suffer hallucinations that remained with her until late adolescence. This entrée into other worlds gave the teenage Patti an air of strangeness and left her alienated from her surroundings – admittedly not difficult in New Jersey. Like a million other 'alienated' teenagers she sought solace in Art. Landing in New York via Pitman, New Jersey – inspiration for her first and highly collectable single, 'Piss Factory' – Patti found work at Scribner's bookstore on Fifth Avenue, and romance of a sort with the fledgling photographer, Robert Mapplethorpe. Mapplethorpe saw the promise in the young Patti and took her in, hoping to help give some order and discipline to her volcanic energies. She, in her turn, helped supplement their income by occasionally shoplifting from her employers, selling the books cut rate to friends and pocketing the cash.

Two years passed, and after a stint in Paris trying to paint while absorbing the century-old emanations of her poetic

mentor, Patti returned to Manhattan and, again with Mapplethorpe, took up residencies: one in the legendary Chelsea
Hotel which had seen the likes of Mark Twain, William
Burroughs and Andy Warhol, and would later witness the
death of Nancy Spungen, and another, across town at Max's
Kansas City. For six months, she and Mapplethorpe haunted
Max's tables, trying to be noticed, and it's curious to wonder
if an equally up-and-coming Debbie ever served her future
nemesis a drink.

Max's proved a bust, but Patti struck pay dirt closer to
home. In the lobby of the Chelsea Hotel she met Bobby
Neuwirth, most famous as Bob Dylan's painfully sarcastic
sidekick in D. A. Pennebaker's revealing 1965 documentary,
Don't Look Back. Neuwirth saw the skinny art groupie
scribbling in a notebook and asked to see her etchings. She
told him that *Don't Look Back* was a tremendous influence
on her, which, given Dylan's self-portrayal as a nasty piece
of business, tells reams about Patti's later reputation as a
hard case. Under Neuwirth's wing, Patti entered the underground, surfacing for a brief spell as collaborator and
cohabiter with playwright Sam Shepard. But the real event
that set her off was her inaugural poetry reading at the St
Mark's Place Poetry Project, in honour of Bertolt Brecht's
birthday on 10 February 1971. Accompanied by Lenny
Kaye* – a New York rock journalist – on guitar, Patti
opened her notebook and performed several poems, one of
which contained perhaps her most famous line, about Jesus
dying for somebody's sins, but not hers.

After a relationship with Allen Lanier, keyboardist for
Blue Oyster Cult, and a visit to the year-old Parisian grave
of rock shaman Jim Morrison, in 1973 Patti found herself

---

* Lenny Kaye was also responsible for the influential *Nuggets* collection of
re-released sixties psychedelic garage/punk bands.

opening for the New York Dolls in the Oscar Wilde Room of the Mercer Arts Center. One wonders what the crowd of glitter kids made of the bony T-shirted androgyny spouting Rimbaudesque one-liners? But her heart was in the right place. All along, seminal rock figures like Brian Jones, Dylan and Keith Richards shared Patti's pantheon with Baudelaire, André Breton and Artaud. More shows followed. And then, in the spring of 1974, the first meeting of what would become a kind of rock and roll mafia took place on the Bowery.

The underground poetry scene in downtown Manhattan was a relatively incestuous small pond and it was not difficult to find your playmates. When Patti bumped into one half of the by now forgotten Theresa Stern, she realized they had a lot in common. Meyers/Hell, like Smith an habitué of the Strand bookstore, invited Patti down to see his band play at a bar on the Bowery. In April of 1974, Patti and Lenny Kaye caught Television at CBGB. Not long after, Verlaine truly found his Rimbaud when he and Patti briefly became an item on the underground scene. The art rock contingent had arrived, and from their three chord Olympus the self-important lovers looked down on the lowly rabble, who nevertheless provided some manpower for their projects.

A month after Patti first saw Television, the Stilletoes debuted at CBGB, opening for TV. By August of 1974, the Stilletoes had been shorn off, Ivan Kral tacked on, and the group's name changed to Blondie – a tag the peroxided Debbie had acquired from admiring truck drivers. Patti by this time had expanded, and had included the late pianist Richard Sohl – who I would later work beside with Iggy Pop – in her act. She also shared a bill at Max's Kansas City, soon to shut down, with Television. In December, Ivan Kral left Blondie, enticed by Patti's charms and possibly the conviction that Blondie wasn't going anywhere. But the ex-

Stilletoe dug in her heels, and in January of 1975, Television and Blondie shared a bill at CBGB. A month later, the Patti Smith Group, four fifths of a fully fledged rock and roll band, debuted there. By early March, Richard Hell had left Television.

Now somewhere around this time, if we are to believe Chris and Debbie, Patti Smith started looking out for Fred Smith's own best interest. She must have been persuasive, because by 20 March 1975 – just weeks after leaving Blondie – Fred played a five-week residency with Television and the Patti Smith Group at CBGB. It was not long after this that Clem came round to the storefront and asked if I thought I could play the bass. But at that point, Clem himself wasn't totally convinced. Two ex-Blondies were now in Patti Smith's back pocket, one in her own group, the other in her boyfriend's. Guitar, bass and piano – Patti's line-up – are nice, but if she really wanted to rock, she still needed a drummer. Patti must have been thinking the same thing, because around the same time that she was giving Fred some friendly advice, she apparently had designs on Clem as well.

In their highly distorted and egregiously one-sided 'oral history' of the New York punk scene, Gillian McCain and Legs McNeil – resident punk of *Punk* magazine – quote Debbie as saying that Patti Smith once turned up at the Blondie rehearsal studio and set her fiercely 'come-hither' eyes on their recently acquired drummer.* Debbie, equally fierce and seasoned by numerous cat fights, blocked Patti's advances, but not, apparently, before she had a chance to get a word in, because not long after Clem started playing with Debbie, he invited me to come along to another audition. This time with Patti Smith.

---

* Legs McNeil and Gillian McCain, *Please Kill Me* (London, Little Brown and Company, 1996) p. 213.

It was in a rehearsal space somewhere in uptown Manhattan, above 14th Street, which, for East Villagers, may as well have been the Catskills. Clem had yet to crop his hair to the moptop he sported on the first Blondie LP and, like Chris, was still hanging on to the remnants of glitter. A weird Rod Stewart shag, like a flaccid octopus, hung around his head, and he chain-smoked Marlboros with a quick, jerky motion. I guess I was there for moral support. I wasn't really a musician, and my clothes were definitely uncool. When I thought about it, all I had going for me were my dark glasses.

Inside the room were some amplifiers, a set of drums and two people: Lenny Kaye and Patti Smith. Not one to mince words, Patti came to the point.

'Which one's the drummer?'

Clem twirled his sticks.

Then she looked at me.

'And what about you?'

I had seen Patti (or was it Richard Hell?) on stage at CBGB and had liked her. But face to face with the modern Rimbaud, I found myself at a loss for words.

Again the look.

'Well? Whadda you play? Hmmm?'

Still nothing.

She looked at Lenny Kaye.

'Maybe sunglasses?'

She laughed. Lenny picked up his guitar and started strumming. In a thin sarcastic voice he sang, 'You'll look sharp / Wearing sunglasses after dark.'

Needless to say, Clem didn't pass the audition.*

▶▶

----

* Clem wasn't the last one who was ready to abandon the good ship Blondie. When Richard Hell and Johnny Thunders put the word out that

My own audition for Blondie went somewhat better. After his brief encounter with Patti Smith, Clem decided to stick to his own pastures and get Blondie on the move again. He told them about me, and after hanging around at a couple gigs, they knew who I was. Clem said I was a poet and that I wrote songs – my repertoire on the clapped out piano was growing – and I guess I looked the part. I was thin. I wore dark glasses. The fact that I couldn't really play the bass was a minor detail. If your standards for rock musicianship were Yes and Emerson, Lake and Palmer, then practically none of us could really play. But that was unimportant. The whole idea behind the early New York scene was that you didn't have to depend on established rock performers to provide your musical sustenance. As Patti Smith and Television were beginning to show an increasingly interested media, if you had the nerve to get up on stage and bang away, you could do it yourself.

So when Clem came round the storefront and asked if I wanted to try out for Blondie, I of course said yes. The only problem was that I didn't have a bass. That's all right, he said. There'd be one at the rehearsal space.

The room was uptown, in an office building on West 37th Street, in the garment district not far from the Port Authority Building where only a couple months earlier I had spent a few afternoons panhandling. Nearby, Eighth Avenue was a favourite haunt of the hookers who worked the Times Square area, and not too long before Crash and I had thought it was a great laugh to photograph each other as we talked to the girls walking their beat.

---

the newly formed Heartbreakers were looking for a second guitar, Chris Stein headed up to their rehearsal space and had a bash. Evidently he didn't fit the bill, and to his unforeseen good fortune, was stuck with Debbie.

What I remember most about that audition was realizing how attractive Debbie was. I hadn't kissed a woman, or girl, since Zelda, let alone slept with one, and neither living with Crash nor my job as a messenger offered many opportunities to change that. I had gone close to a year without sex – no wonder I was reading Henry Miller. Occasionally I frightened some teenager at the Metropolitan Museum of Art – one of the few places I could get in free – by asking if she'd like to read my poems. My appearance and awkward manner probably put them off, but I suspect that if they'd actually read the poems, they'd probably have been frightened even more.

No, I couldn't say that I really knew many women. But now one was definitely sitting a few feet across from me. It's not that I hadn't noticed Debbie's looks before. But sitting across from her, talking, in a small, brightly lit room, was different from seeing her in a dive like White's, where she'd mumble a quick 'Hi' before and after a set. She had a serious case of 'bedroom eyes' and that slightly crumpled look that made it seem that she had just rolled out from under the sheets. Like every male who's seen her in the flesh, I knew I was looking at a very sexy woman. Although I never mentioned it, for the next few weeks I had something like a crush on her.

Chris was there too, done up in his Bela Lugosi best. Clem was very supportive, coaxing me out of my natural shyness, telling them about my poetry and songs. Chris lit a joint, and after it went around, he handed me the bass.

'Whaddya know?'

'Er . . .'

'Can you play A and D?'

'Yeah.'

'Okay. You know the Stones' "Live With Me?"'

I nodded.

'Awright.'

We went to it. Chris had a scratchy, plucky way of playing, as if his fingers hit two different chords simultaneously, one banging into the other. Clem hit a steady beat. I ploughed into the bass, figuring it out with a kind of join-up-the-dots approach. Debbie let the chords churn around for a while before coming in. Casually, in thin T-shirt, torn jeans and tennis shoes she sang, 'I got nasty habits . . .'

Yeah, I thought. I bet she does.

'C'mon now honaaay, donchu wanna live with meee . . .'

About an hour later we stopped. Finally, Chris said, 'Okay, you can play.' Clem got off his drums and moved over to the piano.

'C'mere,' he said. 'Play one of your songs.'

I put down the bass and sat at the upright. The tuning wasn't great, but compared to the one at the storefront, this was a Steinway. I hit a C, got my pitch and sang.

Debbie and Chris nodded.

'Okay. Sounds good.'

'So?' Clem asked.

'So he can play,' Chris said. 'So he's in.'

'Debbie?'

'Yeah. Sure. He sounds great.'

Clem smiled and lit a Marlboro.

Cool, I said, and asked him for one. So that was it. I had made it. Goodbye messenger job. Now I was officially in a New York rock and roll band.

4. MANHATTAN SPECIALS

A lot happened after that audition. For one thing Crash informed me that he was moving to a *kibbutz* in Israel. The spot, apparently, would be safe when Armageddon arrived. According to his sources, that would be pretty soon. He didn't want to see me go up in smoke with the rest of Manhattan, so he was giving me one last chance. If I wanted to come along, all I had to do was say so. He'd get me a plane ticket and set me up with the right people. We could even continue with the band idea – once, that is, the rapture passed and the new millennium was installed. An opportunity like this doesn't happen twice. If I passed it up I would be left with the rest, howling in the whirlwind and gnashing my teeth. What did I say?

'Well in that case,' he sneered, 'you have to be outta here by tomorrow. I'm giving up the place.'

Rehearsals with the band were going well, and I was getting better on the bass. Being homeless would pose a problem. I didn't want to lose the momentum my new life had been picking up, and I thought about it over an egg cream at the Gem Spa. No way at that stage could I have afforded my own place, and I wasn't about to start hustling to make some cash, as I knew others in my situation did. There seemed to be only one solution. A couple days later I knocked on the door of my parents' house.

That lasted a few weeks. The fact that I was playing in a

band didn't go down well, and that it was in New York made it even worse. Understandably, my parents didn't care for me crawling into bed at 4 a.m. after a gig or a night out. Not long after I arrived I received an ultimatum: change my ways, get a job, think about returning to university and forget about rock and roll. I packed another knapsack and left.

For a few nights I crashed at the rehearsal space. Technically *verboten*, I had nowhere else to go. I crashed on another friend's couch in Jersey City, but after a couple nights his mother didn't care for this and I was back on the street. Eventually my plight came up at rehearsal.

'Debbie,' Chris said. 'Gary doesn't have a place to live.'

'Shit.'

Then a thoughtful moment.

'Well, I guess he can live with us.'

▶▶

Chris and Debbie lived in a tiny one-bedroom apartment above a grocery store on Thompson Street, in the interzone between SoHo and Little Italy, the kind of neighborhood you'd expect to see in an Al Pacino film. The glitter clothes and green eye shadow never endeared them to their neighbors, old Italian men who sat for hours in smoke-filled social clubs over beers and espresso, and moustached Catholic women who crossed themselves when they saw Chris's pentagrams. SoHo had yet to become the trendy overpriced neighborhood it is today, and Little Italy was a tourist backwater off the main drag of Greenwich Village. Amidst the pizza parlours, garages and avant-garde galleries, you could still find affordable apartments. Debbie had found the place through a friend, Rosie, one of the original Stilletoes, who lived upstairs. Debbie had been there with her three cats and Chris for a while. Chris had his own place on First Avenue and 1st Street, a welfare apartment that he had

shared with Eric Emerson but was now subletting to Tommy
Ramone of the Ramones.

After living in the storefront, I was used to cramped
conditions. But living with Crash wasn't the same as living
with a couple – especially not a couple like Chris and Debbie.

I have some fond memories of that apartment. Like the
time Debbie sent me out to do the laundry. I had very little
experience of laundromats and thought one spin in the dryer
was all you needed. When I brought the clothes back and
Debbie saw they were still damp, she laughed the goofy laugh
I would hear a lot in the next two years, and made me take
them back. Or when she used to go to Chinatown and return
with a sack full of *bao*, steamed buns filled with pork and
sweet sauce, and she, Chris and I would huddle in their
room and watch television. There was Debbie's 1967 Chevy
Camaro, which she had to move by 7 a.m., or else it would
be towed, and which she had throughout most of the time I
was in Blondie. We use to drive out to Coney Island for an
afternoon, or to Brooklyn to vist Chris's mother, who fed us
and gave Chris little bags of grass that the neighborhood
kids had given her. Getting ready for a show, Debbie would
pull out the ironing board, and after doing her dress, would
iron a shirt for Chris or a pair of trousers for me; a little
later, she would help me fix my skinny ties – at first I couldn't
manage it, but even when I could, I liked her to do it for me,
knotting it through my tab collar shirt.*

Little things like that come to mind when I think of
Thompson Street. But what I remember most about the place

---

* Getting ready for a show was a complex ritual, but no one went to as
great lengths with it as Clem. To achieve the desired effect with his hair
Clem would first cover it with several different kinds of hairspray. Then,
having preheated the oven to the correct temperature, he would bake his
hair to perfection, by kneeling down and sticking his head in it.

are the photographs. I had never seen so many before. It's no exaggeration to say that every vertical surface was covered with a picture of someone or something. After living in the storefront, which was lacking in any aesthetic whatsoever, it seemed 'arty' and bohemian. A bulletin board on one wall had flyers for the Stilletoes, an Elvis record cover, a photo of Debbie in her Camaro, a picture of Billy Doll, the inevitable skull and crossbones, a Rolling Stones button with Brian Jones, and an assortment of other items. The refrigerator was hidden behind a wall of faces: Richard Hell, Johnny Thunders, Eric Emerson, the Dolls, the Velvet Underground. I don't know how much Debbie shared Chris's taste for the occult, but in their little cave she had let it run riot. Crucifixes, magical talismans, voodoo dolls and other mystic impedimenta shared shelf space with images of Warhol, French new wave cinema and Japanese monster movie stills, as well as bits and pieces of junk art that Chris picked up from the trash. As I got to know him I discovered that Chris couldn't pass a rubbish bin or trash can without seeing what was inside, and often he'd return to the little apartment with half a table or a broken mirror, eager to show Debbie the spoils of a recent hunt. The bric-a-brac of the streets found its walk-in display case in that tiny crowded apartment. Chris, I think, had a fear of empty space, and for the most part Debbie humored him, but at times the claustrophobia was so thick you could taste it.

The other vivid memory I have is of shivering myself awake most of the first night I spent there, crashing on a small couch amidst amplifiers, speaker cases, Debbie's cats and Chris's guitars, because I was too shy to ask for a blanket after the two of them had gone to bed.

Like any group, we soon fell into a routine. Debbie would make coffee in the morning or early afternoon, depending on when she got up: Café Bustella, a real New York item like the bottles of Manhattan Special, an absurdly sweet coffee soda we'd get from the deli below. Bleary-eyed, rats' nest hair, she'd fall out of their bedroom wrapped in a housecoat, then pull out a frying pan and make scrambled eggs for Chris and me. Most of the time I had been up already for a few hours, reading or quietly plucking one of the guitars, trying my best to keep out of the way.

I met a lot of people. Some are just names to me now, like a character named Youngblood, and Vanessa, the trans-sexual whose guitar Chris had borrowed and was loath to give up. There was Elda who, with Rosie, had been in the Stilletoes and who, along with being one of Richard Hell's girlfriends, was also the mother of Eric Emerson's children. It was Elda who had invited Chris to one of the early Stilletoes shows, before he played in the band. As Debbie told me, she felt a psychic connection with Chris the minute she saw him. I didn't doubt it then and today am certain it was true. The running joke was that he was Svengali to her Trilby.

Another character I met early on was Tony Ingrassia, a theatre director who had had several off-Broadway successes and who had managed the Stilletoes for a brief period. We would later do the music for his production of Jackie Curtis's play, *Vain Victory*. Along with Holly Woodlawn and Candy Darling, Jackie Curtis was one of the Warhol transvestite actresses that Lou Reed immortalized in his glitter hit, 'Walk On The Wild Side'.

Ingrassia was a large man with thick glasses, bushy eye-brows and a beard. He had a background in the Theatre of the Ridiculous, which under the direction of Charles Ludlam, would be a big success in the seventies. But it was as the director of Andy Warhol's play, *Pork*, that he had made his name. Made up of transcripts of Warhol's tape-recorded conversations, the play received modest notices after its run at the La Mama Theatre on East 4th Street, not far from Club 82. But in 1972 when it played the Roundhouse in London, it was a smash. Not with the London theatre critics, who derided it, but with people like David Bowie, who was just starting on his ascent to stardom. Bowie had always idolized Warhol, and when *Pork* came to town, he was one of its most enthusiastic supporters, getting a whole group of London hipsters down to the show. Before *Pork*, Bowie had been hovering in the afterglow of the Aquarian Age, trying unsuccessfully to develop something other than his faery minstrel look. *Pork*'s gender bending and glitter was a revelation to David, and a few months later he transformed Ingrassia's gilded atmosphere into the world of Ziggy Stardust. In a way Ingrassia was one of the founders of glitter. Bowie's production company MainMan later hired many of the people involved with the show, like Leee Black Childers, a photographer who would later manage Johnny Thunders' Heartbreakers and Levi and the Rock Kats, Cherry Vanilla, a singer and actress, and Wayne County: all of whom I would get to know soon after I started playing with Blondie.

For the most part Debbie, Chris and I got along, and I did my best to be as inconspicuous as possible. In an apartment the size of a shoebox, that wasn't easy. Debbie occasionally got stir-crazy and threw Chris and me out, just to have the place to herself. Then Chris would roll a joint and we'd hit the streets, usually heading across Houston to the East Village.

By this time I was wearing some of Chris's hand-me-downs – black pegged pants picked up from a thrift store, a Canadian Film Festival T-shirt, a pair of patent leather shoes, a white leather jacket. Chris was getting some sort of disability support – 'nut money' we called it, although I never knew what it was for – and had a Medicare card. He let me use it to get a new pair of shades, this time a little less dark.

Chris and I had similar interests. We were both avid sci-fi and monster movie fans; Chris was particularly keen on those tacky Japanese ones made in the sixties. We were crazy about comic books, and we both had a fondness for those few years in the mid sixties when AM radio was overflowing with great songs, from the British Invasion to Motown. Maybe he just liked having a young kid he could pal around with and show off to, like when he would show me the 'best' way to roll a joint, or tell me stories about his acid trips. Chris had been my age during the sixties and had lived through things I had only read about. He had seen people like Dylan on the street. He had been at the New York School of Visual Arts, was great friends with Eric Emerson, had been on the periphery of the Warhol crowd, and the first band he was in had once opened for the Velvet Underground. (More than twenty years later, at a tribute for William Burroughs, I heard him tell the same story several times to Laurie Anderson.) I loved walking around the East Village with Chris. He was always pointing out some place and telling me its history – even if I already knew it.

Chris introduced me to a lot of people. It was almost impossible to walk past St Mark's Place without running into someone. One of the first people I met was Jerry Nolan. I hadn't seen the Heartbreakers yet but Chris knew I was a fan of the Dolls and when we bumped into Jerry in front of the Gem Spa he told him. Another time it was Richard Hell. We even saw Verlaine. Although Chris had no hard feelings about Fred and said hello, Tom was too absorbed to give us much attention. On another occasion I met Tommy Ramone, when Chris went to pick up his rent. I remember that meeting for another reason. Chris had left his stuff at his apartment, and while he and Tommy conducted business, I checked out the bookshelves. Two books I borrowed that day would

make a big impact on me: Aleister Crowley's occult novel
Moonchild, and Colin Wilson's *The Occult*.

Some people I met early on were a group called the
Miamis. Two of them, Tommy and Jimmy Wynbrandt, had
been in the Stilletoes in the very early days and, as Queen
Elizabeth, they had backed up Wayne County during the
Club 82 period. I had my first performance with Blondie
when we opened for them at a forgettable bar called Monty
Python's, a dive on Third Avenue and 13th Street in one of
the sleaziest hooker areas. They were a great 'fun' band,
playing catchy topical songs with a sense of humour, like 'Do
What Patty Does' about Patty Hearst, the kidnapped heiress
turned terrorist, and 'Dada Mama', with the memorable lines
'Dada Mama don't you be so gauche / She just stole my last
brioche.' They covered Frank Sinatra's song 'That's Life' and
were absolutely unpretentious. It's unfortunate that they were
lost in the shuffle when the record companies started signing
up the punk bands. It was at their place that I had a funny
encounter with Dee Dee Ramone.

The Ramones had just signed a contract with Marty Thau
to produce a single and were also being courted by Craig
Leon – who would co-produce Blondie's first single – and
Seymour Stein of Sire Records. Understandably, Dee Dee
was feeling rather pleased. We sat around the kitchen table,
the inevitable joint had gone around, and Dee Dee was
telling us what it was like dealing with record company
people. The usual questions were asked. How much money
did they get? When was the album due? Were they going on
tour?

Somebody asked if the Ramones would still play CBGB.

'Well,' Dee Dee said. 'Y'know, probably. But not that
often. We'd rather do bigger places, y'know, being signed
and all.'

He lounged back in his chair, satisfied with his assessment of things, his pudding bowl hair fringed across his forehead, jeans torn at the knees and regulation black leather jacket hanging open. Then suddenly he leaned forward, put his hands on the table and earnestly assured us that success hadn't gone to his head.

'But I'll come to see you guys play. I don't want to lose touch.'

I hadn't said much and everyone was quiet. Then I sighed, shook my head and commiserated with Dee Dee.

'Gee, Dee Dee,' I said. 'It must be lonely at the top.'

The others laughed. Dee Dee seemed a little put out. I don't think I made a good impression.

►►

It was around this time that I decided to call myself Gary Valentine. Like everyone else who's done it, I took a new name to mark a change in who I was and to signify a break with the past. But while many of the people on the scene had angry violent names – Richard Hell, Johnny Thunders, Alan Suicide* – I didn't feel particularly angry or violent. I was living in New York, was playing in a band, and was becoming what I wanted to be, a pop star, all at nineteen. What was there to be angry about? Valentine seemed like an appropriate name for a teen idol, and I had fantasies of having my face covered in red lipstick from all the kisses I'd receive from my frenzied nymphet fans.

---

* Sucide were one of my favorite acts on the scene and strangely one of my most vivid memories is of a conversation I had with Alan in front of Max's Kansas City sometime in 1976. We got on the topic of cigarettes and I mentioned that at the time I smoked several different brands. He shook his head. 'Quickest way to get cancer,' he said. 'Find a brand you like and stick to it.' Seeing that Alan was a chain-smoker, I imagined he knew what he was talking about. Roughly four years later I quit.

The fans, however, would be a long time coming. I still hadn't met any girls and, judging by the sound of the band, it would be a while before I would have to start beating them away with a stick. At the time I joined, Blondie was more a dream than a reality. For one thing, we barely had equipment. Until we got our record deal I was using borrowed bass guitars and amplifiers. Chris had a string of guitars he borrowed from different people. Clem was the only one with his own equipment. We didn't own a PA and shared the rehearsal space on 37th Street with a bunch of rich kids who played universities and bars in Long Island. 'Shared' isn't quite appropriate for our relationship with them as Debbie and Chris never paid the rent.

At first Chris taught me the songs at the apartment, using a very rough cassette he had made of our set. We'd sit on the couch I used as a bed and go over the songs again and again. Most of the Blondie material then was cover tunes. Chris and Debbie just weren't writing many songs, and a lot of the very early material was leftover stuff from the Stilletoes. We did the Shangri-Las' 'Out in the Streets'; 'Femme Fatale' and 'All Tomorrow's Parties' by the Velvet Underground; 'Crazy Little Thing' from Captain Beefheart; 'Moonlight Drive' by the Doors, 'Come On' and 'Stupid Girl' by the Stones. We did a cover of Verlaine's 'Venus', a song or two from the Miamis, and 'Mercer Street', a song Elda had written. There were a few disco hits too, like 'Honey Bee', 'My Imagination', and a tune known simply as 'The Disco Song', which would later become the smash hit 'Heart of Glass'.

There were a few original songs, and I was impressed that someone could just go ahead and write their own material. By this time I had already written a few songs on the piano at the storefront, but I hadn't recorded anything. I was a quick learner and picked up the songs easily enough. I enjoyed the bass, and Chris and I seemed to work well together. Well enough that my first show with them came up pretty quickly. I don't remember much about it now, except that it was the one and only time that I felt stage fright and, like Stu Sutcliffe from the early Beatles, played with my back to the audience.

►►

Although Chris, Debbie and Clem had played CBGB, the Television/Patti Smith mafia decided to block the new Blondie's immediate return. Patti Smith had made her name away from CBGB and she wouldn't really be part of the scene that would emerge there in the next year, yet her influence and relationship with Verlaine counted. Debbie and Chris may have been paranoid, but it did seem that there was some distinct cold shouldering going on. For one thing, Terry Ork was now booking shows at CBs. Blondie in the old days had been considered passable eye-candy, but as far as music was concerned they were non-starters. Television's and Patti Smith's enthusiastic championing of 'art' created a rarefied and slightly stifling atmosphere, and Ork's datebook often seemed too crowded to allow space for Patti's sole serious female competitor. For the first month or so of my tenure, we were *personae non gratae* at CBGB.

However, by this time, there were some other places to play. There was the forgettable Broadway Charlie's and the equally unmemorable Brandy's, both of which were somewhere around 12th and 13th Street on Third Avenue. And there was Mother's, a gay bar on 23rd Street, across from the Chelsea Hotel. Peter Crowley booked the shows there until he moved over to Max's Kansas City. Max's, which had been closed since 1974, re-opened in 1975 under the management of Tommy Dean. There was also the Performance Studio on East 23rd Street, where the Ramones had been playing since 1974.

We did the rounds of these places, often playing three sets in a night, usually doing the same material for the same audience, making very little money. Most people think a musician's life is about sex and drugs and rock 'n' roll, but most of the time it's about making enough money to eat. If we were lucky, after a show we'd hop into Debbie's Camaro and head to Dave's Pot Belly, an all-night coffee shop on Christopher Street, west of Bleecker in the West Village, and stuff ourselves on cheeseburgers, fries and milkshakes. If the take wasn't good, there was Smiler's Deli on Seventh Avenue and Sheridan Square, for less sumptuous fare like chicken salad sandwiches and chocolate milk. Sometimes we'd head down to an all-night restaurant in Chinatown. Occasionally there'd be a show where we would make some real money. One night we played at a party for the Equestrian Club, somewhere on the upper East Side. We had to play for three hours to a well-heeled crowd and did everything we knew, repeating songs three or four times. Nobody seemed to mind. The food was good and so were the drinks. There were bowls of joints scattered around the tables, and Chris, Clem and I scooped up handfuls and stuffed them in our pockets. We had no pride. We made about three hundred dollars that night, the most money we had seen, and thought, Yeah, this is what it's all about . . .

At that point no one used the word 'punk'. No one was a punk in 1975. There was very little press about the scene, and what there was tended to call what was happening 'New York Rock' or 'street bands'. I had by this time cut my hair short and had started wearing clothes we found in thrift shops and the trash: white shirts, black jackets, skinny ties. I had seen Patti Smith in her oversize white blouse and undone black tie, and liked Richard Hell's shades and split suits. Debbie later said she had planned the sixties retro look from the start, just as she had planned the revitalized sixties AM radio sound. But if you look at the early photos, I'm the only one with short hair and a skinny tie.

Early on, Debbie asked if I thought I could sing a number, to give her voice a rest. I hadn't sung much before but was ready for anything. I picked an old rocker, 'Bad Boy'. It was pretty standard, a simple progression, and was easy to play and sing to at the same time. It was a kick to sing in front of an audience, even if, at that time, it was made up mostly of a few friends and groups like the Miamis. One time though, someone else was impressed. Anya Philips was a friend of Debbie's. She worked with Debbie at White's, but that was just one of her jobs. She was a clothes designer of sorts, a photographer and also a topless dancer – a trade several girls on the CBGB scene picked up in order to make ends meet. A few times Debbie and I went up Times Square to watch friends strip in some sleazy bar to a background of Roxy Music. I later found out that Anya was also into S & M, and that she kept a diary of her erotic encounters. In October 1976, Anya and Debbie would 'star', along with Richard Hell, in *Punk* magazine's 'graphic novel', 'The Legend of Nick Detroit'. (More on this later.) In 1977 she would come off the sidelines and make a brief name for herself as the manager of 'no wave' artist James Chance. I didn't know Anya very well, but even then I thought there was something dark and tragic about her. Maybe it was that she was half Chinese and had a air of Oriental mystery. In 1985, Anya died from cancer.

After the show that night she introduced herself to me. She was wearing black leather, a lot of it, had long black hair, very long fingernails, and was smoking a cigarette in a holder. She oozed sex like a perfume. I had seen a lot of outrageous looking people at Club 82, and didn't twig that this wasn't just a get-up. Anya meant business. After exchanging a few pleasantries, she leaned next to me and asked a very personal question.

'So,' she said in a low voice, 'you know, you're cute. I wonder, are you really a bad boy?'

Later, back at Thompson Street, when I told Debbie that Anya had given me her telephone number and address, and suggested I come by to see her, Debbie laughed.

'Oooh,' she said. 'Anya eats little boys like you.'

Hmm, I thought. She probably does.

Anya shared a large apartment with a friend on Fifth Avenue. Whether she paid for the place from what she made working tables at White's – which I doubt – or from dancing, I didn't know. But it was the swankiest place I had been in yet. The only girls I had known were a few hippie chicks, the sisters and Debbie. Now a leather clad dominatrix had invited me to her apartment.

The general idea was to listen to music, have a drink, relax, and get to know one another. I didn't know what to expect. It may be morbid to fantasize about a sexual experience one might have had with someone twenty-five years ago, who is now, sadly, dead. But if I had had a little more self-confidence and savvy, I might have had one of those wild erotic adventures most people dream of.

Unfortunately, my lack of experience and general shyness got in the way. Early on, Anya realized I wasn't hip to her party games and gave up waiting for me to come on. Her room-mate came back and, after some more talk, Anya said she was tired and invited me to crash on the couch. I did. The next morning, when I left, I got some idea of her disappointment. I didn't want to leave completely empty-handed, so kissed her goodbye.

'Mmm,' she said. 'A good kisser. But I prefer rockers to mods; they're sexier.'

I don't think I made it into her diary.

But my dud night with Anya wasn't my only early erotic failure. One of the first things I did with Chris and Debbie was to go to a party for the photographer Anton Perich at Andy Warhol's Factory on Union Square. I spent the night getting loaded and trying unsuccessfully to convince older women – in their twenties – to take me home. On another occasion, after an all-nighter, I wound up walking in Central Park at 7 a.m. with a girlfriend of Johnny Thunders. We had started out at CBGB and I no longer remember how we ended up in Central Park. Somewhere near the bandshell she broke a heel. She hobbled along for another hour, hanging on to my arm, waiting until she thought a friend who worked uptown would be at her office, so she could borrow a pair of shoes. I made it to Thompson Street and had to wake Debbie and Chris to let me in. At one of our first gigs at Mother's, someone came up to me and started telling me I was cute and asking what I was doing after the show. I didn't have my glasses on and couldn't tell if it was a boy or a girl, and didn't want to take any chances, so I backed away. 'What's the matter with you? You don't have to run away,' my surprised fan asked in disgust. Later I discovered it was a nice girl named Guillemete, who later married one of the Marbles, another unsung sixties retro band that Blondie shared some bills with.

Another group we got to know from playing Mother's was the Fast, two of whose members, Miki and Mandy Zone, later succumbed to Aids. (Eric Li, keyboardist with the Marbles, would die from a heroin overdose.) The Fast had been around since the Mercer days, but by 1975 had shed their glitter skins and developed a very mod look modeled mostly on the Who – a lot of black and white polka dots, bullseyes and arrows. Paul Zone, who later became the group's singer, was the scene's resident fashion plate, and combined Marc Bolanish hair with peg-legged suits and tab collar paisley shirts. One time, around the Christmas holidays, he invited me to his parents' house in Brooklyn for dinner. He brought out a box of untouched tab collar shirts, still in their wrapping, and gave them to me. I was ecstatic. It was that kind of time, when people were very friendly, very young and very happy. We were playing at being rock stars and all helped to keep each other's fantasy going. Later, when record executives started to enter the scene, this early camaraderie would fade. When the Fast played, a whole entourage of their friends from Brooklyn would show up, and in between shows we would run across 23rd Street to the Chelsea Hotel, looking for the ghost of Andy Warhol.

We tried a few things in the early days. For a few shows we worked with a conga player, and did a few others with a flautist. Blondie circa the summer of 1975 had very little direction and our performances were not impressive. Chris would look at his guitar as if it had just materialized out of thin air. Debbie would invariably forget the words and often sang off-key. I had mastered a kind of one-finger approach to the bass, but the material wasn't demanding. Clem was really the best musician of the group. One of the first things we did was record a five-song demo. I had only been playing with Blondie for a few weeks when Alan Betrock, a journalist with the *Soho Weekly News*, and later the founder of *New York Rocker*, approached us. He had seen us play and wanted to record us. Alan, who sadly passed away while I was writing this book, had an obsession with girl groups, as any reader of his book, *Girl Groups*, knows. He was an omnivorous consumer of pop culture and saw something in the early Blondie that other people didn't. Maybe it was only Debbie, but while most people sniggered through our ragged set, Alan thought we had something and was willing to invest in it. One reason he was eager to have us record is that our live performances were so embarrassing.

In June 1975 we headed to a basement in Long Island, to make our recording debut on an eight track machine. (Anyone in a band now and discouraged by their progress should listen to this tape, available now on a Chrysalis Blondie compilation, *Platinum Blonde*.) We did a cover of the Shangri-Las 'Out in the Streets' and four original numbers, one of which, 'The Disco Song', became, as I said, 'Heart of Glass'. Another original tune, 'Platinum Blonde', was more or less Debbie's theme song for the time – a campy number in which she yearns to be just like her heroines, Marilyn and Jean, Jayne, Mae and Marlene. Alan thought it best to tone some of the words down a bit. In the original, at the very end, Debbie would sign off with a plaintive 'Oh I hope I get laid', which Alan had her change to 'I hope I'm okay.' By today's standards, the song wouldn't bat an eye.

On the 'press release' that came with the few acetates Alan made of the tapes I'm listed as playing bass and piano; I had forgotten that I banged out a few honky-tonk chords on 'Platinum Blonde'. I was Blondie's first keyboardist. The photo shows four people who barely know each other. Clem's round bushy hair makes him look like a teddy bear. Chris's tweaked eyebrows, long locks and eyeliner hearken back to the Mercer days. Debbie's platinum blonde tresses slide across one eye like Veronica Lake. She looks like she could be a Gestapo agent's mistress or an airline stewardess. And there's me, with short hair and skinny tie, looking to the future.

It wasn't far away. Just across Houston Street to that grungy little bar on the Bowery.

Blondie, June 1975. Promo shot for the Alan Betrock tapes. I had only been in the band for a few weeks. Note my short hair and skinny tie.

A growing boy needs a healthy diet: chocolate milk and Twinkies. Note inverse pentagrams and cross. Soon after this, I was electrocuted.

Behind every good nun stands a budding punk rocker.

Getting ready to make the scene, circa 1975: Debbie fixes a last minute cocktail, Jimmy ties his shoe, and I decide whether or not to bring the nun. Note Lenin poster on wall and drum case above the cupboard.

The magus in his inner sanctum: the inimitable Benton. Note 'Women Behind Bars' poster and assorted magical paintings, skulls and self-portrait of Chris.

The genius at rest: Chris in a pensive mood, 1975. Note length of hair and 'Blondie' voodoo doll above drum kit.

Team spirit: from the first official Blondie photograph session, 1975.

▲ Lisa's phony *New York Rocker* press card. It rarely worked.

◄ Lisa and me at the Wayne County Benefit Concert, 1976. The woman in the background is a man.

▼ A bad case of the Mumps, 1975. Left to right: Kevin Kiley, Lance Loud, Kristian Hoffman and Rob DuPrey.

► An apt pose for Christopher Street, 1976, with Bleecker Street in the background.

▼ Women Behind Bars: Lisa and Divine in a touching scene, 1976.

▲ Debbie and me on the set of *I Married a Rock Star*, 1975.

◄ Debbie does something Weill: Brecht's 'Bilboa' hits CBGB, 1976.

▼ Chris and me in the dressing room, Max's Kansas City, 1977. Note the freshly painted Cramps graffiti. Jimmy Miami in foreground.

A Spector haunts the Whiskey: Phil Spector in the flesh at the Whiskey A Go Go, 1977. His bodyguard is out of the picture. Note my squint – obviously the effect of too much reading.

The mellow sounds of Suicide. Marty Rev (left) and Alan Vega, Max's Kansas City. Note the Stilletoes graffiti.

My favorite Blondie shot, in the dressing room of the
Mabuhay Gardens, San Francisco, 1977. Note Ronnie Toast
graffiti as Debbie perfects her glass eating act.

The beat goes on: the Mabuhay Gardens, 1977, just down the street
from City Lights Bookshop and Jack Kerouac Alley.

Lisa joins the infantry, while I do my Yves St. Laurent impersonation.
Note magical ring on right hand. LA, 1979.

The Leather Boys.

The genius at work, or, 'Look into my eyes'.

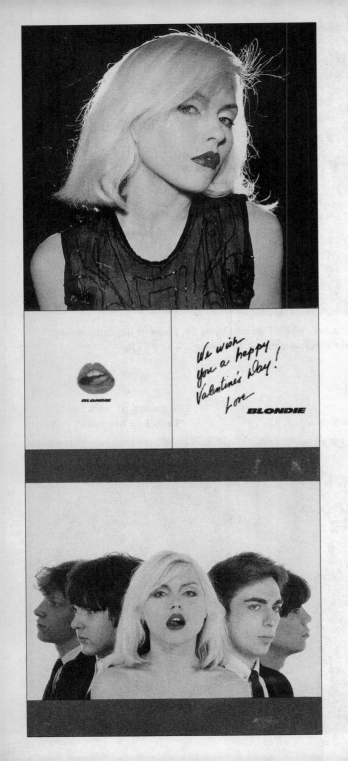

We wish you a happy Valentine's Day! Love

BLONDIE

After the suits got a hold of us: Valentine's Day card, 1977.

February on
Sunset Boulevard,
across the Strip
from the Whiskey.
Clem later got
a ticket for
jaywalking.

Little GTOs:
Debbie and Rodney
Bingenheimer,
1977.

An outtake from the *Blondie* album cover session.

My last session with Blondie, somewhere in Staten Island, New York, 1977. Note chipper expression on bass player.

► Just about to rip it to shreds one night at the Whiskey A Go Go.

►► LA, on the way to the studio. Sadly, we had to walk those last few yards.

▼ In search of the lost chord: rehearsing in LA, SIR studios, 1977.

◄ Poolside in
Beverly Hills.
Next stop, the
jacuzzi.

▼ From JFK to the UK:
en route to
London, 1977.

The Know, LA 1978, in front of the now demolished Hollywood Billiard Hall. Left to right, me, Joel Turrisi, and Richard D'Andrea.

The Know live at Madame Wong's, Chinatown, New Year's Eve, 1979, with John McGarvey on drums.

Another LA basket case,
Hollywood, 1977.

Magick, 1977.

Touched by the presence: tomorrow belonged to us.

5. BOWERY BOYS AND GIRL

When you walked into CBGB in the summer of 1975, you were usually met by Roberta Bayley, an attractive brunette who either took your money or decided you were cool enough to be let in free. Roberta had worked for Malcolm McLaren in London in the early seventies, and had moved to New York just in time to catch the Dolls at Club 82. Later she became one of Richard Hell's girlfriends, and then one of the unofficial photographers of the scene. I didn't know Roberta that well. One story about her stands out. Early on I was told her relationship with Hell ended when she flushed the toilet in their apartment which, evidently, Richard never did. Hell was very particular about this point and Roberta's flagrant violation proved too much, so he threw her out. I don't know how true this story is, but if the atmosphere around CBGB was any indication, it wouldn't surprise me.

After Roberta let you in you passed a dark and mostly unused telephone booth on your left, and a bookcase stuffed with hundreds of old paperbacks on your right. Hilly was something of an old beatnik, and with his original idea to have poetry readings, he tried to affect the atmosphere of a Greenwich Village coffe house. The rows of unread books collected dust and created a faintly literary air, decor many espresso bars indulge in today. In the early days he was somewhat successful, and grand old beats like Allen Ginsberg occasionally made an appearance. What the Hell's Angels who also frequented the place thought of this I don't know.

The bar was on the right, and the tables and jukebox on the left, with the stage set a couple feet off the floor directly in the back, at the end of a long narrow runway. There wasn't a dance floor and most people kept to their seats, so even if the place was packed – which was rare until 1976 – you could usually get a decent view of what was on stage from practically anywhere inside. On the stage itself were strange, turn-of-the-century, life-size black and white photographs lining one wall – a nod, perhaps, to the Bowery's heyday as an 1890s theatre district. Initially the PA was pretty rudimentary. Later, after the scene took off and the crowds started coming, Hilly invested, building a new stage, installing new lights and replacing the sound system.

One of the things to go to make way for these improvements was a pool table. It was off to the right of the stage, in front of the kitchen and the narrow corridor which served as a dressing room, basically a crowded little slice of floor where bands could hang out before they went on. One of my vivid memories of CBGB involves that pool table. I was shooting pool with Clem and a couple other people. Dee Dee Ramone was nearby. He was drinking and getting louder and louder, urged on by his crowd. We said hello when we came in, but maybe he felt he wasn't getting enough attention because soon after we started playing he came over to us and started knocking the balls around on the pool table.

I guess the look on my face must have suggested what I thought. Dee Dee came up to me. With a big smile, and in a drunk little boy voice he said, 'I bet you think I'm acting like an asshole.'

To which I replied, 'No, Dee Dee. I don't think you're acting at all.'

Dozens of stories have been told about the decrepit state

of CBGB, most of them revolving around Hilly's famous dog, Jonathan, known for nonchalantly shitting all over the place. Legs McNeil even interviewed Jonathan about it for *Punk*, which gives you some idea of their coverage. Brecht says somewhere that the world of culture is built on a mountain of shit. If nowhere else, this was certainly true of CBGB.

Strangely, for somewhere that was known as 'the toilet', I can't remember ever using the one there, which was usually jammed with people either vomiting or doing drugs. When it was free the urinal would be so overflowing that it would be criminal to add to it. Graffiti, of course, covered the walls; some of it choice, a lot of it band names but most the usual drivel.

If I needed to pee – which, given the cheap beer Hilly served, was fairly often – most times I'd head outside. An empty lot on the corner housed a rubbish tip that served as a handy spot. That was the great thing about CBGB, the fact that you could move in and out without any problems. Most clubs had a no re-entry policy, which meant that once you left, that was it: you couldn't get back in unless you paid again. The open door policy at CBs meant that if you thought an opening band was crap, you could walk over to the Gem Spa, head to another bar where the drinks were cheaper or even go to Alphabet City to score some dope, and then come back to catch the headliner. Later, when Max's reopened and starting having bands, it wasn't unusual to run back and forth between the Bowery and Union Square a few times a night. Taxis back then were pretty cheap, and with four people splitting the fare it came to practically nothing. Often we would see the Ramones at CBs and then catch Suicide or Talking Heads at Max's, and then head back to CBs for the Heartbreakers, all in one night.

In between sets, you'd move over to the bar and grab a

beer, and someone would play Television's 'Little Johnny Jewel' or Patti Smith's 'Piss Factory' on the jukebox. It was easy to mingle. The place was small enough and on a good night half of the audience was made up of other bands. But in fact, most of the real socializing at CBGB took place outside, in front of the club. Unlike Max's, CBs wasn't a place to hang out. The smell alone would keep you out. The only reason to be there was either to see someone play or to play yourself. So, between sets, everybody headed outside to the street, to hang out in front of the white stucco walls and clam shell awning. On any given night you could find Blondie, Talking Heads, David Johansen, Danny Fields (who had managed Iggy and would later manage the Ramones, and who started writing about the scene for the *Soho Weekly News*), Hell and an assortment of other rising stars crowding around the place, which stood out like a meringue amidst the liquor stores and cheap hotels.

Bums and winos from the neighboring Palace Hotel and other flophouses would mingle with burgeoning punk rockers, asking for change, a drink, cigarettes or a drag on a joint. Usually they were pretty tame, and you even got to know a couple regulars. They enjoyed seeing you and saying hello; maybe they got a kick out of seeing their neighborhood becoming popular. Aside from CBGB, there was Phebe's, a restaurant on the corner of East 4th Street a couple blocks away, where the punk crowd met the campy off-Broadway set, and which I got to know pretty well a few months later when I started dating the actress and *New York Rocker* journalist Lisa Persky.

I first graced CBGB's stage, opening for the Ramones on 4 July 1975. I had already met Tommy Ramone through Chris, and during that weekend got to know the others. Like Chris and Debbie they had been in different bands around the Mercer scene, and also like them they were a lot older than me.

My next appearance was during the legendary Festival of Unrecorded Rock Talent, more or less the start of the golden age of New York punk. Practically all the bands that would emerge out of the Bowery in the next two years made some of their earliest appearances during the festival, which ran from 16 July to 2 August. It was during this time that I got to know most of them: the Ramones, Talking Heads, Television, the Heartbreakers, the Demons, Tough Darts – who later changed the spelling to Tuff – the Shirts, the Marbles. We kicked it off on 16 July with a bill that included the Ramones, Talking Heads and Tuff Darts. On 31 July we played with the Ramones again, and on 1 August with the Ramones and Talking Heads. Two weeks later, on the weekend of 15–17 August, we were back with the Talking Heads, this time supporting the Heartbreakers. I remember that show particularly, because there was a party at the Heartbreakers' loft on Chambers Street afterwards. They weren't successful finding any dope, and as a consolation scored a massive bag of grass instead. I have a distinct memory of Hell and Thunders leaning over a pile of buds, rolling joints and lighting them one after the other. It was only later that I learned that grass is often used as a diversionary treatment for junk sickness.

By that time we had become something more than a band that played on the Bowery. We were living there too.

▶▶

When the band we shared the uptown rehearsal space with finally figured out we weren't going to pay our half of the rent, they threw us out. For some reason, another musician down the hall took us in. He knew we were broke but it didn't matter; I think he just liked Debbie. In any case, he let us rehearse there for a while. Chris and Debbie got their revenge on the rich kids not long after. They were away for a few weeks and in their absence someone broke into their room and trashed the place. Assuming they had abandoned their gear, Chris and Debbie pinched a player-piano from the room and hocked it for fifty dollars, which was quickly turned into some grass and a few groceries.

Eventually the good Samaritan at 37th Street had to ask us to leave as well, and we were strapped for a rehearsal room. Broke as usual, our prospects of renting one weren't too good. Then a fairy godmother turned up, at least for a little while. She was disguised as Arturo Vega, owner of the Ramones' loft, conceptual artist and graphic designer, and possibly the best dressed man in town.

Playing with the Ramones was like opening for a jumbo jet. Most of their songs clocked in at under two minutes, and they invariably started with Dee Dee chanting 'One, two, three, four' before the wash of distorted guitar, thudding bass and clockwork drums came on. I never figured out if Dee Dee's mantra was just part of the act or if they really needed it to start in time. If they did, it didn't always work. Half of the time they'd start, stop, and then Dee Dee would shout 'One, two, three, four' again, only to stop again. Johnny's guitar was so loud that it would feed back as soon as they stopped playing. Most of the time Dee Dee's bass was out of tune. He played it like a jackhammer, drilling 'duh-duh-duh-duh-duh-duh-duh-duh' about half a step sharp or flat of Johnny's wall of sound. Joey, who in some ways bore a distinct resemblance to Hilly's dog – and who sadly passed away while I was working on this book – would droop over the mic-stand like an unwatered sunflower, his terse staccato vocals barely breaking through the waterfall of Johnny's guitar. Tommy's drums were the most stable thing about the act, and he hit them like a metronome. I don't think he ever played a drum roll. A half-hour after they started they'd have gone through fifteen songs. What they reminded me of more than anything else were the Saturday morning cartoons I used to watch as a kid.

Arturo had come to see us a few times and heard we were without a rehearsal space. He had become the Ramones all-round aide-de-camp and was sharing his loft on East 2nd Street with Joey and Dee Dee. We got to know him because he used to come to all our shows wearing a Mexican wrestler's mask. He was easy to pick out because the only other regulars were two very tall Spanish girls who wore flamboyant flower dresses, like something out of *West Side Story*, and a couple of guys who wore dark glasses and had their heads shaved long before it became fashionable.

Arturo, who later became lighting director and graphic designer for the Ramones, had some strange tastes. Aside from the wrestling mask and fish bowls full of Mexican cigarettes stationed all over the place, he was known for his Day-Glo swastikas, a series of paintings he had all over the loft. He also had an SS uniform hanging from the ceiling, alongside a fancy gown. I had heard stories of Artuto and Dee Dee dressing up in that gear, but I didn't think much of Nazi chic. Chris had a swastika armband that, pretending to be Brian Jones, I wore once; on another occasion I did go with him to an auction of Nazi memorabilia at a swanky hotel uptown, just to see the kind of people that turned up. The Ramones had a side that was into Nazi stuff and did songs like 'I'm a Nazi, Baby' and 'Today your Love, Tomorrow the World'. They were funny, but a year later when the Dead Boys – a real late entry in the CBGB sweepstakes – rolled into town in full Third *Reich* regalia, I couldn't believe anyone would take them seriously.

At Arturo's we worked on new material, like 'Love at

the Pier', Debbie's song about the gay pickup scene at the Christopher Street Pier, 'Slip of the Razor', a tune of mine about the joys of suicide, and 'Starbeast', a poem of Toast's I had set to music, on which Debbie played a dinky pre-synthesizer keyboard. But our tenure was brief. When Arturo informed us that having one band running around his loft was enough, it was a disappointment. Debbie and Chris must have felt that, once again, the scene was against them. On top of this the situation at Thompson Street was becoming untenable. The place was just too small for Debbie, Chris, three cats, an assortment of guitars and amplifiers, Chris's ever growing junk-art collection and myself. Obviously, something had to give.

▶▶

Chris returned to Thompson Street one afternoon with a smile and in something approaching a good mood. He told us that not only had he found a new rehearsal space, but a new place for us to live, too. It was, he said, a loft. It was big enough for the three of us to have our own rooms and secluded enough to have the band rehearse. It was cheap and, maybe best of all, it was not far from CBGB.

The place turned out to be an illegal space above a liquor store, just two blocks south of CBGB. The address was 266 Bowery. It was old and filthy and graffiti covered the door. The liquor store below catered to a downbeat clientele, and our next-door neighbor was a restaurant supply shop, filled with second-hand stainless steel counters, refitted griddles and chrome sinks. Around the block on Elizabeth Street, in the bad end of Little Italy, there was a Puerto Rican neigh-borhood where English was definitely not the first language.

Coincidentally, around the same time, William Burroughs moved into his famous 'Bunker' at 222 Bowery, living there from 1975 to 1981. Decent living space in New York was difficult to find, and previously undesirable neighborhoods like SoHo and the East Village became more and more trendy, attracting weekend bohemians who could afford higher rents. Urban pioneers like Burroughs and ourselves discovered some unusual quarters. The Bunker got its name from its unique feature: having once been a YMCA locker room, it had no windows. In an apartment on the Bowery, this was probably no great loss and also lessened the chance of burglars.

In quite a few accounts I've read that Burroughs was something like a regular in CBGB; Burroughs himself has said so. I have to say I never saw him. Having been a big fan of the beats, I would have recognized him. Then again, for someone known as 'El Hombre Invisible', not being picked out in a tiny, half-empty bar shouldn't have proved too difficult.

The rooms in the loft were full of dust and grime, but they were large, and there was certainly enough room for the three of us and the band's equipment. To get to them you had to walk up a long dark rickety staircase. So many bums had pissed against the door that the odor of urine clung to the corridor no matter how many times we cleaned it. Debbie's cats, thinking the scent gave them carte blanche, made their own contribution. Urine, in fact, became an ungoing theme of the place.

One of Chris's friends had a lease on the building, and he was willing to rent the first floor, above the liquor store, to us. He lived on the second floor. For the time being, the top floor was empty, but soon after we moved in another resident arrived, Stephen Sprouse, the clothes designer. Debbie has remarked somewhere that Stephen was in some way responsible for Blondie's mod look. That's not how I remember it.

I don't recall Stephen ever giving me a piece of clothing or suggesting I wear something. What I do remember is that he seemed to take a lot of psychedelics.

From the summer of 1975 to the summer of 1976, the Blondie loft, as it became known, was a headquarters of the New York music scene. The friend who had rented us the place was named Benton. Gay, thin as a rail, with a long mane of blond hair and an eloquent southern drawl, he was extremely intelligent and an artist of sorts, a painter. His single maxim for life was pithy and memorable: 'Learn to love it.' I liked Benton, talked with him and got to know him well. During my stay there, I sat for him a few times, and he even created a few large-size paintings that we used as props for some of our shows, like a painting of a Hulk-like monster that Debbie destroyed at CBGB to a song she and I wrote, 'Kung Fu Girl'. By this time Johnny Thunders had jammed with us a couple times at CBGB and we wanted to give the song to him as a kind of sequel to 'Chinese Rocks', the Heartbreakers' junkie anthem. It turned out to be too good so we kept it.

Benton's real passion was wearing biker gear and fantasizing about Hell's Angels. It would lead to some unfortunate results, but its initial manifestations were only unsanitary. One of the trials that prospective Hell's Angels had to endure was to go without washing for days and to sleep in clothes that other members (no pun intended) had pissed on. Benton and a boyfriend took this to heart and would sometimes lock themselves away, unwashed and urine clad. Benton would also piss into empty Coke bottles. Whether this was part of the Angels routine or whether he simply wanted to avoid Chris and Debbie, whose room was next to the toilet, I don't know. But often his room would be dotted with piss-filled Coke bottles, standing amidst piles of art supplies, cigarette butts, comic books and magazines. He also had the unappetizing habit of shitting with the toilet door open and engaging you in conversation at the same time.

I don't know if Benton had designs on me. When they were negotiating the deal, Chris brought me along to show Benton who exactly would be moving in. A nineteen-year-old waif was probably a handy bargaining chip. If Benton did have ideas, he never made a pass, but he was certainly into a dominance trip. Some things were innocuous, like getting me to clean the staircase, which from all appearances, probably hadn't been swept in twenty years. He would also get me to do his shopping at the Puerto Rican *bodega*. His list wasn't long – usually cigarettes, coffee and sugar. (Benton's sugar intake was phenomenal.) The neighborhood kids would make fun of him, he said, so if he could avoid going, he would. I didn't mind and in any case I often went to the *bodega* myself, to get the cheese sandwiches, chocolate milk and Twinkies that were my staple diet.

Like Chris, Benton was deep into comic books and sci-fi films, and like myself he was also into sword and sorcery, Conan the Barbarian, H. P. Lovecraft and 1930s pulp magazines like *Weird Tales*. He had nabbed a near life-size cardboard display of Conan from some bookstore and had it standing in his room, so that when you walked in you were greeted by a muscular barbarian holding a broadsword. But what we often talked about was magic. Like Chris, Benton was into the occult, but he was more serious about it. Chris was certainly a sucker for anything to do with vampires, voodoo, ghosts and witches. He used to go on about spirits and poltergeists inhabiting the loft. Debbie agreed and would chip in about UFOs, telling me, in all seriousness, that she was an alien. She and Chris would sometimes consult the *I Ching* together, but it always seemed to me that they would do the opposite of what it advised.

Benton was different. He would talk about magic calmly

and intelligently, and relate it to other things I knew, like Nietzsche and Jung, neither of whom Chris had read. Benton even gave me a copy of Nietzsche's *The Birth of Tragedy out of the Spirit of Music*; on the title page he had drawn a fist rising out of crossed thunderbolts. We'd smoke grass and he would read from Crowley's *Diary of a Drug Fiend*. I could tell that it meant more to him than something merely weird or spooky. It was a kind of philosophy of life. At one time he even introduced me to someone who claimed to be one of Crowley's illegitimate sons.

Between Chris's occult obsessions and Benton's impromptu readings of Crowley's infamous Thoth Tarot deck, the place had the atmosphere of a bad Satanist film. An eerie statue of a nun stood in front of the fireplace which often served as our sole source of heat. A cross was painted on her forehead and rosary beads hung from her hand. The fireplace itself was covered in occult formulae. Chris had found an old beat-up doll in the trash and turned it into a voodoo ornament, hanging it over the drum set. Benton had got his hands on a series of weird Tibetan tantric paintings, one of which depicted a group of monks eating one of their fellows, and these adorned the length of a brick wall. The story went that the place itself had been a sweat-shop, a doll factory that employed child labour, and in a cannabis-induced trance, Chris claimed that he had seen one of the ex-employees. After its run as a doll factory, the legend continued, the building had been owned by a New York gangster, Louis Desalvo. Rusty iron shutters covered the back windows, and Chris and Debbie swore that the holes that peppered the glass had been made by bullets. I didn't know. The panes were so cracked and splintered that it was more likely the windows had been targets for the neighbor-hood kids. But Chris and Debbie liked to think they were living in some kind of mysterious place, and that all these weird special things were happening to them.

Maybe they were. One weird special thing certainly happened to me at that loft.

Like everything else in the place, the wiring was faulty. How we got electricity at all was a mystery, but one of Benton's friends had somehow tapped into the liquor store's line and sent the juice up to us, gratis. This was a godsend, because otherwise we could never have afforded to run the amps and PA. I had set up camp in the rehearsal area, which would serve as my room. One day I reached out to move a lamp and ZAP! I had 110 volts running through me. I couldn't move and I couldn't let go of the lamp. A black mass like a storm cloud rose from the back of my skull and headed toward my forehead. I knew when it got there I'd be gone. I figured I had about thirty seconds and tried to call out but could only manage a whisper. There was no way that anyone in another part of the loft could have heard me.

Miraculously, Chris emerged from his and Debbie's room. Calmly smoking the ubiquitous joint, he looked at me, looked at the lamp, then stepped over to the socket and simply unplugged it. I collapsed. For several days after, my arm was numb and I had a tendency to fall asleep sitting up with my eyes open. Whether it was poltergeists, spirits or a previous tenant that tipped him off, I don't know, but that Chris should walk into the room just as I was receiving electroshock treatment seems like one of those unbelievable intercessions you read about in accounts of angels. He probably saved my life, something I had to remind myself of later.

One day Clem came running in saying that one of the winos had frozen to death outside. Chris, Benton and I went out and saw him. He was lying on the sidewalk, his back propped against a door. He was wearing very little and his feet were bare. Maybe someone had stolen his shoes or maybe he hadn't any to begin with. It didn't matter. His toes were turning blue. One of the locals hovered around, muttering 'Someone's got his shoes. See? They took his shoes.' Somebody suggested hauling him inside. All I could think of was Benton's painting of the Tibetan monks eating one of their dead, and was thankful when the ambulance arrived.

Some catastrophes proved blessings in disguise. Once we had no hot water for a few weeks. For Benton this wasn't too much of a problem, but the rest of us weren't so stoic. Debbie and Chris could make runs out to Chris's mom in Brooklyn. I tagged along a couple times, but for the three of us to turn up whenever we needed a shower seemed a bit much. It became clear that if I wanted to wash, I'd have to fend for myself.

Not too long before this, Benton, realizing I wasn't interested in the homoerotic elements of Crowley's magick, nevertheless believed it was a crime that I slept alone. My own attempts at warming my sheets proving fruitless, he took matters into his own hands. A friend of his, he was certain, was the just the right party. His message to her was simple and direct: 'You must come here and sleep with this boy.'

When I first met Lisa Persky, her looks, intelligence and sense of humor were enough to attract me. But there was more: she had her own apartment in Greenwich Village and she wore a black leather jacket festooned with silver studs and a clear plastic cock ring.

Benton wanted Lisa to cut all the preliminaries and just hop in the sack with me, but Lisa took her time. We talked. She told me about herself. We were about the same age, but there the resemblance ended. Her mother had been a beatnik; her father worked for *Playboy*. She grew up in Greenwich Village and when she was a little girl saw Bob Dylan and Peter, Paul and Mary walking the streets. Before she met

John Lennon, Yoko Ono had been the superintendent of Lisa's building, and she remembered little flyers Yoko had put up saying 'Come to the Vagina Painting'. Lisa's mom went and saw the future Mrs Lennon stick a paintbrush up herself and daub the fluid on a canvas. Lisa's mom was divorced and Lisa's stepdad had been a concert violinist. On one of his tours she met Salvador Dali, Pablo Casals and got the Beatles' autographs. She had been to Europe. She left school at fifteen, had been mugged and nearly killed, read her poetry at CBGB, and met Benton working on an off-Broadway production of a play written by her genius playwright friend, Harry Katoukis.

Not bad, I thought, as I reached for one of her cigarettes. But then came the clincher: 'I hear you don't have any hot water here. Would you like to come to my house and take a bath?'

She took a puff on her cigarette. Her breasts heaved under the leather jacket. I looked at Benton. He smiled.

'Yes,' I said. 'As a matter of fact I would.'

'Okay. Here's the address. Do you want to come tomorrow?'

I hadn't bathed for days, but that didn't matter. Tomorrow would be fine.

Lisa lived at 87 Christopher Street, between Bleecker Street and Sheridan Square, on the main drag of New York's gay district. I knew the area from my glitter days with Crash. The first thing that struck me about her building was the shop on the ground floor. It was called the Leather Man. I looked in the window. It was full of S & M gear: leather masks, fishnet vests, silk gloves. A whip. Some studded belts and collars. I later found out she got the cock ring there, and not long after that discovered what she did with it. Later,

Lisa also introduced me to the neighborhood, pointing out the bookstore on the corner of Christopher Street and Hudson Street whose back room was a trysting place for a new gay craze, fist fucking.

She opened the front door and smiled.

'Hi. Glad you came. C'mon up.'

I followed her up a flight of stairs. She had on a red T-shirt, black jeans, a pair of converse hi-top sneakers and was smoking a Parliament. She let me in. If I had thought Debbie's old place was small, this was a matchbox.

'So, you wanna take a bath?'

Lisa had a forthright manner and seemed eager to get down to business. On the way over I had fantasized about how things would proceed. Would we talk for a while and then take a bath and then make love? Or would we talk, make love and then take a bath? Would we take a bath at all? I needed one but if in the throes of hot passion my personal hygiene slipped our minds I wouldn't be put out.

'Well, the bathtub's here.'

She pointed to a large wooden board that I thought was a counter top. She moved the dish rack and lifted the board. The bathtub was underneath.

'Funky, huh? These old buildings are all like this. Here's a towel and there's the soap. I'll be upstairs in my mom's. C'mon up when you're finished and have a drink. It's the apartment right above. Okay? Enjoy yourself.'

Then she walked out of the kitchen and closed the door.

Well, I thought. She'll probably come down after I've been soaking for a while.

While I waited for the bath to run I looked around the rooms. The bookshelves proved interesting. She read. *Les Chants de Maldoror*. The obligatory Rimbaud and Baudelaire. Damon Runyon. S. J. Perelman. *My Wicked, Wicked Ways* by Errol Flynn. A whole shelf of fairy tales. Books on

Dada, WeeGee the police photographer and Man Ray the Wonder Dog.

I was flipping through her albums – Pink Floyd, Supertramp, the Velvets – when I realized the tub must be full. I turned off the taps and started to undress. After I scrubbed my back a second time I started wondering when she'd show up. I had been soaking for a good half-hour. It felt delicious, but the water was starting to cool. Still, the thought of that red head slipping through the door in a loosely hung bathrobe kept me rooted to the spot.

I started to worry.

Had she forgotten I was here?

Another five minutes.

It didn't occur to me that maybe all Lisa had in mind was a bath. This was New York. Greenwich Village. Lisa was a beatnik. Benton told her to sleep with me. I was in a rock and roll band.

The water was definitely cold. I gave up, got out and let the water down the drain.

Then I got dressed and headed upstairs. I knocked on the door. An attractive red-headed woman in her forties answered. I noticed she had a heart-shaped face.

'Oh, you must be Gary,' Jane, Lisa's mother said in a southern drawl. 'Come on in. Can I get you a drink?'

'Sure,' I said. 'Thanks.'

Then Lisa came in the from the other room.

'Man!' she said. 'You sure take a long bath. What happened? Did you get lost?'

I took a sip. She laughed. Well, I thought. At least I was clean.

▶▶

On Halloween that year the Ramones and the Heartbreakers played at a loft party in Soho. There was a whole loft party

scene around this time, when the rents were still low and the
kind of people we knew could still afford to live in them.
Bands would play or there would be poetry readings, or
'experimental' films and videos would be shown. My intro-
duction to the Modern Lovers was at one of these, seeing a
really low budget video of 'Roadrunner', basically shots of
Boston taken with a hand-held camera in a moving car.
Benton told me about the Halloween party and suggested I
dress up. Knowing Benton's ideas about dressing up, I wasn't
enthused. But then he suggested I make my own costume. I
took an old T-shirt and painted 'Helter Skelter' on the front
in bright red, and a black and white bullseye on the back.
Then I tore this in strategic spots and threw a leather jacket
over it.

I got to know both the Ramones' and the Heartbreakers'
material very well that night. They each did three sets. The
Ramones had a decent number of songs and could vary, but
the Heartbreakers didn't have that many tunes. They had
been together about as long as I had been in Blondie and
Richard Hell was the main songwriter. He had a hand in
two anthems of the scene, 'Blank Generation' and 'Chinese
Rocks', but he really wasn't prolific, and although Johnny
Thunders could come up with some classic rockers, he really
wasn't a songwriter. So what did they do? They performed
the same set of seven or eight songs three times in a row. I
saw every one and by the end of the party considered myself
a kind of expert on the Heartbreakers.

Another thing to happen around this time was the filming
of Amos Poe's and Ivan Kral's *Night Lunch*, perhaps the first
punk rock movie. Amos worked as a cab driver when he
wasn't hanging out at CBGB, and he brought his hand-held
camera a few nights and shot the bands. A later effort, *Blank
Generation*, proved more successful. Not financially – I don't
think Amos made a dime from either film – but as a

representation of what CBs was like at its height, *Blank Generation* is the better film.

For *Blank Generation*, Amos came to the loft and shot us clowning around like the Beatles in *A Hard Day's Night*. Our segment ended with 'the boys' pushing Debbie's Camaro up the Bowery. What I remember most about *Night Lunch* is a shot at the bar at CBGB. A lot of the band members were lined up there that night. I cringe a bit when I remember myself; I had taken to wearing a felt John Lennon cap which must have looked pretty naff, especially with the dark glasses.

Around the same time I developed a crush on Tina Weymouth in Talking Heads, and would often go to their shows. This was when they were still a three piece, and hadn't yet got Jerry Harrison from the Modern Lovers on keyboards. Tina was known for her very static look on stage; robot-like and expressionless, she played her bass with short jerky motions, looking as if she was unsure of every step. With her Dutch-boy hair, round face and vulnerable air, I was attracted to her and liked the idea that we both played bass.

Nothing came of it – I knew she was with Chris Frantz – but we did talk a few times. I seem to remember that not long after the showing of *Night Lunch* at CBGB in early November – when everyone turned out to see themselves on the screen – we had a beer together and she told me to get rid of the hat and shades. I did.

Not long after that at a Talking Heads show I returned the favor. Tina never cracked a smile on stage, which I thought was a shame. I liked Talking Heads, especially 'Psycho Killer' and 'Warning Sign'. But like Verlaine they seemed a bit detached, involved in the non-image they were non-presenting, although as far as I remember, they weren't like that offstage. A lot of Talking Heads songs have a black, dance feel, and around this time disco was hot with 'The

Hustle' and 'Shake Your Booty'. During one set at CBGB, when David Byrne was scratching away in some extended funky instrumental and Tina was nervously keeping time, I called out 'Shake your booty, Tina!' She couldn't keep a straight face and laughed, and the audience did too.

It was also around this time that we were temporarily banned from CBs. One awful night, when we were scheduled to go on at 1 a.m., we discovered that Hilly had booked a couple extra bands that he was putting on ahead of us. I told him what I thought of that, very loudly. I don't remember now if we played that night or not, but I was angry enough at Hilly to piss him off and he told us that he wouldn't book us again. Debbie, who usually didn't stand up for herself, admired me for not taking shit from Hilly, and told me so. Unfortunately, when it came to me not taking shit from her and Chris she was less admiring.

▶▶

One of the gang of kids that hung around the Fast was a cute girl named Donna. Like the Fast and their crowd she lived in Brooklyn. She wasn't in a band, but she did play piano. Music must have run in her family, because her brother was a keyboard player too. He *was* in a band, or at least he had been until fairly recently. Milk and Cookies were a nondescript 'clean cut' pop group, led by whizz-kid guitarist Ian North. They played around town but really weren't part of the scene. Right before they left New York to head to England to cut their first record, they did a little spring-cleaning and divested themselves of some unnecessary baggage. One of the items they left behind was Donna's brother, Jimmy.

Jimmy had come to see us play often, and being axed from a group just on the verge of making a record must have hurt. Understandably, he wanted to get back into action and was very eager to audition for us. We desperately needed something to pull our sound together. Chris's guitar playing simply couldn't cut it. Clem and I provided a solid back-beat, but Chris's playing was, well, *eccentric*. He had a lot of interesting ideas but his execution was unreliable. After seeing us with a conga player, a flautist and a few other brief additions, Jimmy knew we needed another instrument. Donna made the introductions. After a show at Mother's she brought her little brother up to the stage. What I remember most about meeting Jimmy for the first time is how liberal he was with his compliments about my songs.

At the time he was living at home and working as an orderly in the emergency room at Maimonides Hospital in Brooklyn. It was an unenviable job. To hear him tell it, he was handling dead bodies, taking knives out of people's heads and subduing epileptics. He worked a long shift and would arrive at our rehearsals or at a gig running on high-octane adrenalin. I liked Jimmy, but later learned that he had a tendency to exaggerate, often, in fact, to invent things. So I'm not sure how many of his hospital stories were factual and how many were lurid inventions.

Initially we thought that a piano would provide the extra layer of sound we needed, but Jimmy didn't have a piano. What he did have was an ancient Farfisa organ, the kind that garage bands in the sixties like ? and the Mysterians used. By seventies standards it was rinky-dink, but we liked it. We were in any case veering more and more towards a distinct retro sixties sound, so Jimmy's obsolete keyboards were exactly what we needed. After a few rehearsals we realized it would work, and just as important, we all got along. Jimmy was a year or two older than me, and at the time he had pretty-boy looks and enthusiasm. We liked the same kind of music and he brought in his taste for groups like Procol Harum. With Clem we made up the youth side of the group.

The CBGB ban was still in effect, so our first shows with

Jimmy were at places like Mother's, Monty Python's, and Brandy's. But one of the first things we did together didn't take place at a club. Debbie had kept up her old Stilletoes connections and had heard that Tony Ingrassia was putting on a performance of Jackie Curtis's play *Vain Victory*, one of those absurd campy affairs, full of double entendre gay humor, like the one line I can recall:

'I'm so hungry I could eat you!'

'You'll do no such thing. Have another Saltine.'

Always hankering after the Warhol crowd, Debbie thought it would be a *coup* to get involved, so she got in touch with Tony and said she wanted to be in his production. He gave her the part of Juicy Lucy, one of the 'House of Wax' girls. The action took place on an ocean liner, the *Vain Victory*, and some of the other people involved were Cherry Vanilla, Tony Zanetta and Leee Black Childers. Tony decided the play needed some live music and corralled the rest of us into providing it. I don't remember a lot of what we played. The one thing that stands out is a version of a Coca Cola television commercial popular at the time. Coke's tag line back then was 'Things go better with Coca Cola, things go better with Coke', and during a scene in which somebody is sniffing some of the kind that doesn't come in bottles, we broke into a few bars of that theme. The play ran for several performances and was held in a loft space in Tribeca. Just before opening night Chris found four identical blue sharkskin suits at a discount clothes store on Broadway. We wore these for the performances, which were usually sold out. Clem and Jimmy cracked dubious jokes about some members of the cast, and I remember some unwanted attention from Cherry Vanilla but on the whole it was a good experience.

The production warranted some notice in the gossip columns written by high-ranking members of New York's gay

mafia. Danny Fields's column in the *Soho Weekly News* was
a case in point. Our contribution to *Vain Victory* garnered us
our first mention in his weekly round-up. But *Vain Victory*
has a warm place in my heart for another reason.

Benton had invited Lisa to the last performance. We had
known each other long enough and had to decide if we were
going to sleep together. At the end of the show everyone
was excited. Champagne made the rounds. Then word went
round that there was a party uptown. I saw Benton, and
hovering behind him, Lisa. She had on her leather jacket –
the one with the studs and cock ring – and a kind of
motorcycle cap. I told Benton about the party and gave him
the address. Then I turned to Lisa.

'There's a party for us uptown. You wanna come?'

'You taking me?'

I saw Debbie and Chris heading to the door.

'Gary,' Debbie called. 'We're heading to the party. Do
you want a ride?'

'Can I bring someone?'

'She'll have to sit on your lap.'

'Did you hear that?'

'Yeah. Let's go.'

We pushed through the crowd and tumbled out to the
street. It was cold. Early winter had hit and all I had on was
that sharkskin suit. Finally Debbie pulled up and I climbed
in. Lisa followed, planting herself on my lap. Then Jimmy
and Clem squeezed in and Debbie hit the gas. Lisa fell back
against me. We looked at each other and started making out.
Twenty minutes later we reached the address. Somebody told
us and we reluctantly pried ourselves apart.

I don't remember where it was held, but the place turned
out to be swanky – several floors up in an apartment building
on the Upper West Side. As this was my first closing night
party, I intended to make the most of it. Bottles were opened

and glasses were handed to me and I felt obliged to enjoy myself. The place was packed with Warhol clones and off-Broadway types. People danced. I was congratulated. 'Great music.' 'Cool suit.' 'When's your next gig?'

I became increasingly loaded and realized I had lost track of Lisa. I started moving from room to room, asking for the redhead I had arrived with. No sign of her. I was about to give up, figuring she got bored and left, when I decided to make one last sweep. And that's when she popped up.

'Are you tired of this?'

'What do you have in mind?'

'Do you want to go to my place?'

We headed out the door and grabbed the elevator. The ride down was a bit abrupt and as soon as I hit the street I felt it coming. I leaned against a mailbox and heaved. Charming, I thought, as a cold sweat covered my forehead and the vomit kept pouring out. I hunched over the gutter, shivering. After a few minutes it stopped but I was dizzy and could barely walk. Lisa flagged down a taxi and huddled me in. When we got to Christopher Street, she pulled me out and dragged me to the door. Just as we were coming in we ran into her father, who had dropped by to visit her mother. I reeked of vomit, had the spins and my legs were made of rubber. 'Pleased to meet you,' Mort, Lisa's dad, said.

When we got inside Lisa deposited me in the bathroom. Gradually the room stopped rotating. In the meantime she kept herself busy. When I walked in from the kitchen, I saw her under the sheets. Apparently she had decided to heed Benton's advice.

▶▶

Sometime before Christmas Clem went to England to visit his girlfriend Diane, who was studying at Oxford. The rest of us settled into the loft. Lisa and I started seeing a lot of each other. After *Vain Victory* we did a gig or two, but with Clem gone we wouldn't be able to perform, which meant that we missed out on the CBGB Christmas Rock Festival. Instead of taking a break we used the time to write new songs and really work Jimmy in.

On 24 December 1975, Christmas Eve, I turned twenty.

There wasn't much of a celebration. I spent my twentieth birthday alone at the loft. It was cold. After a fiasco with the oil burner we rarely had heat. A couple days earlier I scavenged the streets for firewood, but the few table legs and crates didn't burn well and were used up pretty quickly. I wore my coat, scarf and sweater and could see my breath. I smoked cigarettes and read the copy of *The Birth of Tragedy* Benton had given me.

Earlier in the week I had found a stack of silk screened Jimi Hendrix posters. I don't know whose they were, and no one laid claim to them. There must have been about a hundred of them. Bored, I crumpled one up and threw it in the fireplace, struck a match and lit it. Jimi wouldn't mind, I thought, and the brief flame felt good. By the time I got through half of them it was late and I went to bed.

6. SEX OFFENDERS

The 1975 Christmas party at Max's Kansas City was one of the big social events of the scene. Micky Ruskin, who ran the original Max's, was a brilliant entrepreneur and he had created a legend. The Velvet Underground had done their last shows there. Iggy Pop had famously cut his chest to ribbons on stage one night. Alice Cooper had been arrested for saying 'tits' during his act. The Dolls had been regulars. Even the telephone booths were notorious, well known as convenient spots for impromptu oral sex. I had heard a story about one that mentioned Debbie and David Johansen – but maybe they were just making a call.

When Tommy Dean took over Max's in the fall of 1975, he wanted to recreate the atmosphere of the original Max's, to corral the prominent hipsters as Mickey Ruskin had. Unlike CBGB, which was primarily a place to hear bands, Max's was a hangout, a place to see and be seen. Tommy may have had the best intentions, but he lacked Mickey's touch. When the flock of celebrities and late-night carousers he expected didn't arrive, he thought he would have a go at the disco market. But the spinning globes and flashing lights were just reheated Club 82, and that angle didn't work either. It wasn't until the arrival of Peter Crowley – who had been booking the acts at Mother's – that the one serious rival to CBGB's dominance as a venue for the new music arrived. The fact that Crowley was also Wayne County's manager may have had something to do with the frequency with which Wayne appeared on Max's stage, and with his extended run as the house DJ. Another favored act was Suicide. Marty Rev's electronic dissonance and Alan Vega's primal scream therapy was a surprise success at Max's – not least to Suicide themselves.

The 'real' Max's had always been downstairs, and the esoteric centre of that was the infamous 'back room', where besotted rock stars tossed chick peas and coke spoons at each other. Late in its career, Mickey had opened the upstairs room as a venue for live acts. The bulk of these were showcases for record execs eager to get through a night of blow and Jack Daniels. The original crowd of Warholians and Manhattan artists resented the new arrivals, but the trend caught on and toward the end of its run Ruskin's Max's was booking the likes of Patti Smith and Television. By late 1975 the joint that had catered to Mick Jagger and Truman Capote was opening its doors to the rabble from the lower East Side.

In many ways, Max's was a better place to play. The sound system was better, the stage was bigger, it had a dressing room and it didn't stink. But to me there was always something second best about it. Until Hilly started taking his press seriously, CBGB was just an unpretentious bar where bands could play and people could hang out. Max's couldn't give up its history – or at least Tommy Dean couldn't – and there was always an air of 'rock club' about it. At one point Peter Crowley took to putting portraits of 'the stars' on the walls – Thunders, Hell, Debbie, Dee Dee Ramone and, of course, Wayne.

For a while there was a kind of unwritten law that if you played at CBs you couldn't play at Max's within two weeks and vice versa. But it didn't take long for Hilly and Peter Crowley to figure out that the pond was pretty small and it wouldn't profit either club to starve out any of the fish. This amiable *détente* was seriously challenged by the infamous fracas featuring Wayne County and the Dictators' 'Handsome' Dick Manitoba – on which more shortly. This led to a self-righteous Peter Crowley informing Blondie that we had to be either a Max's or a CBGB band. His ultimatum was fortunately withdrawn before we had a chance to be the one group on the scene to be banned from both of its main venues.

All of this, however, wasn't on anyone's mind that Christmas Day 1975. Wearing a shocking green suit belonging to Chris that was too tight on him but fitted me perfectly, I arrived at Max's that afternoon hungry and ready to celebrate. Of the party itself I don't remember much, aside from a group photo of the orphans who turned out for a decent meal and some holiday cheer, and Jimmy Wynbrandt's remark as I walked in: 'Look! It's Brian Jones.' Food and drink were ample. I don't recall Hilly ever doing anything as lavish. Having seen the kitchen at CBGB, I'm not sure I would have wanted him to.

Debbie and Chris were away, and with Clem in England it was up to Jimmy and me to represent the group. In the party photo we're there with the regulars: the Ramones, the Fast, Richard Hell, the Marbles, the Miamis, Arturo Vega, Robert Gordon, the ubiquitous Wayne County and the super-groupie Sable Starr. The photo was taken by Leee Black Childers, who was more or less Max's house photographer, in the same way that Roberta Bayley filled that spot for CBGB. Leee was good at getting photos. One collage of his, featuring everyone on the scene, now resides in the Rock and Roll Hall of Fame in Cleveland, Ohio.

After *Vain Victory* we had got to know Leee pretty well. He came to a lot of our shows and was always taking snaps of me. Naive as I was, I didn't know there was anything to it, but on a drive to upstate New York, I twigged that Leee's intentions were more than journalistic.

On the weekend of 26–28 December, the Heartbreakers and Mink DeVille played Mother's. I went to one show. New Year's Eve I spent alone at Lisa's, with a bottle of wine and a stack of records. She had invited me over but was then dragged out to a party by a friend. The party was at an ex-boyfriend's and I wasn't in the mood to meet an old flame.

When I turned up at the loft the next day Debbie and Chris had returned. Debbie told me they had a surprise. Leee Black Childers had telephoned and asked if we wanted to go to Ian Hunter's house that evening. At that time Ian lived somewhere in upstate New York, I forget exactly where, but it was an hour or two out of town. Back then I thought it was very kind of Leee to invite us, but now I realize Debbie's Camaro must have had something to do with it.

Jimmy was on his way and I don't remember if Leee turned up at the loft or if we picked him up. What I do remember is that he wound up sitting in the back between Jimmy and me. Given Leee's predilection for handsome young men, it must have been a happy new year indeed. At one point he stretched his arms out along the top of the seat, a natural enough thing to do on a long drive. I don't know what was happening on Jimmy's end, but Leee's right hand must have found a comfortable spot on my shoulder, because it stayed there, indulging in less and less furtive squeezes for most of the ride.

I didn't mind too much. A year ago Ian Hunter had been one of my rock heroes, a role model even. Just how much damage I did to my eyes through emulating his dark glasses I'll probably never know. My hair reached its greatest length because of him. I had seen Mott the Hoople a year or so ago at the Uris Theatre on Broadway when their opening act was Queen. Mott's covers of 'All the Young Dudes' and 'Sweet

Jane', as well as originals like 'Violence' and 'All the Way to Memphis' were favorites. I liked Ian Hunter's lyrics and even thought he was a more 'serious' songwriter than Bowie.

I thought there would be a party at his house, but when we arrived I was surprised to find that, aside from a couple friends, we were the only guests. It was my first really close encounter with a rock star, and the first thing I noticed was that he *did* wear his dark glasses indoors. I had opted out of wearing mine, thinking that would be like visiting Richard Hell in a ripped T-shirt.

After some drinks we wound up in the basement, where Ian had set up a small recording studio. He must have done pretty well for himself, although I don't think Mott the Hoople had been that successful in the States. But it was a large house and the studio was well equipped: he had a piano, several amps and a drum kit. After more drinks he asked if we wanted to play. He sat at the piano; Chris picked up a guitar. I'm not sure if Debbie joined in or what Jimmy did. I sat at the drums. We diddled around on a few basics, and then Ian mentioned a new song he was working on, 'All American Alien Boy'. I gathered he was experiencing some problems with American immigration and was getting his frustration out in song.

I was gobsmacked. Here I was, jamming with a rock and roll hero in his own home on one of his brand new songs. I was playing drums in his studio, and there he was, a few feet away from me, that mane of wild hair cascading over his shades. After that, the fact that Leee continued to fondle me on the long ride back to the city was negligible.

▶▶

The six weeks Clem spent in England turned Blondie from a well-liked but hardly respectable garage band into a serious act. Six days a week Jimmy, Chris, Debbie and I got together and worked on new material. Blondie was never an innovative band, nor were we ever an art rock group – Chris and Debbie's later pronouncements aside. There wasn't a concept; we just remembered those few years in the 1960s when it seemed nearly impossible to turn on the radio and hear a bad song. We didn't want to bring back the sixties, we wanted to come up with songs that were that good. Songs you could hear once, and walk away humming. Songs with hooks.

Hits.

Sitting at a table one night at Max's, I thought I heard one.

I got up, rushed back to the loft and picked up a guitar. The next day I had the chorus, melody, hook and the lyrics for the chorus. I played it for Debbie. She asked if I had lyrics for the verses. Not yet.

'Let me have a try,' she said.

All during this time, I was still returning to New Jersey for court appearances. The rape case went on for several months. At one point I arranged to take a blood test in order to prove – or disprove – paternity. But when I arrived at the clinic I had to cancel. I didn't realize I'd have to pay for it and had no money. Eventually, after Zelda's mother failed to appear in court several times, the charges were dropped. It wasn't my intention to write an autobiographical song about my experience with Zelda, but for some reason Debbie took that as a theme. According to her the song was about 'a poor kid' who had 'a sixteen-year-old girlfriend who was a hooker. He had fallen under her influence and she had gotten knocked up when he was seventeen.'* Zelda wasn't a hooker, but the essentials are correct. The 'poor kid' was me

---

* Debbie Harry, Chris Stein and Victor Bockris, *Making Tracks: The Rise of Blondie* (New York, Dell Books, 1982) p. 26.

and the song was 'Sex-Offender', later changed by Richard
Gottehrer to 'X-Offender'.

Six months after I wrote it, it would get us a record deal.

When Clem returned from England we threw a party for
him at the loft. It turned out to be the first big punk social
event of 1976.

More people came than to any of our gigs. One was
Nancy Spungen. I didn't know her well, but I had seen
Nancy around at the clubs, and we talked a few times. It
always struck me that she wasn't well liked, not even by
herself. The next time I remember seeing her was a year later,
in London, at the Music Machine, by which time she had
picked up an English accent. A year and a half later she
was dead, and her boyfriend Sid was in jail, charged with her
murder.

Another character at the Blondie party was Neon Leon,
reportedly the last person aside from Sid to see Nancy alive.
Neon Leon had a band. They really weren't considered a
serious part of the scene but they did have a blonde bass
player, whose name, I think, was Cathy.

I was introduced to Cathy by Anya Philips at another
party, this one on Greenwich Street in the West Village. She
was sexy in an obvious Jayne Mansfield kind of way. She
wore low-cut leopard skin tops and very tight jeans, and I
think she worked as a topless dancer somewhere in Times
Square. Sex-starved and twenty, I was taken with her charms.
At the same party some people turned up later, saying Jerry
Nolan had just been taken to St Vincent's Hospital after
some drunk had shoved a broken bottle into his groin.

Cathy was at the Blondie party that night too. As
was Lisa. We hadn't committed to each other yet, and
I was interested in getting to know Cathy a little better.
Lisa twigged that this was the case and asked if I wanted
to come back to her studio. I didn't. She got the message

and left. The party was in full swing. Clem had brought back the first Dr Feelgood album and it was a hit. We kept playing it over and over and everyone loved it. The place was packed with the cream of New York punk – Hell, Thunders, the Ramones, Talking Heads, Suicide – except for Patti Smith and Tom Verlaine, who inhabited a rarified atmosphere of art and snobbishness and didn't mix much with the rest of the bands.

Meanwhile, Cathy had told me about a box of comic books at her place that she didn't want anymore. She wondered if I was interested in them. Benton, who had seen Lisa leave, quickly figured out why she had. It was obvious he disapproved of my philandering. After a few more gazes at Cathy's ample décolletage, I told her that yes, I *would* be interested in seeing those comic books.

'How about now?' she said.

Good idea, I thought, and said let's go.

When Benton noticed we were leaving. He came over to me.

'Are you going home with that *girl*?' he said, in a particularly nasty way.

'Yes.'

'Well make sure you get those comic books!'

▶▶

At the beginning of 1976, both *Punk* magazine and *New York Rocker* started publishing.

Punk was the brainchild – or brain-dead child, depending on your tastes – of John Holstrom and Legs McNeil. Before its release, flyers plastered all over the East Village announced 'Punk is Coming'. Most people thought this meant just another band from New Jersey, tring to cash in on the scene. It proved to be another sort of johnny-come-lately. CBGB had been in full swing for at least six months before *Punk* saw the light of day. *Punk* had a boorish wit a few notches below that of its mentor, *Mad*. It was also highly selective. Where *New York Rocker* covered *all* the music coming out of CBGB and Max's, *Punk* specialized in a fanatically narrow canon of hard core punk bands: the Ramones, Richard Hell, the Dead Boys and the Dictators.

These last two were latecomers to the scene. Like Holstrom and McNeil, both flirted with a nasty brand of right wing sensibility. Also like Holstrom and McNeil, they were into getting very fucked up and acting stupid.

The Dictators were an upstate New York band that had released an album even earlier than Patti Smith, *The Dictators Go Girl Crazy*, on Epic. Their themes, like those of Cleveland's Dead Boys, were mother's milk to McNeil and Holstrom: booze, cars, cheap sex, junk food and volume. The Dictators' first offering fell dead in the water in 1975, and they found themselves without a label. It wasn't until the summer of 1976 that they started playing CBGB.

The Dead Boys didn't arrive until that summer either, decked out in swastikas and iron crosses, reeking of the MC5 and Alice Cooper. By that time the 'fuck art, let's rock' mentality had blossomed, symbolized by Hell's departure from the Heartbreakers earlier that spring. (More on this shortly.) This left an increasingly numbed Thunders in full control – after a fashion – and an exodus of many of the original audience.*

Although the Dictators weren't my cup of tea, I didn't mind them too much and we even did a few shows with them. But the Dead Boys were another story. I just thought they were stupid. Their original material was minimal, and they pandered to a mostly out-of-town crowd with rock's

---

* Thunders' heroin intake, heavy to begin with, soon became legendary, earning him the sobriquet of the 'Dean Martin of junk'.

lowest common denominator: excess. Their biggest claim to
fame is that Stiv Bators, lead singer and Iggy Pop clone, got
a blow job on stage at CBGB. To me they were the first sign
of the mental dry rot that would arrive in full with UK bands
like the Damned. With *Punk* and the Dead Boys, the end of
the New York scene had started. The shades of Rimbaud
were gone.

Punk was divisive in another way. As with the Warhol
crowd a generation earlier, you were cool if you were in, and
not cool if you weren't.

Debbie and Chris, it turned out, were determined to be
cool.

New York Rocker was another story. Alan Betrock was a
true pop fanatic. Unlike *Punk* he had no axe to grind and
wasn't partisan. His basic aim was to spread the word about
what was happening on the Bowery, wise record companies
up to the new music, and get these bands *signed*. He had
certainly been on the scene much longer than Holstrom and
McNeil. Alan had written for the *Soho Weekly News* and
had put out his own magazine, *The Rock Marketplace*.
He had seen Television in its early stages and had been at
Club 82. His motivation for putting out *New York Rocker*
was, I think, love; I'm not sure he ever made a dime from it.

For the first year of its existence – a run of eleven issues –
Alan staunchly sang the praises of the bands making the
rounds of CBGB and Max's. When he left as editor, both
the scene in New York and the ambience of the new music in
general had changed. By the spring of 1977, all of the first
wave CBGB bands had record deals and had more or less
left the nest. The vacuum was filled by a new generation of
bands, whose central influence was the punk flowing over
from the UK. The atmosphere at CBs had changed. A harder
more aggressive sensibility surfaced, carried in by out-of-
towners decorated with safety pins. When Andy Schwartz

took over in April of 1977, the front cover was dedicated to the Clash, the first time a non New York band had a cover photo.

In its early days, *New York Rocker* was as much a fanzine as *Punk*. With one difference: the fans writing for it were often members of the bands being written about, a step up from filling in as each others' audiences. For the first issue Debbie wrote a piece on the Miamis, while Tommy and Jimmy Wynbrandt – Tommy and Jimmy Miami – wrote a piece on us. A passionate piece about the Heartbreakers was penned by one half of a briefly revived Theresa Stern. In it, Richard Hell shows he has no qualms about patting his own back: 'Hell is that master rock conceptualist . . .' At the time there was more coverage on what was happening in New York written by correspondents for the UK publications *NME*, *Melody Maker* and *Sounds*, than by *Rolling Stone*, *Crawdaddy* or *Creem*, so he could be excused some home grown propaganda.

I was biased toward *New York Rocker* in another way as one of its writers from the beginning was Lisa Persky. It also gave ample coverage to yet another incident in my 'year of living dangerously'.

►►

In February 1976, the new and improved Blondie made its debut at CBGB. Hilly's sanctions against us were lifted. We headlined the St Valentine's Day weekend, with the Miamis as openers. Actually, we split the support duties, but to headline at least one night at CBGB was a major breakthrough for us.

We debuted our new material. This was a real step ahead, but it also proved another wedge in the crack opening between Chris, Debbie and me. All of the new material got good response: 'In the Sun', 'Rip Her to Shreds', 'Look

Good in Blue'. But one of the best received songs of the new set was 'Sex-Offender'. This just happened to be a song on which I played guitar instead of Chris. I also played guitar on another new song of mine, 'Scenery'. Naturally, Chris wasn't very happy with this.

Chris was an interesting guitarist, but he was never very together on stage. He had a tendency to crack under pressure. He would throw tantrums, yell and scream, and often become violent. One time at the loft he completely lost it and destroyed a coffee table. I can't remember what we were talking about. We were sitting on a rickety old couch we had found in the trash, and Chris became enraged and started slamming the coffee table with his foot, over and over. He pounded on it like a hammer, went red in the face and slammed the thing until it collapsed. This was only one incident. After these fits, Debbie would pull me aside and remind me that Chris was, after all, 'a genius'.

The CBGB debut a success, the natural thing was to repeat it at Max's. We booked a gig at the end of the month. It was a leap year. The date was 29 February, a Sunday night. I don't remember who the support was, but at the time that was the least of our worries. The Friday night before the show, Clem, Benton and I were arrested and put in jail. We weren't let out until a half-hour before our soundcheck.

That was a close call. The fact that the arresting officer almost killed me was a minor inconvenience.

A friend of Benton's, a crazed individual called Mike at the Mike, a schizophrenic who thought he was a stand-up comic – Benton was always bringing home weirdos – had landed a part in a production of *The Tempest*. I think he was Caliban. Benton invited Clem and me to a performance. I don't remember much about the production, but I think we felt relief when it was over. As soon as we got outside, one of us lit a joint.

To smoke grass in public in New York back then was not unusual. Many people did, and there was little trouble. The police had more important things to do and most people were adequately discreet. We casually took a few puffs and walked down the street, thinking nothing of it.

Suddenly I heard a maniacal voice shrieking, 'No! No! This can't happen! Not in my neighborhood!' Then some madman was trying to clap a pair of handcuffs on me, an off-duty policeman who lived on that street.

I had no idea he was a policeman and fought him off. He chased me into the street. A crowd gathered. Benton and Clem looked on, uncertain what to do. I called for help. The cop grabbed me again and I hit back. He threw me into some trash cans, lifted me up, and threw me to the asphalt. My head hit the street and everything went black and white. That black cloud I saw when I was electrocuted returned. This time it reached my forehead.

When I surfaced a few minutes later, a crowd of people were standing over me. I couldn't move, was barely conscious and couldn't speak. But I could hear. 'Is he all right?' 'Do you think he's an epileptic?' 'Should we stick a wallet in his mouth?' I thought I was in one of the Scientology adverts popular at the time, which showed a group of people standing around someone and asking him if he was 'all right'. The cop had radioed for backup and it arrived. Someone asked if I wanted to go to a hospital. I was coherent enough to realize that if I did I probably wouldn't see Benton or Clem again. I garbled out a 'No.' The next thing I knew I was wearing handcuffs, sitting next to the two of them in a police car heading for jail. We were in three different jails that weekend, entertained by New York's finest, charged with possession of a controlled substance, loitering and resisting arrest.

At the 10th precinct on 19th Street, the madman did his paperwork and we went through the usual routine: mugshots, fingerprints, statements. My head pounded from its recent meeting with West 18th Street, and I could barely talk and walk. Incredibly, not a single doctor looked at me. Then they took us to the 30th precinct, on 151st Street in Harlem, where we were finally put behind bars. By this time I couldn't see. The police had taken my glasses and refused to give me painkillers, suspecting that I might slit my wrists with the broken lenses or overdose on two Excedrin.

After spending the night in Harlem, on Saturday morning they took us to the Tombs on Centre Street, the depths of New York's jails. The other inhabitants of our cell were a gang of Puerto Rican kids who had obviously been through this wringer before. Benton was in his leather jacket, tight jeans and motorcycle boots. With his flowing blond mane and Southern drawl, he was hard to ignore. Clem was in his mod best. They took one look at us and said, 'These guys must be in a rock and roll band.' Clem kept up a mantra of, 'Shit man, this sucks,' with minor variations thereof, which Benton countered with his all-purpose maxim, 'Learn to love it.'

The cops didn't know what to make of us. One kept telling us that the protest days were over and suggested we go to auto mechanic school. Others made fag and hippie jokes. I was concerned that Benton might taunt one into enacting one of his masochistic Hell's Angels fantasies. The situation was grim. I told *New York Rocker*, 'We slept on wooden benches. You couldn't lay in one position for more than ten minutes. If you wanted a pillow you had to take off your coat. If you took off your coat you froze.'*

At one point Clem asked a black guy for a cigarette. The guy eyeballed him.

---

* 'Blondies Behind Bars' *New York Rocker* Vol. 1 No. 2, March 1976, p. 4.

'Hey man,' he said. 'You look like Mick Jagger. You want a cigarette? You gotta sing for it, man.'

Clem took a deep breath and let rip. 'I can't get no satisfaction, I can't get no . . .'

I didn't think he looked at all like Mick Jagger. Unbelievably, he got the smoke.

You see some strange things in jail. In the back of one cell, I noticed something odd. Crumpled up against the wall and obviously getting over a bad bout of smack, I saw a guy I knew from the third grade who had made a habit of beating me up. I reflected that there was some justice in the world after all.

We managed to reach Chris and Debbie and told them not to cancel the show until the last minute. As Saturday passed without a sign of a courtroom, it struck me that that last minute was approaching fast. On the Sunday of the show, we spent the day in a holding pen waiting to see the judge. Chris and Debbie had managed to get us a public defender. Finally, after watching everyone else have their day in court, we were brought out five minutes before the judge left for the day. The arresting officer admitted he had failed to identify himself as a policeman, and that was it. The case was thrown out, although we were put on six months' probation. Not a word about my skull being nearly cracked open. We went straight up to Max's for the soundcheck and later did the show.

▶▶

One of the people at Max's was Lisa. After my fling with Cathy we decided to be in a 'relationship'. As I hadn't been in a relationship before, I figured it meant she was my girlfriend, and I started spending a lot of time at her studio. After waking up a few times at the loft with cockroaches crawling over her, she thought it was better that way. In any case, there was more privacy there.

One of the first things I did in my new status as Lisa's boyfriend was go to a performance of a play she was in, *Women Behind Bars* by Tom Eyen. I didn't know what to expect. The only thing I knew was that the star, Divine, had made a name for himself in John Waters' classic trash film, *Pink Flamingos*, famous for its last scene when Divine scoops up a pile of dog shit and eats it. Later, when I got to know Divine, I asked him the obvious question. 'Yes,' he said. 'It really was shit.' Five years later, when I toured with Iggy Pop, I had an opportunity to confirm this. On the tour bus, one of Iggy's favourite videos was *Pink Flamingos*, and he played it constantly. I think Divine was telling the truth. It really was shit and he really did eat it.

The play was running at the Truck and Warehouse Theatre on East 4th Street, just up from Club 82, a few blocks from CBGB. After Club 82 and *Vain Victory*, I had some idea of camp theatre. Nevertheless, what I saw on stage was a surprise.

Women Behind Bars was a send-up of fifties women's prison films like *I Want To Live* and *I Wake Up Screaming*. Divine played the sadistic sexually voracious lesbian prison matron. Lisa was the innocent framed by the system – as well as by her boyfriend. I don't remember any redeeming social value, just a lot of bad jokes and raunchy gags. When Paul, Lisa's boyfriend for whom she has taken the rap, visits to make sure she won't give him away, he's attacked by the sex-starved inmates and orally gang raped. During a fight, a prisoner shouts a warning about a knife hidden away in a vagina, to which her friend replies, 'Don't worry, Cheri, I've got a twat blade too!'

But Lisa was in it, so I sat there open-minded. Her big

scene was up. Desolate and crying, she confides in the prison matron. Divine – eyebrows arching and with a knowing wink to the audience – 'consoles' the young thing. Frightened, alone, abandoned and innocent, Lisa succumbs to the lecherous matron's designs. She rapes her. Literally. Before I knew it, Lisa's clothes were torn off and her white skin was glaring in the footlights. And there was Divine, hulking over her with a broom handle. A similar scene happens later in the show. Twice nightly for the run of the production Lisa was naked and raped with a broom handle, usually to a packed house. Four times with matinées. By the end of the play, the sweet innocent is transformed into a hardened criminal. On her release she meets a gangster who sets her up for a heist. He grabs her breast. 'Not bad tit.' She grabs his crotch. 'Not bad cock.'

Within a few weeks everyone in Blondie had seen the show, as had many members of other bands. A couple months after we started going out, it seemed that practically everybody on the scene had seen my girlfriend naked. Twice, in fact. We were a hit. Lisa introduced me to Divine. We had lunch at his apartment and I met some of the other John Waters people: Mink Stole, Cookie Mueller, Van White (the makeup artist), Billy Edgar and David Lochary. Divine was friendly, warm and funny. One of his favourite sayings was, 'There are two kinds of people in the world. My kind of people and assholes.' We got to know him well enough to work together on a production of *Medea*. Lisa and I played the ill-fated children, with Benton as our tutor and Divine in the title role. We did it in yet another loft, this time on Bleecker Street and Broadway. What I remember most is Benton dragging us across the floor on our knees. He was a great believer in method acting. The scene was rehearsed several times. When I complained that my knees were beginning to hurt he snapped back, 'You're about to die. They're *supposed* to hurt!'

►►

Having a glamorous woman for a lead singer, it's under-standable that Blondie would have some gay fans. One time we played at a Gay Pride celebration on an outdoor stage on Christopher Street, near the piers. There was a massive crowd, thousands of people. The Village People were becom-ing huge at the same time – the summer of 1976 – and I remember many crazy costumes. We did the old sixties hit, 'Heat Wave', and it went over so well we had to do it again. I also remember Tony Ingrassia's displeasure when Jimmy and I declined to sign a petition for some gay cause or other. At a table on the corner of Christopher Street and Sheridan Square, Ingrassia spotted Jimmy and me walking by. He called us over, showed us the petition and asked us to sign. Jimmy and I looked at each other, then shook our heads. 'Sorry, Tony,' Jimmy said. 'We can't.'

Ingrassia looked at us in astonishment.

'Why not?'

'We don't want people to think we're gay,' Jimmy said as we ran off.

There was a reason for our not signing. After seeing one of our shows, a photographer friend told Benton that he wanted to photograph Jimmy and me. We thought that was perfectly normal; people were photographing us all the time. He came to the loft and shot us in one of the rooms upstairs. We wore our usual gear: tab collared shirts, skinny ties, black trousers. Then he handed us a couple leather jackets, real motorcycle stuff, lots of zippers and snaps, and took a few shots.

A couple days later, Benton showed us the prints. There we were in the leather jackets.

'You two look *fabulous*,' Benton said.

He was right. It *was* a good photo. Jimmy and I look about fifteen years old. I have my arms crossed against my chest, facing straight ahead, the belt looped tight around my waist, the short leather a snug fit. Jimmy is behind me, leaning slightly forward, a fringe of hair falling across his forehead, a striped polo shirt visible under his leather.

Jimmy asked what the photographer was going to do with them.

'I think he's selling this one to the *Advocate*.'

The *Advocate* was the biggest gay newspaper in New York.

Jimmy and I flipped.

'The *Advocate*! He can't do that! We'll be ruined!'

'Well, that's what he said.'

We got his telephone number. No answer. We got his address. He wasn't in. Frantic, we knew we had to catch him before our faces were plastered over the biggest gay magazine in town. We were twenty and had our careers to worry about. And I was practically living on Christopher Street. For the next couple days I was worried that I would suddenly become very popular in the neighborhood.

In the end it turned out to be a false alarm. We found the photographer and he assured us he wouldn't publish the photo without our consent; it was for his personal collection. Benton was having us on. But it scared us enough to avoid anything else that might give people the wrong idea.

▶▶

In the spring of 1976, the rivalry between CBGB and Max's started to hot up. Max's had its own event, the Easter Festival of New York Rock, which ran from 11 to 22 April.

Note that neither festival used the word 'punk'.

We did a Sunday night, opening for the Ramones. Debbie

introduced a little highbrow *schtick*, doing a rendition of Weill and Brecht's 'Bilboa Song' from *Happy End*. She also wore her famous zebra skin dress, which was really an old pillowcase Benton found in the trash. Stephen Sprouse got his hands on it and *voilà*, instant legend. A sabre-toothed necklace, heavy mascara and wild frizzy hair completed her jungle look.

Not all the regulars played. Television and the Miamis sat this one out. Talking Heads cancelled at the last minute, but enough showed to make it a real event. Besides Blondie and the Ramones there were the Heartbreakers, Suicide, the Marbles and, of course, Wayne County. Second-rung bands like the Planets, the Shirts, Honey Davis and John Collins filled the empty spaces. And Pere Ubu, along with Devo one of the more interesting bands to arrive from Ohio, made their New York debut. Later, when Max's, following Hilly's lead, released a compilation album of New York rock, the best track would turn out to be not by a New York group at all – although Suicide's 'Rocket USA' was a close second – but by Pere Ubu. 'Final Solution' is one of the classics of the time.

It was also at this festival that Richard Hell informed Johnny Thunders and Jerry Nolan that he was leaving the Heartbreakers. I saw their last show. Chris has the classic photograph of the night. Hell is in the dressing room, sitting forlornly on the ratty couch. Shades are on, cigarette is in hand, his bass leaning in a corner, a pout of petulant weariness looking into the void. After six months, the most exciting band of the scene was no more. It was a shame they were never properly recorded.

By the time of the Easter Festival, the A & R people had started to show up at CBGB and Max's. The Ramones had a deal with Sire at the beginning of the year. What a proper Heartbreakers album might have sounded like is something we'll never know. Maybe Hell realized that contracts were going to appear soon, and he admitted that what he really wanted was his own band. I couldn't blame him, although neither the Voidoids nor Johnny Thunders' Heartbreaker were half as interesting or powerful as Hell and Thunders together. When Hell left the Heartbreakers, it was the end of the 'art rock' union that had started with Patti Smith and Television two years earlier. Hell found Thunders and Nolan too 'brutish'. They thought Hell a poseur and egomaniac. Here was the second nail in the coffin of the golden age of New York Rock.

But if the scene was starting to mutate into its final phase, things were looking up for us. As with our 'new improved' debut at CBGB, we went over well at Max's. Well enough for Lisa – who was generally objective and not easily pleased – to give us a rave review in *New York Rocker*. According to her, at the Easter Festival, 'Another band's incubation period has ended and the award for the loveliest Easter Egg goes to Blondie.' Remarking that we had finally jettisoned the 'between song dreck', Lisa went on to comment that, 'all of Blondie did much to convince us that they are now deserving of more concrete recognition than they have so far received'.

Note the 'all'. This may be the first time the idea that Blondie was a group and not just a singer raised its contentious head. Among the five of us the understanding was that we were equal members of a band, *not* that we were a backup group for Debbie and Chris – although I did call them Ike and Tina from time to time. That the press would see this otherwise, we accepted. Anything to get in print. But we all contributed equally to the sound, the material and the look.

Around the same time we did a show for German television. A German actress named Gaby talked us into supporting her for a show at CBGB. We thought it was a bad idea at first. The songs she wanted to do were enough to make it unappealing. The Stones' 'Starfucker' was one. But then she mentioned the money. Suddenly it seemed a good idea. The crew set up and shot us backing her and Debbie as they went through a few numbers. What I remember most about it is getting cramp in one hand, and my fingers freezing up as I played. In between songs, Gaby – who was actually very attractive – massaged my digits rather skilfully. Lisa, who was in the audience, didn't care for that, although after the business with the broom she should have been the last one to say anything. I never saw the video and have no idea what it looked like or what may have happened to Gaby.

The biggest event around this time was the New York Party on 30 May 1976 at the Manhattan Centre in aid of Wayne County's Legal Defense Fund, after his notorious fracas with the Dictators' 'Handsome' Dick Manitoba. More than anything else, this briefly divided the New York scene into Max's people and CBGB people. At the center of it was Handsome Dick's broken collarbone, and Wayne County's bruised ego.

There are varying accounts of what happened. I wasn't at Wayne's show at CBs that night, so I'm not an eyewitness, but I heard all the stories at the time. To this day, Wayne maintains he was provoked beyond reason; Dick claims Wayne attacked him.

According to Wayne, Handsome Dick started heckling his show, calling him 'drag queen', 'queer' and other assorted names. Wayne invited him to come up on stage and say it to his face. Dick obliged and got up, holding a beer mug. Wayne knew Handsome Dick had been a wrestler and was, understandably, worried. He says he was sure Dick was going to attack him, so Wayne made a pre-emptive strike. He grabbed his mic-stand and swung it down on Dick's collarbone.

The mic-stand had a heavy circular metal base.

When Wayne heard Dick's collarbone crack, he was worried. Dick reeled back and hit his head on a table. A few seconds later he was back on stage, fighting with Wayne. Wayne, by the way, *was* in drag, and his clothes and wig were wet with Dick's blood. He was, by his own account, high on amphetamine.

In his book, *Man Enough to Be a Woman*, Wayne claims that Handsome Dick heckled us the night before, calling Debbie a slut. It's possible, but I don't remember. In any case, Wayne's band kicked into the next number as Wayne kicked into Dick, until finally an ambulance came and took Handsome Dick away.

It became a cause célèbre. The *Village Voice* ran a piece with the heading 'Mad Drag Queen Attacks Poor Defenseless Wrestler'. The gay mafia struck back with vindictive articles attacking Dick – probably the first and last time they ever did. Wayne claims he went to his job as DJ at Max's dressed in a wig, moustache and beard, hoping to fool the cops, who had a warrant for him. It didn't work. They found him and brought him down to the Tombs. Remembering my own experience there, I didn't envy him. I wasn't that fond of Wayne's act – although he *did* do a classic Patti Smith pastiche – but I liked him. At least he was always nice to me. And I knew that Handsome Dick and a lot of the *Punk* crowd had a nasty, almost gay-bashing mentality. But I think Wayne could have handled it with more tact. If you're going to break the collarbone of every drunk that heckles you, you're going to wind up with a lot of hospital bills.

Aside from Wayne being arrested and Dick spending time in hospital, the major effect of this incident was to divide the scene. You were either Wayne's friend or Dick's. Although we had no beef with the Dictators, it was prudent to be Wayne's friend. After all, his manager booked Max's.

In any case, the New York Party was the biggest punk gathering so far.

It was held at the Manhattan Center on 34th Street and

8th Avenue. The participants were an amalgam of the punk and camp worlds that were more or less Wayne's milieu. Aside from Blondie, there were Richard Hell, Thunders, Nolan and Walter Lure – the four Heartbreakers – untogether again for the first time. Dee Dee Ramone made an appearance for the Ramones; Joey wouldn't perform because he was a friend of Handsome Dick. Mink DeVille, Tuff Darts and Suicide also turned up. On the campy side were Jackie Curtis, Cherry Vanilla and Holly Woodlawn. Divine and the cast of *Women Behind Bars* also performed. This marked the first and only time that Lisa and I shared a stage. What I remember most about the show is that at the same time there was a massive Sun Myung Moon meeting at a hotel down the street. Getting to the Manhattan Center, we saw a tremendous crowd pouring down the block. I thought, Wow! Wayne's really drawn some support. Then I saw the banners and the Moonies. But there was a decent crowd for Wayne, even though he didn't pull in enough money to cover his legal expenses. What those expenses might have been, I don't know, as Handsome Dick eventually dropped the charges. No one got a party together to help cover Dick's medical expenses.

Later, a lot of people, Blondie included, apologized to Dick for supporting Wayne, who really wasn't the victim he claimed to be. Strangely, the bad press helped the Dictators, who started playing at CBGB not too long after the event, and then landed their second recording contract. Leee Black Childers – who became the Heartbreakers' manager after Hell quit – took Thunders and Co. to London toward the end of 1976. Old ties are rarely broken. Leee phoned Peter Crowley and told him that he had to get Wayne over there. Peter did, and Wayne was one of the first New York rockers to get a taste of what was cooking across the Atlantic. Pretty soon the rest of us would find out, but by the summer of 1976, we had a lot else on our minds.

7. SO YOU WANNA BE A
ROCK 'N' ROLL STAR?

One of the things to hit the Bowery in the summer of 1976 was angel dust. For about a month, smoking PCP was the new hip thing to do.

Chris liked it. He told me it enhanced his telepathic powers. Gave him ESP. One of the cats, he said, was really Chairman Mao.

That would be Chairman Meow, then, wouldn't it?

Chris was so keen on angel dust that he brought a few joints of it to CBGB one night, told everyone it was grass and got a lot of people blasted. It was his idea of a joke, like dosing people on acid without them knowing. They didn't know what to expect and a few weren't taken with Chris's sense of humor.

I had a puff one night at the loft. It was probably the most gruesome two hours of my life. I felt someone had emptied a vacuum cleaner into my brain. I tried to play the piano but couldn't remember how to move my fingers. The worst thing was when I looked at Debbie. She had smoked some too, more than me. She smiled. She looked like a skeleton. I saw her face, but it was a skull. That was bad enough. But the smile was worse; it meant she liked the stuff. How anyone could enjoy this was beyond me. I had somehow entered hell and it was a very dirty place and was thankful when the shit wore off.

Benton was another devotee. For some reason he really got into it and for a while it threw him into the deep end. This was when the urine business really got out of hand. The Coke bottles were piling up. He'd be in his room for days. His biker boyfriend joined him and brought his two Irish setters. The dogs got a whiff of the piss and like the cats started shitting and pissing. By this time Stephen Sprouse had vacated the top floor. Benton's Hell's Angels fantasies began to escalate and in some PCP-induced ecstasy he smashed a full-length mirror in his room. He just left it. The shards remained on the floor, reflecting the chaos overtaking the loft. Benton and his boyfriend decided to leave the second floor and move upstairs. One day, when the angel dust had really settled into them, Benton's boyfriend made his way to the roof and began to scream his lungs out. He had visions. He went on for hours and we were worried that he might prove violent. But the crisis passed and he just crashed out.

Benton's tarrying with the angels was more costly. Whether it happened by chance or by design, dusted out of his brains he found himself on East 3rd Street, the Hell's Angels block. Literally, they owned the street. A row of choppers stretched from Second to First Avenue. I generally avoided the vicinity. Like most wild animals, they kept to themselves unless provoked.

Benton, I think, provoked them.

In any case, he didn't walk down East 3rd Street for a while.

They beat him. Badly. I came back to the loft one afternoon and stopped by his room. He had curled up in his lair to lick his wounds. His face was black and blue, his eyes puffed and swollen. He looked as if someone had stuck a bicycle pump under his skin and inflated him.

The whole atmosphere at the loft changed after that. We

still had a couple months to go. But by the end of that summer, Blondie would move on.

I was spending a lot more time at Lisa's studio on Christopher Street. *Women Behind Bars* was still going strong and Lisa continued to write for *New York Rocker*. She interviewed the Ramones, Suicide and the Miamis, and wrote a piece on Jonathan Richman's show at the Town Hall. By this time Jonathan had dropped the garage punk sound of the first Modern Lovers album and had got onto his health food kick, singing songs like 'Here Come the Martian Martians' wearing gym trunks and a sweatshirt. When *Women Behind Bars* did a run in Washington, DC, Lisa reviewed some of the local talent. *New York Rocker* also used a lot of her photographs.

I got to know more people through Lisa, like Lance Loud of the Mumps. Lance had become nationally famous a few years back when he announced on television that he was gay. His family was the subject of a documentary series, *An American Family*. The crew set up their cameras in the home of the Loud family of Santa Barbara, California, and filmed them for a year. The idea was to capture an 'average' American family as it went about its day-to-day business. Either the selection process picked absolutely the wrong family, or the Louds were indicative of an average more exceptional than the makers expected. Along with Lance announcing his homosexuality, during the program his father's drinking problem became apparent and he and Lance's mother broke up. Lance took advantage of his notoriety, headed to New York and started the Mumps. Around the time she met me, Lisa had been dating their guitarist, Rob DuPrey. One night at CBGB, Rob cornered Lisa and asked who it was: him or me. It turned out to be me. Rob was angry, but we soon became friends. He was a great guitarist and I became a big Mumps fan and, after that,

Blondie and the Mumps played together often. Lance was never a very strong lead singer, but they had witty songs and were more musical than most of the other bands. Their intelligence probably worked against them and, like the Miamis, the Mumps are another of the great unsung bands of the golden age of CBGB.

Lisa's studio was in a perfect location. On warm summer nights, we'd walk across town on Bleecker Street, past the Pink Tea Cup and John's Pizzeria, Bleecker Bob's record shop, the Bitter End, the Village Gate and other famous folk-bars, cross McDougal Street not far from where Bob Dylan had lived, pass Mercer Street and the old headquarters of the yippies and finally arrive at the Bowery and CBs. We never had a lot of money. Everyone was just getting by and we lived on very little. Clem and Jimmy lived at home and so always had a meal, but the rest of us had to struggle. Debbie made jewelry, soldering pieces of stained glass on to belt buckles for fifty cents a shot. Chris still collected his disability money, so he was a little better off. I did some temp work and made my share of the pittance we collected at gigs last as long as possible.

Lisa and I were known as a couple and would run into people everywhere. In September of 1976, *Phonograph Record*, one of the few non-scene magazines to pick up on what was happening in New York, ran a ten-page feature on 'New York Street Bands'. (It still wasn't called punk.) In the 'Layman's Guide to the Who's Who of the New York Underground Kingdom' – listed alphabetically – Lisa and I clock in at number 42: 'A Guinevere/actress/critic and a Lancelot Blondie-bassist comprise the scene's favourite love birds.'* One of our favourite things was to head to the photo booths at Times Square and take dozens of shots of ourselves

---

* *Phonograph Record*, September 1976, p. 32.

wearing sunglasses, turtlenecks or skinny ties, kissing or trying our best to strike artistic poses. We haunted second-hand clothes shops, hunting for anything faintly mod, jackets with narrow lapels, pointy-toed shoes. One time we hit a gold mine: in Hoboken, just across the Hudson in New Jersey, we found a shop that had what seemed like an endless supply of old peg-legged trousers, skinny ties and tab collar shirts in paisley and polka dots. They were just sitting in the back room, still in their wrappers, and the shop was letting them go for practically nothing. We'd head to the Path train and spend a morning rifling through the inventory. We built up a collection of sixties accouterments: my *Man From U.N.C.L.E.* badge, a Batman tie, 007 cufflinks, Beatle boots, Ray Bans. I tracked down albums by the Seeds, Beau Brummels and Zombies, collected comics and ransacked bookstores – places like the Strand and the old Weisers Occult Bookshop at Cooper Union. My interest in magic had grown and I was studying it very seriously. We were twenty. It was fun.

Lisa had some curious neighbors. The window in her bathroom opened onto an airshaft and when you were inside you could hear voices from the other apartments. One character was convinced that the CIA had installed a radio in his head and was transmitting messages to him, telling him what to do. You'd hear him say 'Fucking CIA! Don't want no radio in my head. Fucking CIA!' That could go on for hours. Another neighbor we thought was screwing his dog, although thankfully we never saw him in the act. The dog's name was Koloo and we'd hear the neighbor saying 'Koloo, Koloo, Koloo' with increasing intensity and frequency. He'd work himself up to a frenzy, then cap it off with a long breathy groan. This seemed to happen practically every day. Eventually Lisa and I heard it so often we forgot about it, although we did wonder about the poor dog.

A friend we made at this time was John Browner, who a

couple years later would write the first punk rock crime novel, *Death of a Punk*. He was a friend of Rob's, a great fan of the Miamis, and shared our taste in clothing. John soon became another member of the growing skinny tie brigade. People started picking up our look and pretty soon at all the Blondie shows we'd see a roomful of people dressed like us. It got to the point where'd there'd be two crowds at CBs: people in torn jeans and leather jackets, there to see the Ramones, and people in black suits and skinny ties, to see Blondie. The band who would open for anybody was developing a following of its own.

Two very dedicated fans were a couple of very nice but not altogether brilliant guys from the Bronx named, improbably, Vinnie and Tony. They saw us one night, immediately fell in love with Debbie, and wanted to manage us. Not for a minute did Debbie seriously consider the offer, but she appreciated their efforts and attention, as well as the assorted treats the two very liberally bestowed upon us. They actually did do a few practical things – took out advertisements for our shows, even had buttons made up – but their intentions were doomed from the start. Vinnie and Tony were so besotted with Debbie that they ignored her when she told them that they weren't the right managers for the band. They just wouldn't take no for an answer, and Debbie didn't press the point. They were out of their depth, like two characters from a Woody Allen film, but they were persistent.

One night they threw a party for us at their apartment in the Bronx. When we got there they had dozens of balloons stuck to the walls. After drinks they handed us darts and told us to throw them at the balloons. It was a party game; there were little party favors in the balloons. We each took some darts and had a go. Pop! I hit a balloon, and picked up what was inside. It turned out to be a quarter gram of cocaine inside a small paper packet. I threw another dart. Pop! There was a chunk of hash. Pop! Some quaaludes. Pop! More coke. Pop!

Pretty soon everyone's darts were flying and we were bumping into each other, trying to get at what hit the floor. Like kids with Pokémon cards, we wound up trading with each other. I wasn't keen on quaaludes and swapped mine with Chris and Debbie for their hash.

►►

Craig Leon had been hanging out at CBs as early as the summer of 1975. He worked A & R for Sire Records, Seymour Stein's label, and was good at his job. Seymour was looking for new blood and sent Craig out to talent scout. Craig had heard about Patti Smith and headed down to the Bowery to see what all the excitement was about. He soon found out.

One band that particularly excited him was the Ramones. He reported back to Seymour that he just had to sign them. They would, he said, be the next Bay City Rollers. It's incredible, but a band that practically every rock historian puts with hard core punk bands like Iggy and the MC5 actually thought of themselves as the new Beatles, or at least the new Herman's Hermits.

Seymour didn't know. He wasn't sure that what he had heard on stage at CBGB could be translated onto vinyl. And if it could, whether the kids would go for it. Craig persisted. It took a while but eventually, in January 1976, the Ramones signed with Sire Records. The fact that Craig promised Seymour that he could bring an album in within a week at next to nothing may have been a deciding factor. Anxious to get his hand in on some producing, Craig labored at capturing the Ramones' Chinese wall of sound at night after taking care of his A & R duties during the day. Craig was as good as his word. Like the Ramones' songs themselves, their time in the studio was exceedingly short. Seven days after they started, they had an album.

A few months later, *The Ramones* burst on an unsuspecting – and generally unimpressed – public. Even *New York Rocker* gave it only a fair to middling review. The production, it thought, was rushed, the sound unfinished. But the important thing had happened. A CBGB band was signed and had released an album. Pandora's box was open. Now was the time of the great punk gold rush.

Seymour was undaunted by the lukewarm reaction to the Ramones' debut. The mid seventies were still a time when record labels would work with fledgling groups, helping them through their adolescence. Sire was a new company and Seymour had visions of it becoming *the* New York rock label. He put out feelers to all the bands. Television were courted, but passed when it was clear that Seymour couldn't provide the kind of advance Verlaine was looking for. Other bands were less demanding. Eventually, Sire nabbed the Talking Heads and Richard Hell.

But during the months that Seymour was dithering about signing the Ramones, another player got in on the act.

Marty Thau had already had a brush with the scene via the New York Dolls. Before the Ramones signed with Sire, Marty convinced them to do a single with him. Nothing came of it, and the Ramones ended up with Seymour. But according to Marty, his old friend Jerry Nolan gave him a ring one day and told him that he should check out some of the other bands at CBs. Marty did. Jerry was right; something was happening down on the Bowery. Then Marty had a bright idea. After failing to get Seymour Stein interested in an act he was working with, Marty decided to call Seymour's partner, Richard Gottehrer. Richard had been in a sixties group, the Strangeloves, and made a name for himself as the composer of the Angels' sixties hit 'My Boyfriend's Back'.

He had also produced another sixties top ten number, 'Hang on Sloopy', by the McCoys. By the mid seventies he had done some recording with progressive groups like Focus and Renaissance. When Marty telephoned, Richard was working with a Scottish bagpipe player.

He had also split from Sire Records and was looking for a new partner.

Marty thought he would clue Richard in to what was happening. He also told him to forget about the bagpipes.

Marty's original idea was to do a live album, capturing the best of the Bowery sound at its source. This notion came to him in spring 1976. Through no fault of Thau's, the eventual product, *Live At CBGB*, turned out to be a disaster. By the time it was recorded, during the month-long second CBGB Underground Rock Festival 5 August to 6 September, most of the top groups had already secured contracts and their tracks – which were of top quality and represented a high moment in CBs history – couldn't be used. What remained were a string of second-rung acts that had nothing to do with the scene and good groups like the Miamis who were adversely affected by the bad reviews the double album generated. None of the bands that had made CBGB what it was appeared. No Television, no Talking Heads, no Richard Hell – and no Blondie.

When Marty Thau eventually got Gottehrer to take a look at what was happening at 315 Bowery, Richard was surprisingly impressed. True, the musicianship was amateurish, the material rough, but it had that indefinable something that is the secret ingredient of good rock and roll. When Richard saw that his ex-partner Seymour was scooping up some of the better acts at CBGB, he decided that if he wanted to be a part of this, he had better act fast. Instantly, as a matter of fact.

Pretty soon after his first visit to CBGB, with Marty Thau

and Craig Leon, Gottehrer formed his own production company, Instant Records. One of the few who were left out of Seymour's initial foray into CBs was Richard Hell. In June 1976, Hell signed with Instant Records, who eventually sold Seymour on adding Richard to his list.

Next in line was us.

Twenty-five years on, exactly how we wound up signing with Instant Records is a bit hazy, but no doubt Gottehrer's history with girl groups had something to do with it. Debbie was like the Shirelles and Ronettes rolled into one and 'Sex-Offender' had 'AM hit' written all over it. I had wanted to write a song like the ones I had grown up listening to, and I did. By the time Thau brought Gottehrer down to see us, we had built up a big following, unbelievable considering the handful of friends who made up the Blondie camp just six months before. Skinny ties and polka dots bounced amid the dog shit and broken bottles. I was pogoing up on stage, something that eventually got on Chris and Debbie's nerves.

'Sex-Offender' was the last number in the set, and people waited for it. Clem would start up the beat while Chris and I exchanged guitars. I grabbed his Stratocaster and then, remembering a tag I used to hear on the radio when I was a kid, would say, 'And the hits just keep on coming!' Then Clem would break into a roll and I'd hit the opening E chord.

Gottehrer loved it. He told Marty Thau. Thau met with Debbie and Blondie had a recording contract. Leon and Gottehrer came down to the loft to work with us in some pre-recording sessions. It was then that Richard convinced us to change 'Sex' to 'X'. He also neatened up a couple lyrics and added Debbie's spoken intro which, I have to admit, I've never liked. No matter. In June of 1976, we were in the studio, recording 'X-Offender' and a song of Chris's 'In the Sun'.

We recorded our first single at Plaza Sound Studios in

Radio City Music Hall, around the corner from Rockefeller Center, in the heart of Manhattan. Craig Leon produced. Gleaming glass skyscrapers, wide open plazas and gushing fountains were the backdrop. For a band that spent most of its time stepping over winos, this was an improvement. For myself, it was a kind of triumph. A little more than a year ago I was trying to get to these office buildings on time so I could pocket the subway token.

The studio had a impressive pedigree. It was built for Igor Stravinsky and was suspended from the rest of the structure so that it was virtually vibration free. This meant that a whole orchestra could play without the sound reaching the Music Hall below. The Rockettes rehearsed their routines nearby in a similar room. I used to see them on my way to recording sessions, cramming into the elevator in my shades and skinny tie with four or five dancers all done up in flamboyant revealing costumes. In between takes we would head to the roof of the Music Hall, and look out on the crowds on Sixth Avenue. It was fantastic. Everyone was excited. We'd dress up for the sessions as if we were playing a gig. Lisa came and took photographs. Clem and I could barely believe our luck, and ran around the rooms pretending to be the Beatles.

Craig wanted to get a Phil Spector effect, and this meant creating a massive wall of sound. He also wanted to get as authentic a 'surf' feel for my guitar as he could. He set up my amplifier at the end of a long hall, way out of the studio, and cranked up the volume, making the guitar sound as if it were recorded in a cavern. Chris was unhappy about playing bass, groaned most of the time and threw temper tantrums. But 'In the Sun' turned out well too.

Everyone was impressed with the results. Marty and Richard decided that instead of putting the single out as an independent release, they would sell it to an established label.

What we needed was someone with national distribution who specialized in singles and could get the record on to the radio and into the shops. Private Stock was a Top Forty company, whose big gun was Frankie Valli, ex-lead singer of the Four Seasons, a nauseatingly innocuous quartet with a string of sixties hits. He also happened to own a big chunk of the company. Marty knew Howard Rosen, who was the director of promotion for Private Stock. He called Rosen and said he had something to play for him. Thirty-five listens later, Rosen conceded that 'X-Offender' had a hook something like Bruce Springsteen's 'Born to Run', and concluded that it could work. A short time later, the first Blondie single appeared, on a label that had made its name with MOR hits. So much for punk rock.

When 'X-Offender' came out, everyone was amazed, especially us. No one who heard it could believe this was Blondie. Wayne County played it constantly at Max's. It was on the jukebox at CBGB. Other bands congratulated me. Lisa and I must have listened to it a hundred times. I gave copies away to her mother, her father, friends, auto-graphing singles left and right. I saw it in shops like Bleecker Bob's on Bleecker Street and Human Being on Second Avenue. It got radio airplay in New York and points west. Rodney Bingenheimer from KROQ in Los Angeles played it over and over again and telephoned Debbie in New York to tell her how much he liked it. *New York Rocker* gave copies of it away as a subscription offer. We started to get more magazine coverage as well, with *Creem* featuring Debbie in their 'Creem Dream' centerfold, and some good reviews in the English press. What everyone had fantasized about was starting to happen. We were becoming rock stars.

But although 'X-Offender' achieved cult status, and was bought by punk rockers in the US and UK, it failed to break into the Top Forty, putting us in the tradition of the New

York Dolls and the Ramones as a band with great promise but as yet little financial return. The deal Marty Thau had made with Private Stock gave them an option to do an album. Normally, if a first effort fails, a record company hesitates to throw more money at the band, but the single had cost a pittance and we received practically no advance, so Private Stock could easily write off the expense. There was also enough of a buzz about the new music to suggest that somebody out of CBGB was going to hit big. Recording an album with us wouldn't cost much. Private Stock decided to do it, but first one of their shareholders had to check out the product.

In the summer of 1976, punk rock met easy listening when Frankie Valli walked into CBGB and listened to one of our sets. We even did a Four Seasons number for the show, 'Big Man in Town', a nod, I guess, both to Frankie and our own ambitions. Either he liked what he heard or Debbie turned on the charm. Probably both. Around the same time, the *Soho Weekly News* published a letter from Debbie, expressly stating that Blondie was *not* a punk band. No doubt Private Stock was a bit concerned about the bad connotations of punk and wanted Debbie to reassure them that Blondie was essentially wholesome Top Forty material. The fact that Debbie had already appeared as *Punk*'s 'punkmate of the month' was conveniently overlooked.

In August we were due back at Plaza Sound but before heading back into the studio we did a couple gigs. One was at the Stone Pony in Asbury Park, the club where Bruce Springsteen had been discovered. Asbury Park is a seaside resort town in south Jersey. Evidently the new wave hadn't hit the beach, or if it had it was a washout, because the audience didn't quite know what to make of us. Then in early July we played the Ratskellar, Boston's answer to CBGB. In many ways, Boston had a head start on the punk/new wave market, producing Jonathan Richman and the Modern Lovers and another early group, The Boys, a year or so before CBGB really got going. Boston had its own punk scene and that summer, new wave central was the Ratskellar, a basement dive in the center of Kenmore Square. What I remember most about the show is driving back to New York, and getting into the city at 7 a.m. on the 4th of July. That year it was the bicentennial celebration and Manhattan was packed with tourists. We had driven through the night and I hadn't slept. A regatta of sailing ships were due to travel up the Hudson as part of the celebration, and hordes of patriotic visitors were making their way to Battery Park and other points along the river. Lisa went with Chris and Debbie to take in the sight, but I could barely keep my eyes open and decided to crash.

But then a new crisis popped up. Benton decided to kick us out of the loft.

Exactly why he wanted us to leave is unclear. Probably seeing us go from poverty-stricken wannabes to poverty stricken justmightbes was too much for him. It didn't affect me that much. The band would have to find a new place to rehearse, and that would be a hassle, but I had already pretty much moved into Lisa's studio and now it would simply become official.

Chris and Debbie were harder hit. They had to find a new apartment. They wound up moving to the top floor of a brownstone on 17th Street. Not too long after they moved in, they had a fire. Chris and Debbie thought Benton's magic may have had something to do with it. But I had read enough to know that Chris was often playing around with things he didn't really understand – copying out magical spells and formulae because he thought they looked cool. If there was any occult hanky-panky going on in their new apartment, it may have been self-inflicted.

Benton did have good reason to be angry, though. Before they left the loft, Chris, Debbie and the others graffitied the walls. In their eyes Benton had become just another person out to get them and so, as far as they were concerned, revenge was justified.

▶▶

Craig Leon had produced 'X-Offender' and 'In the Sun', but when it came to the album, Richard Gottehrer took over the controls. Working with Richard was different from working with Craig. Craig had an idea of what the music at CBGB was about. I wasn't that sure about Richard. I felt that he got too personally involved in the music, almost like a kid who wanted to play with our toys. It seemed less that he wanted to capture our sound than that he wanted to create it himself. I'd come into the studio and he'd be banging away at the drums or hitting the keyboards, and we'd often have to wait for him to finish before getting down to work. He bounced around with boyish enthusiasm and seemed hurt if you didn't want to play with him. He didn't seem to understand our style and couldn't resist showing us how to play a part, even when we knew how to play it well enough. He'd also resent it if one of us didn't like an idea of his, and seemed surprised if we had any ideas of our own.

It's true that musicianship wasn't our strong point. I remember one session, when Chris was trying to do a guitar solo. He kept making the same mistake, over and over, muttering 'Fuck!' and 'Shit!' into the microphone. After about a dozen attempts, I heard Richard say to Craig, 'He can't play it,' and Craig answer, 'I know.'Chris seemed close to an emotional breakdown and, under pressure at the studio, he'd frequently freak, fling his guitar to the floor and storm out. The session would have to stop until Debbie could calm him down. Generally this would happen if one of us disagreed with him.There was an awful amount of disharmony among us and Chris and Debbie saw any criticism or difference of opinion as a challenge to their authority. Discussions would invariably end up as arguments. Jimmy, seeing that Chris often got his way after a tantrum, started to throw fits himself. All the unvoiced tensions began to break through the cracks. Sometimes whole days would be lost because of some ego clash.

I threw a fit of my own one afternoon at Gottehrer's apartment. During the final mix, Gottehrer wanted to talk with me about 'Scenery'. I played guitar on this as well, a twelve-string, and had written it alone, without Debbie. I wasn't happy with Debbie's vocal, and felt she was holding back. She just didn't seem to give it her all. When I got to Richard's apartment on the Upper West Side, he told me that he thought 'Scenery' would have to be pulled from the album. It didn't 'fit with the rest of the material'. I didn't agree with him and told him what I thought: the real reason it was being pulled was that it was another song of mine and I played guitar on it. Chris wouldn't want two tracks with me as guitarist and composer. That was why Debbie did such a weak vocal. He said I was crazy. I raved about how this would wreck my career. He asked me to leave. I did, but not before telling him what I thought of him.*

Not everything to do with recording that first album was so melodramatic. A lot of sessions were fun. Lisa came and did a photo spread for *New York Rocker*, getting a shot of me playing the Rickenbacker twelve-string. Ellie Greenwich, who co-wrote Phil Spector hits like 'Be My Baby' and 'Da Doo Ron Ron', came to the studio and sang backup on 'In the Flesh'. Cousin Brucie, a NY disc jockey I had grown

---

* It's now included with other rare Blondie material on a Chrysalis compilation, *Blonde and Beyond*.

up listening to, did a television promotional slot with Debbie. Brucie wore a Plaza Sound T-shirt, and, to the tune of 'Rip Her to Shreds', Debbie tore it off him live on TV. Richard Hell, who had started working with Gottehrer, came to the studio one afternoon and jammed with Chris and me. And at the end, we threw a party at the studio, inviting Hell, the Ramones, the Miamis and the people from *Punk* for some cheap drinks and a first listen. It was a lot of work and it cost us all sleepless nights. But a month after going back to Plaza Sound, *Blondie* was completed, and everyone, more or less, was happy.

It would soon become clear that Private Stock had no idea what to do with us. First they decided to hold back the album until January. Until then, we had to keep our momentum going. We did the usual spots, Max's and CBGB, and even played at a kind of mini festival in the East Village. With the Dictators and a few other bands, we played the Quando Gym on Second Avenue, an old church building that had been leased by a Puerto Rican neighborhood group. The place was in really bad repair, with holes in the walls and part of the roof missing. The Dictators were headliners, but the event was so disorganized that we didn't hit the stage until about 2 a.m. This turned out to be the perfect time. The crowd loved us. When we finished practically everyone left so the Dictators, who came on after us, had hardly any audience. This didn't endear us to them, and they also remembered that we had played at that benefit for Wayne County back in the spring.

Around the same time Legs McNeil called Chris and said he wanted to use the band in a project he had going for *Punk*. 'The Legend of Nick Detroit' was a *noir* graphic detective novel featuring Richard Hell in the lead role. Legs invited us down to the 'Punk Dump' on Tenth Avenue, the office he shared with John Holstrom and Ged Dunn. He showed us round the place, then took us to some locations in the neighborhood and talked about doing some photo sessions.

A couple days later Chris called me at Christopher Street. Legs was shooting for the Nick Detroit issue on the Staten Island Ferry. Did Lisa and I want to be in it? I asked if Legs had told him to invite us. 'Yeah,' Chris said. 'Sure.'

When Lisa and I got down to Battery Park it was as if half of CBGB had turned up. I don't know what the people who ran the ferry thought. A crowd of us in either skinny ties or ripped T-shirts crawled up the gangplank and filed past the families out for a quick turn past the Statue of Liberty. In the autumn of 1976 what would emerge as the punk look was still rare and we must have seemed a really strange bunch.

It takes a good half-hour to get from the Battery to Staten Island. You get a good view of the Statue of Liberty and downtown Manhattan, with the twin towers of the World Trade Center looming over everything. Earlier that summer, Lisa, Jimmy and I had joined thousands of other people around the base of the Trade Center during the filming of the remake of *King Kong*. We were part of the crowd that gathered around the great ape after he fell from the top, shot down by the air force, still clutching on to Jessica Lange.

The first couple hours on the ferry went by without incident. I knew photo sessions took time, and that these things tended to drag on. But after we had sailed from Battery Park to Staten Island and back several times and Legs hadn't yet spoken to us, I started to get impatient. It looked like everyone else had been given their parts. Was there some problem? Why hadn't he even come up and said hello?

The ferry set off again. Lisa and I had another rotten coffee. Finally, heading back to the Battery once again, I approached Legs.

'Hey Legs,' I said. 'When are you going to use Lisa and me?'

In true punk fashion, Legs had beaten the heat with a few cheap beers and seemed the worse for wear.

'Huh?' he said. 'Oh, ah, wow, man. I don't think I *am* gonna use you.'

'What?' I shouted. 'We've been waiting on this ferry all day and you're not going to use us! Chris called me and said you *wanted* to use Lisa and me. That's why we came.'

'Wow. Did he? Ah, I don't remember telling him that, man.'

'You gotta be kidding!'

'No, I don't think so, man. There just aren't any parts for you. Sorry.'

I told him he was an asshole. Lisa was mortified, more at my outburst than at having wasted the day. When the ferry docked at the Battery we got off. Later, Legs wound up using us anyway. In the final product there's a scene of me stuffing twenty-dollar bills down Lisa's cleavage, sitting at the bar at CBGB. I don't know if he wrote us in just to be nice. It probably wasn't his fault anyway. Knowing Chris, he probably didn't think that we'd have anything better to do, and just said that Legs wanted to use us just so we'd go. Debbie turns up in the issue too, as the leader of a Nazi lesbian gang. Don't know what Frankie Valli thought of that.

Sometime before December we shot the album cover. That proved almost as harrowing an experience as making the record itself. For a while the idea of having only a shot of Debbie on the front and the rest of us on the back was mooted, but the clamour was so great it had to be dropped. Each of us had different ideas and no one could agree on anything. Time was running out, so Private Stock secured the services of Shig Ikeida, the Japanese fashion photographer, and told us we had to get it done. One afternoon we all piled into Shig's West Side studio. Debbie brought a trunkload of get-ups, but one idea for the boys was fairly clear. We decided to pull the blue sharkskin suits we had used for *Vain Victory* out of the mothballs. Private Stock was fairly liberal in providing refreshments, and during the shooting everyone got progressively loaded. My own specialty was White Russians. The session went on and to relieve the boredom Jimmy and I started to tease Chris. I don't remember how it started, but we got on some roll about how we were going to kill him. It was stupid, but we were fairly drunk and it really was in good fun. Chris didn't see it that way and decided to throw one of his fits. He wouldn't pose and started screaming at us to stop teasing him. The shot that was eventually chosen for the cover, with Debbie at the front and the rest of us lined up behind her, was taken quite early on. The one on the back was taken toward the end; by that time, the five of us were more or less plastered.

Ronnie Toast provided some stream-of-unconsciousness liner notes. With that, and some short notes of thanks, the packaging for *Blondie* was done. But Private Stock thought we needed a little extra something. They asked Debbie to do some more photo sessions. Debbie was generally very easily swayed by the people around her, and although she later regretted it, she agreed to the sessions. The result was the kitschy shot of Debbie in the see-through blouse, which became the promotional poster for the album. We all hated it, including Debbie. She may have hated it most of all, as it made her look like yet another sex kitten, but why she agreed to be photographed like that is unclear: she must have realized that the record company would use the shots. As time went on she was less tetchy about using her sex appeal to sell records, and some of the other promotional material was equally embarrasing. According to the Private Stock 'biosheet' on the band, I was a 'nineteen-year-old natural born poet, comic book freak and soon to be college dropout,' whose 'curly blond hair, skinny ties and newly cultivated knack for songwriting' made me 'the perfect rock and roll teen idol'.

A couple weeks before its release, Private Stock sent out review copies. Reports were good. Lester Bangs liked it. Writing for the *Village Voice*, Lester said that 'The Spectorish "X-Offender" contains the best roller rink organ since the Sir Douglas Quintet', and 'the best surf guitar break since "I'm Set Free."' The *Soho Weekly News* was equally enthusiastic. The album had 'expressive, exciting tunes . . . you remember and sing along with them after one listen'. Later reviews would be equally glowing. My own favorite was John Rockwell's brief report in the *New York Times*. In his column 'Pop Life', for 24 December 1976, Rockwell wrote that Blondie's first album was 'a most appealing disc debut indeed'. Debbie has a 'peroxide sex-pot image' and sings with 'graceful, pretty assurance'. The band plays 'spiffily' and the songs are full of 'clever pop twists'.

Nothing fantastic, but the timing was right. Another year had rolled around. Another birthday had arrived. I was twenty-one. Lisa and I read the review that morning in bed at the studio. It was a nice way to start a new year. I still wasn't quite a rock star. But at least this Christmas Eve I didn't have to burn Jimi Hendrix posters to keep warm.

8. OFF THE ROAD

1977 got off to a cold start for Blondie. At midnight we were on stage at the Bethesda Fountain in Central Park, playing 'Time Is Tight' by Booker T. and the MG's. The temperature hovered around the freezing mark. Crowded in front of us were thousands of absolutely frozen, absolutely blasted people, lit up by searchlights. It had been a cold December and during the night it snowed. Then the snow turned to icy rain and the ground was ankle deep in slush. It was a dramatic sight. Shafts of light coursed across the clouds and shot through the frozen trees.

Debbie had got the gig through the Parks Department. The money was good: $1,500, a tremendous amount for us. And it was good publicity; the performance was being televised on the *Joe Siegel Show*, something half the country would be watching, so we got to plug the album. It was hard work. Debbie wore a fur coat over her minidress. The boys wore their leather jackets. I had to cut the tops off of my gloves so I could play. But they didn't help much. My fingers were frozen and it was impossible to get them warm. Massive burners were off to the sides of the stage, but they did little against the cold and the fumes were sickening. The stage was covered in a kind of tent, and the exhaust from the burners collected within it, making the air nauseating. In between freezing and keeping my mind on playing, I remember wondering if I was going to pass out.

At midnight, people dressed as giant white hands descended the staircase to the fountain – the march of time – and then the ball came down in Times Square. The crowd got the message and went wild. After the show we crawled through the traffic in Debbie's Camaro, cutting through the throngs of people in Times Square as if we were underwater, moving in slow motion. It seemed to take forever to get downtown. At around 3 a.m. I found Lisa at a loft party on Broadway at Cooper Union. We kissed.

A couple weeks later the album came out. There were good reviews. The *Sunday News* liked it and called it the 'very best album to come out of the CBGB crew'. *Newsday* was impressed too. Excited by the favorable reception, we kept up the pace. We did a string of shows throughout January, opening for John Cale at My Father's Place in Long Island, and headlining at Max's with the Cramps – one of their earliest New York appearances. The Max's show was memorable because we packed the place beyond its capacity, breaking the record held by the Ramones. For a while we became the biggest money-making band on the circuit, and for the first time we had to turn people away from a show. I remember the Cale show for another reason. I was looking forward to it because I had always respected Cale's work, both on his solo albums and with the Velvet Underground, and was chuffed that we would be sharing a bill with him. But when I met him that evening, my enthusiasm sank. Maybe it was just that night, but Cale seemed odd. When I was introduced to him he shook my hand. At first it didn't seem like anything, just a strong grip. He looked at me and grinned. Then he squeezed and squeezed until it was clear he was trying to hurt me. After a while he let go. He did the same to Lisa. Both of us were disappointed that meeting him had turned out to be a disaster.

The shows were good, and we used them to work in a

new cover tune, 'Palisades Park'. Palisades Park was an old amusement park on the Hudson that had its heyday in the sixties. The song was written by Chuck Barris, a sixties pop songsmith who had become a TV producer in the seventies. Barris was responsible for such seventies drivel as *The Gong Show* and *The Dating Game*. Covering his hit made it clear that Blondie was no nostalgia band; we had our roots in the worst pop culture of our own decade as well.

Penthouse gave the album a favourable review, calling Debbie a 'youthful Marilyn Monroe', a remark that must have made her day. Roy Carr in the *NME* gave the thumbs up from across the pond, although he annoyed the band by erroneously reporting that Chris and Debbie had 'hired' us in 1976 to record 'X-Offender'. But the little bruises didn't seem to matter. We were definitely on our way. Somewhere around this time we made our first nationwide television appearance, on the *Don Kirshner Rock Concert*, a late-night music show, years before MTV. We did 'X-Offender' and 'In the Flesh'. I wore my *Man From U.N.C.L.E.* badge, a black turtleneck, played guitar and jumped around like a madman. (If anyone needed any convincing that I was not long for the band, that video would do it.) Chris was obviously not pleased to be playing bass and Debbie was intimidated by the camera. But it didn't matter. From third on the bill, Blondie was suddenly the toast of New York. Our shows were selling out. The album was in store windows. Record company execs were being nice to us. And Debbie turned up in embarrassing gossip columns like Henry Schissler's 'Rock-arama' in the *SoHo Weekly News*, which assured its readers that she was a 'warm, interesting individual whose career is on the up and up'.

Surely we had arrived. What was left to do?

▶▶

The press release from the desk of 'Famous Toby Mamis', a sixties radical turned LA publicist, read 'Blondie to Make Hollywood Debut'. 'Blondie, the sensational New York-based group who are the most talked about new band of the new year, will be appearing at the Whiskey A Go Go February 9 through 12. This appearance will mark Blondie's first venture out of New York since its inception, and is timed to coincide with the release of the group's first album, "Blondie", on Private Stock Records.'

The man responsible for this was someone Debbie had known in a past life, when he had managed her brief career in the late sixties as a hippie songstress in a group called Wind in the Willows. Aside from the untruth about never being outside of New York, it wasn't bad. We hadn't had many press releases sent out about us, in fact we hadn't had any. So if this one fiddled around with the truth, well, who were we to quibble? We were thankful somebody was bothering to do anything for us. It was a new sensation. Suddenly there was someone else there, helping our career. We had signed the contracts with Private Stock with as much insight into the business as Elvis had when he shook hands with Colonel Parker. We needed someone to help us, someone who believed in the music and would fight for our careers, someone we had faith in and could trust, someone who was on our side.

Unfortunately the man who turned up was Peter Leeds.

My experience with managers was absolutely nil, but the minute I saw Leeds I knew I didn't want to work with him. Unfortunately, neither Chris nor Debbie thought much of my misgivings, much to their later regret. Leeds I'm sure had me pegged as a troublemaker from day one.

His plan was simple. We had conquered New York and there really wasn't anything left to do there. We had to leave our comfortable East Village nest and head out into the world. The natural destination was Hollywood. To me, it seemed that without conferring with the rest of us, Debbie and Chris agreed that Leeds would manage us. He in turn made arrangements with a publicist and tour manager, booked five flights to LA, and got us some shows in Hollywood, San Francisco and other California cities.

When I heard about the deal I was of course excited. California? I had barely been out of the Tri-State area. Of course I wanted to go. I was especially keen on seeing San Francisco. But Chris and Debbie were a bit disingenuous about the rest. We were going to see 'how it went' with Leeds, they said, and if we liked him, we'd sign. It appeared to be a fait accompli. As far as I was concerned Chris and Debbie had made it a habit of late to keep us as uninformed as possible.

Nevertheless we packed our bags and got ready to go. Lisa, who wanted to break out of the campy off-Broadway scene and get into films, would come along and see some Hollywood agents. On a freezing 7 February 1977, the Blondies plus one girlfriend, wrapped in tight black jeans and skinny ties, left a winter bound New York for the warm California sun. When we got to JFK, a porter grabbed my bag, gave it a heave and groaned.

'Hey, whaddayou got in here, bricks?'

My magic studies had become quite serious, and my bag was filled with books on tarot, kabbalah, astral projection and the Golden Dawn. But it was heavy for another reason. I was very particular about my clothes, and had to have absolutely wrinkle-free shirts, a perfect crease in my trousers, and uniformly smooth skinny ties. Unaware that our hotel would supply one, I had packed Lisa's iron.

I had never flown before and recorded the fact with some excitement in my journal: 'It is February 7, 1977, and for the first time in my life, I am flying.' Long before smoke detectors

and non-smoking flights, we passed the time by taking a few
puffs in the toilets. Chris had learned an old trick to keep the
smell of the grass from getting out. You put your face down
in the sink, lift the plug and exhale, and the suction pulls the
smoke down the drain. I don't think you can do this now but
back then it seemed to work. In any case, I spent a lot of
time looking at the clouds and thinking, Wow. I'm 40,000
feet in the air.

My first impressions of LA were dazzling. The light, the
palm trees, the heat in February, the vast open spaces and
endless freeways were about as different from the Bowery as
we could imagine. Leeds had booked us into a hotel, the Bel
Air Sands, just outside of Beverly Hills. (The place doesn't
exist now.) The owners were concert promoters and Leeds had
wangled some deal with them whereby we'd play at some
disco they had running on Catalina Island, about twenty miles
off the coast, in exchange for our rooms and a 'modest' tab. It
seemed a fair exchange, and the promoters were happy. A
couple weeks later their mood had changed. The concert never
happened and our tabs were anything but modest.

The first day we arrived we were hit with jet lag and made
an early night of it. But the next morning I was up early,
eager to get a look at Hollywood. Lisa was staying in our
room, making calls to agents. I had no idea what LA was
like and thought I could get a bus or subway downtown
before the rehearsal for our debut show at the Whiskey A
Go Go the next night. I went to the desk and asked how
I could get to the city.

'Where?'

'You know, downtown, where all the shops are. The
center of town.'

'I don't know where you mean. Do you have a car?'

'No.'

'Well, you're not gonna get anywhere in this town without a car.'

'Well, could I walk?'

'You're about ten miles outside of Hollywood.'

'Bus?'

'Uh uh.'

'Subway?'

'Nope.'

For the first time I realized that not every town was like New York.

►►

On 9 February we headlined at the Whiskey A Go Go on the Sunset Strip, with Tom Petty and the Heartbreakers as support. Aside from the Ramones, who had played the Roxy and the Starwood the year before, we were the first of the CBGB bands to head to LA and our reputation travelled before us. Rodney Bingenheimer had been a mainstay of the LA rock scene with his English Disco since the mid seventies, and he had been playing the album on his KROQ radio show endlessly. Rodney was famous for his fondness for nubile nymphets and was, I think, a bit disappointed when he realized that Debbie had hit puberty way back. Nevertheless he was wild about the band and invited us on his show. We took him up on his offer and had a great time playing records and being interviewed.

Robert Hillburn of the *Los Angeles Times* liked us too, and gave the album a rave review. So when Blondie hit the stage at the Whiskey, the crowd was expecting something good. In early 1977, punk – or 'new wave', as Seymour Stein was starting to call the new music on his label, hoping to lose the bad connotations – hadn't yet hit the West Coast, and the dominant sound was good old hard rock and heavy metal. A few blocks down the Strip from the Whiskey, clubs like Gazzari's specialized in Led Zeppelin clones, and were more typical of what was happening in LA than the likes of Patti Smith and Richard Hell. The Rainbow, right next door, was the hangout of the real Zeppelin and a hundred other well-heeled rockers, and was glam central. LA was the home of the music *business*, with A & R men taking time off from their coke spoons to do poolside deals and sign the most recent Aerosmith soundalikes. Art rock, street rock, punk rock – whatever you want to call it – fitted in here about as well as my skinny ties and black suits amid the tennis rackets and suntan lotion.

There were a few bands on the scene, like the Quick and the Runaways, both of whom we met and got to know, and who would help us trash our rooms at the Bel Air Sands. And entrepreneurs like Kim Fowley. Fowley had a history going back to the sixties with oddball numbers like 'Alley Oop'. In the flower power days he staged 'love ins' and produced novelty hits like 'Nut Rocker', by B. Bumble and the Stingers. In the early seventies he had got his hands on the Modern Lovers and produced a few demos for them, before Jonathan Richman went off the deep end and started writing songs about abominable snowmen in the market. Recently Fowley had hit big with the Runaways, an all-girl teen group who scored a minor hit with 'Cherry Bomb' and who were being touted throughout LA as the Next Big Thing. Their ticket to success, according to Fowley, was that they were sixteen-year-old girls playing guitars and singing about fucking. Their age was questionable but the lyric content was pretty clear. Fowley struck me as violent and strange, someone who wanted to appear intimidating, the kind of person who would say outrageous things, then stare at you unblinking, hoping for a response.

Phil Spector, who we also met, was another case. He came

to our show with an 'In the Flesh' button – one of Private Stock's promotional ideas – pinned to his jacket. He was wrapped in a long black cape, wore impenetrable sunglasses and was accompanied by a bodyguard. With our 'girl group wall of sound', it was natural that he should be interested in us. He made everyone else leave the dressing room and launched into a long and meandering monologue, peppered with remarks like 'Who the hell do you think you're talking to?' whenever one of us wanted to say something. Paranoid would be a mild assessment of his character. He wouldn't let any of us leave and had his bodyguard stand in front of the door. Later he invited Chris and Debbie to his house to talk about producing our next record. He wouldn't let them leave there either. Apparently he did the same thing to the Ramones.

There really wasn't much of an underground scene happening in LA, but what there was turned up at our shows. We met the local *cognoscenti*, like Pleasant Gheman, a seventeen-year-old groupie who would later write for the *LA Weekly*. There were Phast Phreddie and De De Fay, who put out one of the earliest rock fanzines, *Back Door Man*. De De interviewed us after a show, and quoted me as saying that 'Nineteen sixty-nine was the last year and a new year hasn't happened yet,' a remark that turned up in a few other places. Richard Cromelin used it in his profile on us for *Sounds*,* and it was featured two months later as the lead quote for the first article on us in *Rolling Stone*. Robert Hilburn from the *Los Angeles Times* came to one show and wrote a lengthy and laudatory review. Richard Creamer from *Creem* did a photo session, and *New York Rocker* later ran a two-page spread of us at landmark LA sites like Hollywood High School and the Griffith Park Observatory, both of which

---

* 'At last, the Sound of 1970', *Sounds*, 16 April 1977.

featured in the James Dean teen *angst* classic, *Rebel Without a Cause*. We even saw a bit of Hollywood when Tim, an artist friend of Lisa's, took us around the sets for *Star Wars*. There were tons of other interviews, on radio, TV and for national papers.

When we did our first week of shows with Tom Petty we noticed two things about the audience: they were about five years younger than the crowd who came to see us in New York, and they were dressed in styles about five years out of date, wearing bell-bottoms and fringed jackets. When we returned to do a week opening for the Ramones, everyone was wearing Beatle boots and skinny ties. We were treated like royalty. Fans took us for drives in their convertibles, and it was on one of these joyrides that I heard 'X-Offender' on the radio for the first and only time. Girls asked me to autograph their breasts. Our faces were up over the old Liquorice Pizza Record Shop on the Strip* and the management of Tower Records told us to take whatever we liked. Everyone else grabbed scads of records, but all I wanted was a copy of Television's first album, released only that week.

The Whiskey had been a major venue in the sixties, hosting groups like the Doors and the Byrds, and we met a lot of people from that time. Peter Kantner from the Jefferson Airplane came to our dressing room and congratulated us. Ray Manzarek from the Doors told Jimmy how much he enjoyed his playing. My own favorite was when Roger McGuinn from the Byrds introduced himself to me. The Byrds were one of my favourite groups from the sixties, and I was more and more influenced by their sound. I loved McGuinn's twelve-string guitar and had tried to echo it on the abortive 'Scenery'. When I met him he didn't look at all

---

* Later that year, cartoonist Matt Groening would find work there prior to making it big with *The Simpsons*.

like he did in 1966, but that didn't matter, *I* did. He came up to me and said, 'Hey, where'd you get that suit? It looks like one of mine from about ten years ago.'

A lot of other rockers were floating around. Ron and Russell Mael from Sparks threw a barbecue for us on their balcony patio. I met Brian May from Queen at a party in some hotel room; the same one, I think, where Clem opened a closet and found a half-naked girl handcuffed inside. Michael Des Barres, who had been a teenage movie star in the sixties with his role in *To Sir With Love*, and whose ex-wife Pamela would later write best-sellers about her time as a groupie, was then singing with a group called Detective. He hung out at our shows and became friendly with us. I didn't know it at the time, but a member of his band, Nigel Harrison, the bass player, was also getting friendly with Chris and Debbie, but more on him later.

Sable Starr, the renowned groupie who had already bagged Johnny Thunders and Richard Hell – as well as a string of other rock notables – sank her claws into Clem for the duration of our stay. Malcolm McLaren was in town, trying to secure yet another deal for the Sex Pistols, and turned up at our show. McLaren wasn't having much luck with the record execs, and his chances of finding a friendly face in our dressing room weren't much better. One of the nights we split the bill with the Ramones, Malcolm was running around, trying to ingratiate himself. He made some remark that Johnny Ramone took offense at. Johnny stood up, looked at Malcolm and said, 'Are you talking to me?' before chasing him out of the room, brandishing his Mosrite guitar like an axe. I later made one of my all-time great *faux pas* with McLaren. At the Powerburger across the Strip from the Whiskey – a fast food stand that no longer exists – I introduced him to a friend as Malcolm McDowell.

The boys threw themselves into LA decadence with style.

After scrounging for pocket money on the Bowery, the warm California sun just went to their heads. It became a habit to invite people back to our hotel and treat them to steak dinners, wine and booze, running up a tab like the pros. Lisa got a call for work from an agent in New York and headed east, so I was left a relatively free man. I indulged a bit, but disappointed a groupie by not sleeping with her while Jimmy and another girl got it on in a bed next to us. Pretty soon I tired of getting routinely blitzed, but Jimmy became big friends with Joan Jett from the Runaways and Danny Wild from the Quick, and the three of them threw parties every night.

LA rockers knew how to do everything on a lavish scale. The big party favors back then were quaaludes, known as mandrax or mandies in the UK. With a few drinks, a couple 'ludes had you out in record time. (Patti Smith sings of them in 'Ask the Angels'.) I passed, but everyone else was into them. One night at the Rainbow, Jimmy was so out of it that he crawled the length of the club, picking through the carpet, looking for a 'lude someone said they had dropped. It was, as the Iggy song has it, 'Fun Time'. Things got out of hand. Bored out of his mind at the hotel, Clem decided one night that he didn't care for his chocolate mousse and smeared it on some other guest's door. The guest didn't care for this. Clem told him to get lost. Only profuse apologies from an exasperated hotel manager kept Clem from getting his head handed to him. Another night Jimmy wasn't so lucky. During yet another all-night bash a guest in the room next to Jimmy's knocked on the door and asked him to keep the noise down; oddly enough, he and his wife wanted to sleep. Jimmy told him to take a hike. The guest grabbed Jimmy who made the mistake of hitting back. Soon the guest had Jimmy by the hair and was making a racket against the wall with his head. Eventually the police had to come and pick up the pieces. By this time the hotel management had had enough and moved us out of our rooms to a group of bungalows away from the main building. There was some problem with their Catalina disco and the show was off. They asked us to pay. Leeds fast-talked the hotel managers and we stiffed them for the bill.

But not all the goings-on in Tinseltown were fun and games. Halfway through our stay, Leeds decided to show his hand and get us to sign a contract with him. All the while we were out in Bel Air, Leeds had been staying at the Sunset Marquis, a nicer hotel and, what was more important in a town like LA, about as centrally located as you can get, a few blocks down the hill from the Strip. He called Debbie and Chris. They tapped me on the shoulder.

'Come on,' they said. 'We have to meet with Peter.'

Leeds had made a few attempts to win me over, telling me I was a poet and giving me a book on Jung. But I wasn't buying it. He was precisely the kind of person I instinctively knew to stay away from. Even Debbie said she didn't like him. Why, then, I wondered, did she even think of having him manage us?

'Well, nobody else offered.'

Brilliant.

I hadn't heard about the contract, let alone seen it, until we went to his room. Leeds sat at a table, a pile of papers in front of him. After some inane chit-chat, he smiled a nauseating smile, pushed the papers toward us and suggested we got down to business.

'What business?' I asked.

'Signing the contracts.'

'What contracts?'

He tapped the sheets.

'These contracts. With me. To be your manager.'

A cold sweat broke out on my back and a shock ran up my spine.

'I'm not signing anything until I show it to a lawyer.'

'Oh, don't worry. That's been taken care of. Debbie's had a lawyer look at it. It's fine. Just sign and we can get on.'

'Debbie didn't mention any lawyer to me.'

'Debbie?'

'I . . . ah . . . we . . . I talked to a lawyer on the phone. He said if we trusted Peter we should sign. Anyway, Peter says that if we don't like it, we can get out of it easily.'

Right.

'Well, actually I *don't* trust Peter, so I *don't* want to sign.'

'Gary, stop making trouble,' Chris piped up. 'Just sign the fucking thing.'

'No way!'

'If you don't sign,' Leeds said, 'I'll go to go back to New York and leave you here!'

'Fine with me!' I shouted. 'We have the gigs. We'll get paid. We have our return tickets. I'm sure we can find somewhere to stay. Go back to New York if you want to.'

'Gary,' Debbie shrieked, 'just sign the fucking contract!'

'No!'

All three in unison: 'GARY! SIGN THE FUCKING CONTRACT!'

This went on for two hours. At one point Leeds got up and locked the door. Eventually, after much browbeating, pleading, threatening and promising, I caved in and signed. Big mistake. The sky should have darkened. I hold God personally responsible for not letting out a crash of thunder and kicking up a gale when I picked up the pen. But to everyone's regret, I put my name on that wretched document. Later that week I gave Leeds some indication of my willingness to work with him by throwing a fire extinguisher down a hallway at the Whiskey when he made a suggestion about dropping one of our songs. I got the idea from Jimmy, who had thrown my bass across the dressing room one night when he was pissed off about my jumping around.

'Handle the business,' I said to Leeds. 'We'll handle the music.'

My days, as they say, were numbered.

Leeds did do some work though. He got us some shows at the Mabuhay Gardens, San Francisco's answer to CBGB, a Polynesian restaurant turned punk palace in North Beach, a few blocks from the City Lights bookstore and other haunts of the Beat era. Up there we met the Avengers, one of SF's home-grown punk bands, and Jonathan Postal, a photographer who also had a great, clever band, the Readymades. Jonathan took my favourite shot of Blondie, catching us in the dressing room at the Mabuhay before a show. The walls were perfectly clean when we arrived, but such virginity incensed Chris, who quickly scribbled some inane graffiti on the white plaster. Jonathan gave me a print of his photo, and we stayed in touch. The SF scene was pretty small at that point, but a year or so later, when I came to play the Mabuhay with a different band, it, like all the other scenes around the country, had exploded.

One reason for this punk explosion was the influence from across the sea. By this time Malcolm McLaren's obsession with Richard Hell's ripped T-shirts* had spawned the Sex Pistols, and most of the new bands sprouting up in cities outside New York were looking to England, not the Bowery, for inspiration. It was almost as if at the start of our success, the New York bands were already old hat.

Toward the end of our LA adventure we got some news

---

* His obsession went as far as to ask Hell to join the fledgling band, but Hell had his own T-shirts to tear.

that bowled us over. David Bowie and Iggy Pop had heard our album in Berlin and loved it. Iggy was getting a US tour together to promote *The Idiot* album, with David as his incognito keyboardist, and both of them wanted us as the opening act. It was Iggy's comeback tour, more or less. He had had been out of action for a few years, sunk in obscurity and drugs, until Bowie resurrected him. Now he was ready to make a grand return.

Of course we said yes, and Leeds negotiated a deal. We prepared to go as soon as we returned from LA. We were in New York for little more than a week before we had to hit the road again. Lisa and I had a brief reunion, during which I denied the reports of my fling with an LA groupie that had filtered through the grapevine. Then I packed another bag and was ready to go. Only this time I left the iron behind.

On 11 March, after a 2 a.m. sold-out show at Max's, a sleepy Blondie piled into a Winnebago mobile home and headed north to Montreal, Canada, the first stop on our first North American tour. From New York to Montreal is roughly four hundred miles, and by the time we reached our hotel we were fairly blitzed, a condition most of us would maintain, with brief intervals of lucidity, for the remainder of the tour. On 13 March we played our first show with Iggy and David at Le Plateau Theatre. Rick Gardiner was their guitarist, with Hunt and Tony Sales on drums and bass. Hunt and Tony's father was the comedian Soupy Sales, and when I was a kid in the sixties, I used to watch his television show on Saturday mornings. When I told them this they said that practically everybody they met said the same thing.

Bowie and Iggy were very friendly and treated us like pros. Aside from the shows, we didn't see much of David. He was driven to each gig by Tony, his bodyguard, in the same car that he used in the film *The Man Who Fell To Earth*. Like ourselves, by the time David got to the hotel all he wanted to do was crash. Iggy was more accessible. Both of them gave us advice about performing. Iggy seemed genuinely touched when I told him about listening to his albums, and how I learned how to play guitar from 'Search and Destroy'. Four years later, on another tour, I would get to know him better, but this time around I kept a bit of distance. The others were less reserved. Jimmy was always crowding up to Iggy and David, trying to get their attention, desperately wanting to hang out with the big boys. I thought it better to be discreet, although at one soundcheck I got a smile out of Bowie by playing the bass line to his song 'Width of a Circle' from *The Man Who Sold The World*, an album I used to listen to constantly when living with the sisters.

Pretty soon into the mammoth drives between cities, we realized that travelling by Winnebago was not as great an idea as we thought. From Montreal we headed to Toronto, then Boston. There's only so much grass you can smoke and this was way before Walkmen and laptops, so you were left to your own devices. I read. The others slept. We argued. It was like living at the loft again, only this time we were barreling along at seventy mph. You'd crash out for five hours and wake up only to see you were still on the road. I hadn't seen much of the country outside of New Jersey and at each stop made a point of getting up early to see something of the different cities. Philadelphia, Detroit, Cleveland, Chicago, Milwaukee, Portland, Vancouver, Seattle, San Francisco, San Diego, LA. By now it's pretty much a blur. But a few events on the road stand out.

On 18 March we played the Palladium in New York. Sometime in 1976 the Academy of Music closed down and in early 1977 reopened as the Palladium. All that had changed was the name, and the neighborhood on 14th Street was the same as it had been three years earlier when I saw the Dolls for the first time. It was the biggest venue we had ever played in New York – aside from Central Park – and to do it opening for a punk god like Iggy was a *coup*. People were clamouring to get on our guest list. Our dressing room was jammed. A lot had happened since I first saw the Lipstick Killers back in 1974.

Next was Philadelphia, and then a two-night stand at the Agora Ballroom in Cleveland, Ohio. Cleveland had its own scene and everybody who was in it came to our gig. A crowd of kids hung out outside the club. We signed albums and invited everyone back to the hotel. At the hotel bar, these strange nerdy guys kept telling me how great we were, and handed me a copy of their single. They had a band, Devo, short for devolution. I thought the name was brilliant. I promised to listen to their 45 as soon as I could. Somewhere along the line I came across a record player and we listened. It knocked me out. 'Mongoloid' and 'Jocko Homo' were fantastic. I especially liked the chorus 'Are we not men?' because I knew it had come from the 1930s film of H. G. Wells's novel *The Island of Doctor Moreau*. Later, back in New York, I saw one of their earliest shows at Max's. There were about twelve people in the audience and the singer, Mark Mothersbaugh, did the show with his leg in a cast.

After a visit to a White Power headquarters, where Chris picked up a few trinkets, we left Cleveland and hit Detroit, then Chicago. Somewhere along the way Mikal Gilmore, Gary Gilmore's brother, interviewed us. Chris was more interested in talking about his brother than in the interview. In Chicago Iggy invited us to go to an all-black blues club with him. David's bodyguard Tony had tracked it down. Usually they didn't let whites in, but seeing who we were, they made an exception. We all filed in – Blondie, David and Iggy – the only white people in the place. The next morning I got a surprise. I got a telephone call from Lisa, who I had assumed was in New York. When I hung up and went down

to the lobby, she was there. She had a week off from filming
a television movie and thought she would come for the show.
Her father, who worked for *Playboy*, had given her his 'key',
and that night she took Clem and me to the Playboy Club,
where we were served drinks by bunnies. I remembered that
Debbie had done this for a while and wondered what she had
looked like in her suit and bushy tail.

After Chicago was Milwaukee, then Portland and Vancouver. In Seattle we stayed at a waterfront hotel, famous
for all the rock stars who had crashed there. The place had a
gimmick: you could rent poles and go fishing from out of
your window. We saw polaroids of the Beatles and the Stones
with their lines hanging out of their rooms. Seattle was also
the home of Jimi Hendrix, and Hendrix's grave was a place
of pilgrimage for all visiting rockers. Debbie and Chris opted
out of a visit. In fact, during most of the tour they stayed
apart from 'the boys', trying to distance themselves, and kept
up their pretense as 'stars'. But Clem, Jimmy and I spent an
afternoon paying our respects. Clem had been a big Hendrix
fan and he didn't want to pass up a chance to get close to a
hero. He got closer to Jimi than he might have liked. On the
way back from seeing Hendrix's stone, Clem fell into an open
grave.

Seattle was another town with its own scene, and was the
site of the biggest party of the tour, an event which has gone
down in the local rock legends. After our show, a gang of
local punks invited us to a loft party. They were in bands,
and they all used this same little loft room as a rehearsal
space. They were also devout Iggy fans and had Iggy graffiti
scribbled over the walls. They were desperate to meet Iggy
and pleaded with us to bring him to the party. Iggy was
friendly, but said he was tired and that he didn't feel up to it.
I could tell he really wanted to go; he just wanted these kids
to try harder. In any case, Jimmy, Clem and I went.

It was wild. A hundred grungy kids crammed into a space the size of a small bedroom, with a handful of amps, some guitars, a stage made of crates, a drum set and a tiny PA. They were so excited we had come, they kept handing us joints and bottles of beer. Pretty soon we started jamming. I grabbed a guitar, Clem got on the drums and Jimmy got hold of a bass. We were banging out anything we could think of, old Dolls' tunes, stuff by the Velvets. Some kids grabbed their guitars and started playing. Ten minutes later, the room was one big cloud of noise and smoke, like a scene in some rock and roll underworld. Then the door opened and the kids got the surprise of their lives.

It was Iggy.

We stopped playing and the place went silent. Iggy sat down, the kids scrambling over each other to get as close as they could to their hero. They handed him a beer. He went into some rap, laying down some improvisational poetry, a stream-of-consciousness sermon. The kids hung on every word. They stared at him, as if they couldn't take in that he was really there.

Iggy stood up and jumped on the stage. The kids called out 'Raw Power' 'Search and Destroy' 'TV Eye'. But Iggy wouldn't do his own songs. He looked at me. I started playing. Clem did too. We did Stones' tunes, songs from the Doors, old blues numbers, and then some long droning jam with Iggy rambling on poetically. He took off his shirt. Sweat ran down his chest, dripping on to the stage. The kids in the room were sixteen, seventeen, and here was Iggy, giving them a free, absolutely wild concert, right before their eyes. It went on for at least an hour. It was the high point of the tour, a privileged moment, and I'm sure the people who were there still remember it today.

After Seattle we hit San Francisco, playing the Berkeley Theatre. The punk scene had grown since we were last there, and the place sold out as soon as the concert was announced. After the show, the Tubes gave a party for us. When Jimmy, Clem and I got there late, the bouncer wouldn't let us in. We explained that the party was for *us*, but he wasn't buying it. Clem was pissed and kicked the door. The bouncer chased him. Then Jimmy decided to go one better, and put his foot through the plate glass. The owner of the house didn't care for this and wanted to blow Jimmy away. A fight started up, during which Penelope, lead singer of the Avengers, threw herself on someone and bit him. While all this was going on, David and Iggy turned up and David magnanimously agreed to pay for the door. This placated the host. In the long run, Penelope got the worst of it. Apparently whoever she attacked, got back at her. Later we heard that during an Avengers gig at the Mabuhay, someone ran up on stage and bit her.

The last stops on the tour were LA, where we played the Santa Monica Civic Auditorium – a show promoted by legendary rock entreprenuer Bill Graham – and then San Diego. In two months we had criss-crossed the country and could use a break. Instead, Leeds booked us into the Whiskey for another week. This time he forgot about the Bel Air Sands and got us rooms in the infamous Tropicana Hotel on Santa Monica Boulevard, home of Iggy, the Doors and a hundred other rock casualties, more or less the Chelsea Hotel West.

As it turned out, there was another punk band in town too. One Sunday night on Rodney's radio show, we got to meet the Damned.

Rodney was a true rock and roll hero. He lived, ate and breathed the stuff, usually washing it down with gallons of Tab, an artificially sweetened soft drink. He sported an early seventies shag and looked like a three-quarter-size Rod Stewart. When we first met he was holding court at a booth in Denny's Coffee Shop on Sunset Boulevard. He had a phone installed and would take his calls while munching on cheeseburgers. Evidently the crowd of teenage girls that hung around him didn't spend much, and the owners eventually asked him to move office.

Rodney was one of our earliest supporters and was chuffed to have us on his show. When he heard that the Damned were in town too, he thought he would broker a meeting between the New York and UK schools of punk. The Damned were the first UK band to play CBGB and they had had an effect. Now they were bringing safety pins and shock tactics to LA.

Rodney talked with Debbie, played some tracks from the album, and interviewed each of us. Chris told the listeners to quit school and kill their parents. I played 'Blank Generation', from Hell's Stiff EP. Clem pulled out some classic surf tracks. We told jokes. It was a fun evening. Lisa took a roll of shots.

Then the Damned arrived.

It was like something out of an old rock and roll film, when the two rival gangs meet. We knew next to nothing about them – aside from the fact that they were signed to Stiff Records – and thought 'Fine. What the hell?' when Rodney told us they'd be showing up too. We felt confident after our shows, were relaxed and at ease, but when the Damned turned up the atmosphere got tense. It was clear they had chips on their shoulders. We were from out of town, but they were from another country, even another planet. Dave Vanian, the lead singer, dressed like a vampire. You got the impression they felt they had to try harder. Their management must have told them to spread the word: be obnoxious. So they were. They drank and were pretty pissed upon arrival. They made various outrageous remarks, said everyone in the US was a wanker, and picked the loudest, most abrasive music to play. Then one of them did something stupid. Captain Sensible spat at Lisa.

I couldn't believe it. I knew that spitting was a big thing in the UK, but to have this jerk gob at my girlfriend was too much. I had my hands on his safety pins by the time the others dragged me off. I'm not a violent man, but if it hadn't have been for Clem and Jimmy holding me back, he would have been Captain Senseless for the rest of the night.

For our farewell show at the Whiskey, Hunt and Tony Sales got a band together and opened for us. Then, for the encore of our set, Debbie thought it would be a good idea to have a jam. I thought that was fine but didn't like her choice of tunes. Debbie wanted to do 'Anarchy in the UK'. For someone who *wasn't* a punk, it seemed an odd choice. But as would become standard Blondie practice, Debbie was just jumping on the current bandwagon. The other song they picked was Iggy's 'I Wanna Be Your Dog'. Everyone but me thought it was a good idea and went ahead.

Clem demanded to be the vocalist and screamed through 'Anarchy'. He smeared mustard on his suit, and then emptied an ashtray over his head. Jimmy showed Rodney how to play the one repetitive piano note on 'Dog' and Joan Jett got up and played guitar. Clem had Debbie on a leash. She was on all fours and he walked her across the stage. Then Hunt Sales rushed over to Clem from offstage and wrestled with him for the microphone. It all collapsed into sheer noise, but everyone involved thought it was great fun. All I could think was that this really wasn't what I had in mind when I thought about being in a band.

▶▶

When we got back to New York toward the end of April, it seemed a changed city. With the tour and our two LA stints, we had been on the road for close to three months, the longest I had been away from Manhattan since I moved there. After playing the Palladium and working with David and Iggy, places like CBGB and Max's seemed small, and I was out of sympathy with the new breed that had moved in. The Dead Boys and the Damned had made an impact, and the audience at CBs and Max's was mostly headbanging weekend punks, tumbling in from Long Island and Jersey. Excess and stupidity seemed on tap, and the whole scene started to take on a depressingly incestuous character.

Writers like Lester Bangs decided that they were punk rockers too, and started to perform at CBGB. But Blurt, Lester's 'band', was little more than an excuse to indulge his ego. Legs McNeil would do the same with a group of his own, as would Richard Meltzer with Vom – short for vomit. There were few reminders of the past. At a Voidoids show sometime in May, Hell started the set with a bit of self-conscious irony. 'Summer's on its way,' he said, unbuttoning his jacket. 'It's time to make bigger holes in our T-shirts.' I liked Hell's wit. But this kind of remark was mostly lost on the punks who were turning up in droves and who had started following the English practise of pouring beers over their heads.

In any case there were other things on our minds. We had to start thinking about the next record. Our contract called for a second album before the year was out and that meant new material. I started writing songs, several of them, all at once. One in particular I wrote for Lisa. During the Iggy tour we discovered we were having the same kind of dreams or found we were thinking of each other at the same time. Although we were thousands of miles apart, we were still in touch. Thinking of this one afternoon, it all came together in a song, 'I'm Always Touched by Your Presence, Dear', dedicated to Lisa.

It was just in time. By the end of the month we got the

word from Leeds. Television's first album, *Marquee Moon*, was a surprise hit in England and they were going on tour in the UK in May. The promoters wanted a 'CBGB package' and Television were looking for another New York band as an opening act. It looked like we were going over with them. Blondie hadn't shared a bill with Verlaine and Co. since 1975 – understandably, given the ill-feeling Debbie and Chris had toward them and Patti Smith. But apparently all that was forgotten. In the late spring of 1977, two of the bands that had first put CBGB on the map would be bringing the sounds of the Bowery to England.

We left New York on 16 May and arrived at Heathrow the next morning, just in time for the Queen's Silver Jubilee. In England the economy was bad and getting worse. Punk was flourishing and the Sex Pistols were just about to release 'God Save the Queen', a single calculated to piss off as many people as possible. Leeds had booked us into a decrepit hotel in Kensington, courtesy of the meager tour support given us by Private Stock. The place had recently been taken over by a family of Arabs and they were just learning the ropes of hotel management. I'd see them rushing about the foyer in robes and turbans and had difficulty understanding a word of what they were saying. It was like an early version of *Fawlty Towers*. Even the telephones didn't work. Whenever Leeds or Mamis, our press agent, had to make a call they ran outside to a phone box. That, plus the size of an English sandwich – an unpleasant revelation – gave me some idea that the standard of living in England circa 1977 was roughly equivalent to what we were used to on the Bowery. I wrote in my diary and kept in touch with Lisa by figuring out how to accept collect calls from her in the phone box.

The first couple days were a blur of interviews, sporadic

sightseeing, and clubbing. We knew that the New York scene had made an impression on the English press, but we weren't prepared for the aggressive tone of much of the journalists. It had an effect. At most of the interviews Debbie seemed flustered, and Chris would try to answer all the questions by shouting us down if we started to speak before he did. The main thing the journos wanted to know was whether we were punks or not. Most of the writers had no idea what we were about and the articles that appeared were odd. A big piece on us in *Melody Maker* was really just one long slag off. I don't think the writer saw our show or even heard the album. He went on and on about what we looked like and how apolitical we were. According to him, Debbie had good teeth and I had the 'looks of a child-rapist'.* Strangely, in a *Sounds* article around the same time, Richard Cromelin called me the group's 'token normal'.

We had better luck with the fans. Eddie Dugan interviewed us for *Sniffin' Glue*, one of the earliest punk fanzines. A couple of really young kids, a guy and a girl, interviewed me for another fanzine, whose name I forget. I liked them and thought they were friendly. They asked the usual questions, but I was more interested in talking about magic and the occult than punk rock. We talked for a while, then Mamis cut the interview short. The kids had started asking questions like 'Is it true that people like Wayne County and Cherry Vanilla came here because they couldn't get anywhere in New York?'

On the 18th we went to Dingwalls in Camden Town to see Wayne, and the next night Clem, Jimmy and I were at the Music Machine – now the Camden Palace – to see the Heartbreakers and Siouxsie and the Banshees. I hadn't seen so much spiked hair or so many safety pins in one place

---

* Brian Harrigan, *Melody Maker*, 28 May, 1977 p. 46.

before. At some point we met Siouxsie. She was very friendly. But that's more than I can say for Billy Idol. I had read an interview with him in some magazine and thought he had made some intelligent remarks. I forget what he said – something about the future of music – but I felt he was a kindred spirit and wanted to tell him. Siouxsie introduced us, and after the preliminaries I pulled Idol aside and told him what I thought about what he said.

He looked at me with a kind of sneer. 'Oh *really*, man?' he replied superciliously. 'Did *I* say *that*? I *really* don't remember.' Then he turned around and started talking to someone else.

Oh brother, I thought. What a jerk.

Later that evening we ran into Nancy Spungen and kidded her about her English accent. This was just around the time she hooked up with Sid Vicious. Nancy had been involved with Jerry Nolan in New York and had followed him to London, but was told to keep away because of her bad influence. By this time Nancy was a heavy heroin user and had the uncoveted distinction of being the person responsible for introducing junk to the UK punk scene. We later saw Leee Childers – who had given Nancy the boot – and said hello to Johnny Thunders, who was probably happy to see her. Wayne was the DJ that night and he played some tracks from our album. It was beginning to feel like we had crossed the Atlantic only to see the same people we saw at Max's.

Towards the end of the night, Clem, Jimmy and I headed outside and hung around the statue of Richard Cobden near Mornington Crescent tube.* A crowd of punks stood outside the entrance to the Music Machine and, half-pissed, we looked at them, just taking in the scenery. Then Clem saw

---

* I now live nearby and pass the spot almost every day, wheeling my sons in their pushchair.

someone. At first he wasn't sure. Then he knew it. It was Johnny Rotten.

'Hey Rotten!' Clem bellowed. 'You're a faggot!'

Rotten stopped and looked around.

'I said you're a faggot, Rotten!'

Johnny couldn't tell where the voice was coming from, and he turned his head from side to side, looking like a rat caught with the cheese. Finally he saw us and flipped us the finger. So much for US–UK friendship.

On the way home we got into some pub before last call and ordered more pints than we could possibly drink, so we followed the reigning custom and started pouring them over each others' heads. By the time they kicked us out we were all plastered and sopping wet, and had no idea how to get back to the hotel. Then another American who was at the pub offered to drive us. I got my first view of Big Ben, cruising past it near midnight, pissed and stinking of beer, lying on the floor of his car.

The next morning we headed for Bournemouth, a pre-tour stop for us. We were headlining a show there before meeting up with Television. The five of us, plus Leeds and our driver, crammed into the minibus. After the Winnebago, this was a change. We hadn't been this intimate for a long time. I hated having Leeds in the bus. He constantly made inane remarks, would tell us to stop smoking hash, and had no sense of humor.

We had brought our regular roadie from New York, but thought it good to get a native as well. Keith Crabtree had such a thick Yorkshire accent that we could hardly understand what he said. He took the piss out of us and made fun of our Americanisms, saying things like 'Far much!' and 'Too fucking out!' After a while we got used to it and just started saying these things ourselves.

In Bournemouth we played at the Village Bowl. Squeeze,

who had yet to make a name for themselves, opened for us. Even after LA, we were unprepared for the energy the Brit kids threw into concerts. They went wild. Maybe it was Bournemouth, the sea air, but they just went crazy, like nothing we had ever seen in New York. Some of them even tried to pull Debbie from the stage. One of the advantages of having a bad economy is that you're forced to take your fun seriously. Wow! we thought, after the show. If this is what this tour's gonna be like, it'll be great! Filled with high hopes, we crammed back in the minibus the next morning and started the long haul to Glasgow, the first official stop on the tour.

We arrived the day before our show. The Ramones and the Talking Heads, who were doing their own UK tour, were playing Strathclyde University that night. We went to the show, which was held in a gymnasium on the second floor. Just as in Bournemouth, it was packed with kids jumping up and down and generally going crazy; so much so that the police had to close the show early for fear that the floor would collapse. We hooked up with the Ramones and Talking Heads afterwards and just looked at each other. We couldn't believe it. We had crossed an ocean and driven from one end of a country to the other, but we all felt we hadn't left CBGB. During a Patti Smith European tour the year before, Lenny Kaye had announced, 'It's worldwide!' That's how we felt that night. Lenny was right. It was worldwide. Today the Bowery, tomorrow the Highlands. Well, maybe.

Television turned up the next day and we did our show at the Apollo Theatre. It was not our best. Opening for Television was a mistake. Our styles were about as different as they could possibly be and, as we soon discovered, Television – or more specifically Tom Verlaine – had no feelings of camaraderie with their old New York chums. But all this was nothing compared to the atmosphere around the tour, generated by the reception *Marquee Moon* had got in the UK. The English music press saw it as a religious event. Verlaine was a god, come to save rock and roll; seeing Television perform was a kind of mystical experience. Compared to that, our little garage band seemed like a joke. This is what most of the British music press felt and, pretty much, this is what they said. To Debbie and Chris, it seemed that the long arm of the CBGB mafia reached even as far as Scotland and, to some extent, I had to agree with them.

When we arrived at the Apollo for our soundcheck, we got our first indication that this tour was not going to be as pleasant as the one with Iggy. All of our equipment was pushed into a tiny space at the front of the stage. Verlaine had decided that we were to work within this restricted area. Our brief encounters with him made it clear that he wasn't particularly happy to have us on his tour. After that soundcheck, the feeling became mutual.

The Apollo can hold three thousand people, but only about five hundred turned up for the gig. There seemed to be two distinct camps: late hippies who sported beards and flannel shirts, there for Television, and a handful of kids in skinny ties, there for us. Whether it was the cold shoulder from TV, the vast empty hall or nervousness, our show was a disaster. We opened with 'Kung Fu Girls', a song Debbie punctuated by striking martial arts poses. Trapped in that meager stage area, Debbie's movements seemed silly. We did most of the album, plus some new numbers like 'Presence, Dear'. During our set, people would shout 'Marquee Moon!', anxious to hear Television. Our sound was rotten and the PA monitors cut out at the beginning of 'X-Offender'. To make things worse, Debbie did what one should never do on stage: stop the band. Chris was so disgusted with playing bass that he threw my new short-scale Rickenbacker to the floor. (I had got it to ease their worries about my decapitating Debbie with my old Fender Precision.) All of this was duly noted by the rock press. Both *NME* and *Melody Maker* panned us. My only comfort was that the *NME* writer found my jumping around the only interesting thing on stage. He wrote: 'I'd got a little tired by this time of Debbie's antics, and since there wasn't much else going down in the visual department ... it was left to Gary Valentine and his spastic dancing to keep us enthralled.'* Another review, which I've been unable to track down, said I looked like a Dalek. Piss-take or not, this was handy ammunition when the fights between Chris, Jimmy, Debbie and I broke out over my pogoing.

Not all of these were in the dressing room. Frequently Jimmy threw temper tantrums and directed his frustrations at me. Chris would do the same. Both of them seemed to get a kick from throwing my bass around. Debbie would try to calm them, and Leeds appealed to my reason. But the signs were clear. The family that was at best dysfunctional was coming apart at the seams. Some of this violence seeped out. At some hotel on the road Jimmy got into a stupid fight with Richard Lloyd, and they came to blows. Clem got into kicking his drums over at the end of our set, and tossing lighter fluid on his cymbals and setting them aflame. He also took to smearing mustard on his suits and emptying trash cans over his head. He did this at one hotel and then went to the desk to ask to hire a car. Needless to say, at every hotel we left trashed rooms when we checked out.

But not everything was depressing. Although Verlaine was arrogant, I sat through each of Television's performances, every night, and came away convinced that they deserved the praise the British press was heaping on them. Watching them also confirmed something I had been feeling for a long time: that no matter how good my situation in Blondie, what I

---

* Alan Jones, *Melody Maker*, 28 May 1977, p. 48.

really wanted was to have my own band. Sooner or later, I'd
have to leave.

But even with these heavy thoughts, I was such an Anglo-
phile that just to be in places with names like Sheffield and
Manchester was exciting. In each town I'd take to the streets,
hunting down bookshops and taking in the sights.* In Liverpool we went to the site of the Cavern Club, looked out on
the Mersey and went to Liverpool station, the opening scene
in the Beatles' film *A Hard Day's Night*. Even Verlaine was
drawn into some unconscious fun. At another unmemorable
hotel, Tom, Jimmy, Clem and I were in the elevator, heading
to the lobby. The door closed and Verlaine was nearest the
buttons. We waited. Verlaine had the air of a bemused poet
about him, vague and slightly out of touch. Anyone else
would have hit the button and got the lift moving, but Tom
just stood there, staring into space. We waited. After a few
moments, when it was clear that Tom wasn't moving, Jimmy
said, 'Going down, Tom?' and nodded at the buttons. We
laughed, and I think even Verlaine cracked a smile. I don't
remember if he pushed the button.

Back in London we checked into Bailey's Hotel and got
ready to play the Hammersmith Odeon. Our act had got
better with each performance and we were ready for this one.
The show had sold out immediately and the promoters had
to add an extra night. Clem, Jimmy and I got there late. As
our taxi pulled up I felt a thrill at the crowd gathering around
the entrance. Here I was in London, all ready to play for

---

* I haven't been back to either since, and so my youthful American
romanticism hasn't had a chance to be bruised. My Anglophilia began in
1964 when like a million other kids I saw the Beatles on *The Ed Sullivan
Show*. Later, a progressive-minded 4th grade teacher would allot the last
half-hour of every Friday to letting a group of us bang away at cut-out
cardboard guitars, lip synching to the latest British Invasion 45s.

several thousand people, at what would be one of the most memorable shows of the time.* The gig in Plymouth with the Cortinas also went well and the last show of the tour was in Bristol. It too was a success, even though I had a sort of disaster that night. At the very end of the set, thinking I was heading backstage, I took a step and walked off into mid-air, falling flat on my back. I could barely move, but the others lifted me up and threw me back on for our encore. We did 'Little GTO'. Strangely, that was the one night I didn't wear my dark glasses.

We spent a couple more days in London after that, taking in the sights, going to clubs, checking out Kings Road, being interviewed, buying Beatle boots at Annello and Davide, visiting Stiff Records headquarters and meeting Jake Riviera. Then it was time to go home. I had been on tour for the last four months, but when I got to New York, I'd really have to face the music.

When we got back to New York and started rehearsing, it was clear that something had to give.† Chris, Debbie and I just weren't going to last much longer. There were too many fights. Debbie and I could barely be in the same room together. I resented her trying to control me; she resented the fact that I kept reminding her she was ten years older than me. I wasn't the only one unhappy with the set-up. Jimmy and Clem had their own complaints, and both of them thought it wouldn't hurt if they covertly threw their interests

---

* Since moving to London I've met several people who were at the Hammersmith show. They all say it was one of the best.
† We had been through a couple rehearsal spaces since leaving the loft. One we shared with Mink DeVille, and got to know them quite well. Another was broken into and our guitars stolen.

in with mine for a while and saw what happened. Clem was always unhappy with Chris. Depending on his mood, Jimmy would fluctuate. The upshot was that for a brief spell Clem, Jimmy, Rob DuPrey from the Mumps and I got together at Rob's loft and worked on my songs. We thought we could possibly form a band with me as the front man. Jimmy would get all worked up about it and make grandiloquent gestures, but I think a new song of his showed what he really felt. It was called 'I Didn't Have the Nerve to Say No'.

By mid June and a Blondie show at the classic sixties club, the Village Gate, on Bleecker Street, it was clear I was on my own. It was the last time I would perform with them for nearly twenty years. At the same time, Lisa, determined to escape the dead end of off-Broadway and inspired by her television success, decided that if she was serious about acting, she had to head west. She told me she was moving to LA. It was up to me if I wanted to come. If I didn't, she'd miss me. I could have the studio. But she was going in July.

I thought about it. I knew I wanted to be with Lisa, and I knew I wanted to leave Blondie. I also knew that, hard to believe, I was tired of New York. CBs, Max's, the whole scene just bored me now. LA would be different at least, a challenge. The best thing was to be honest with the others. I talked to them and told them how I felt. My plan was to work on the next album and then leave the band. With all the fighting, it seemed the only reasonable thing to do. Two albums and some more songs under my belt wouldn't hurt.

The next person to tell was Leeds. I went to his office. We had arranged a meeting, but he wasn't there. After an hour or so I got fed up and left a note, spelling out my decision.

Whether she had picked the day for its symbolic connotations or not, Lisa's flight to LA was on 4 July, Independence Day. I went with her to JFK. We'd be recording by September, I told her, and I would probably be with her by November. December at the latest. All right, she said, and boarded her jet. I took the subway back to West 4th Street and went to the studio. Almost as soon as I walked in, the phone rang. It was Leeds. He said I was fired; I don't remember what I said. I hung up and called Debbie. She wouldn't speak to me. I asked Chris what this meant. I thought we had agreed that I would record the album. I worked on all the material, helped Chris, Debbie and Jimmy arrange the songs, and had written two songs for it myself.

He was non-commital. He said maybe, just maybe, if I apologized profusely to Debbie, she might change her mind.

Apologize? After they'd just had Leeds do their dirty work?

I didn't think so.

I wasn't fired. I quit.

Later that night I called Lisa and told her what happened. Then I started to pack. I'd need about a month to deal with everything, and would head to LA in August.

Word got around fast. A week or two after my resignation I got a call from Australia, where *Blondie* had done surprisingly well. The Saints were looking for a bass player. They heard I had left Blondie and wondered what I was doing. Was I interested in playing with them? I thought about it for a second and was gratified they called. I hadn't been to Australia. But I passed. I had nothing against them, but I hadn't left one band just to join another.

Just before I left, New York suffered a massive blackout. There was looting in the Bronx and Harlem, but in the Village it was like a party. People carried candles in the street, and ice cream shops were giving their stock away before it melted. John Browner and I took the Path train to Jersey City, which still had electricity, and had a meal in a restaurant straight out of *The Godfather*. A few days later Rob DuPrey helped me take the dozen or so boxes of books

I was shipping across country to a post office. I had a little emergency of my own, just before I left. One night the bathtub in the studio got backed up with hundreds of cockroaches and flooded. That was another mess I had to take care of. Then, after a brief visit with my parents who I hadn't seen in two years, sometime in early August I packed my bag, got on the train to JFK, got on a plane and was heading west myself.

9. IN THE KNOW

That time around, LA was as different from New York as I could imagine. After a couple weeks I found myself wondering how I ever thought I could live there. The perpetual sunshine wearied me, the lack of public transportation was a pain, and the long distances were a real obstacle.

Another problem was that punk, UK style, had come to town and had really hit big.

►►

Lisa had found a room in a house with four other people. For the next two years, that's where we lived. We were broke, lived on cheeseburgers when we had the money, and went hungry when we didn't. Occasionally we had a decent meal courtesy of Lisa's mom's credit card. We entertained ourselves by staying up till 4 a.m. watching movies like Ed Wood's classic *Plan Nine from Outer Space* on the *Cal Worthington Show*.* Lisa eventually got enough cash to buy a 1966 Mustang, and she barreled along the Hollywood Freeway, making the rounds of Twentieth Century Fox and

---

* Cal Worthington was a used car dealer, who hosted a late-night movie show famous for his promise, 'I'll eat a bug to sell you a car.' These were also the days of *Mary Hartman, Mary Hartman*, the first 'postmodern' soap opera. We went to films too. I think we saw *Star Wars* at least a dozen times.

Warner Brothers. She got work* and made some money, but it wasn't enough to keep us going. *Blondie* had gone gold in Australia – I even had the gold record – but I hadn't seen a penny from it and never would. At one point I got a call from Toby Mamis, speaking on behalf of Peter Leeds. Blondie had recorded 'Presence, Dear' for their *Plastic Letters* album and Leeds knew that it was going to do well. He also knew I was broke. Dear kind-hearted Peter offered to buy my interest in the song for a princely five hundred dollars. I told Mamis where he and Peter could go. But reality hit. I'd have to get a job.

I applied to a 7–11 but failed the lie detector test. I tried a bookstore, but that too proved fruitless.† For a while I worked the spotlights for the Roxy, a landmark club on the Strip. This wasn't too bad. The work was easy, the pay was decent and at least I was involved with music. But the bands were horrible – a week of Don Maclean and 'American Pie' and I was ready to puke. I endured it for a couple months, sitting through nights of Gil Scott Heron and washing my head out with Rocky Erikson and the Thirteenth Floor Elevators. The end came one night during a Bill Withers show. In the middle of his big hit 'Ain't No Sunshine When She's Gone' – the bit where he says 'I know, I know, I know' like a Philip Glass record – instead of having the spot dead on Bill's face, I had a crescent of light cutting off the top of his head. I got my pink slip that night and was without a job.

I applied to an adult bookstore but decided it was too

---

* Eventually she would act with directors like Francis Ford Coppola and Rob Reiner in films like *The Cotton Club*, *Peggy Sue Got Married*, *When Harry Met Sally*, as well as many others.
† The only good thing to come from it was discovering Colin Wilson's book, *The Outsider*. See 'How Colin Wilson Changed My Life: Or, I Had Fame, Wealth, Women Were At My Feet – And Then I Read *The Outsider*' in *Abraxas* No. 13.

creepy and didn't show. I tried temp work but that didn't last. By now it was December and holiday season. I got a job at a Sav-On, a kind of discount drugstore, hauling Christmas trees out to old ladies' cars. The work was boring and I had to wear a little Santa vest, all jolly red with fluffy white trim. My fellow workers grew suspicious when they saw me reading P. D. Ouspensky on our lunch break.

Eventually, the fates sent me an angel. One night I got a call from Craig Leon. He was in LA, producing an album for a singer-songwriter, Moon Martin. Moon Martin? I hadn't heard of him, but that didn't matter. Did I want to play bass? Phil Seymour from the Dwight Twilly Band was playing drums and Craig could probably set up a session with Dwight himself. I didn't have to hear this twice. The next morning I turned up at the Sav-On and said I was leaving.

The manager was pissed. 'You can't leave. It's almost Christmas. We need you.'

I probably could have stayed another week. But I just hated that vest.

Working with Moon Martin wasn't the same as recording the *Blondie* album; it was a little like working with Woody Allen – if Woody Allen had ever played a rock star. Moon wasn't a particularly happy guy. He had written some minor hits and, I thought, had an attitude. The job wasn't ideal but the pay was decent and it was good to be back in the studio. I enjoyed working with Craig again, even though in the final mix my bass lines are nearly inaudible. And I enjoyed meeting the late Phil Seymour, whose song, 'Precious to Me', would be a Top Forty hit a few years later.

A couple years back Phil and Dwight, two Oklahoma boys, had had an early hit with 'I'm on Fire'. They played a big beat sound, lots of guitar and reverb, a combination of Beatles and rockabilly. Craig arranged for me to meet with

Dwight, and out of this Dwight, Phil and I wound up in the studio. My cassette of this jam found its way into some black hole, but I remember enjoying the session. There was even some talk of working together, but nothing came of it.

Phil and I usually got to the studio before Moon and shared a joint – probably the only way we could have got through the sessions. There was a pinball machine in the foyer that was rigged to give free games, and we wasted time and brain cells trying to top each other's score. In another studio Cheap Trick were recording an album, and during breaks they'd come out and have a whack at the pinball machine as well. I got to know them and we wasted a few brain cells together too. I seem to recall that Bun E. Carlos was pretty good at it.

Christmas Eve that year I was twenty-two. After working with Moon, my few months of enforced inactivity were over. We had kept to ourselves and didn't go out much, and in any case what we heard about what was happening didn't tempt us. Like the disastrous Punk-Rock Fashion Show held at the Hollywood Palladium on Halloween. That it had 'punk rock' in the title was enough to keep me away. That Blondie were one of the headliners was another reason. (I guess by this time Debbie had had third thoughts and decided she *was* a punk after all.) It was one of the first big gatherings of the punk crowd in LA, and reports were that it was a failure. The Clash had been advertised but didn't show. Richard Hell was flown out from New York as second best; he stayed just long enough to pick up his fee then decided he didn't want to play after all and went back to New York. San Francisco's Avengers were flown down as third best, to play with Blondie, the Weirdos – a local punk band – and Devo. Blondie were the real big draw and everyone left after their set, leaving the Avengers without an audience. The fashions, I gathered, were equally successful. The company promoting the event evidently thought they could make a quick buck cashing in on the new thing, and the buttons they put out advertising the show said as much; they showed a ghoulish character named Uncle Punk stepping out of a coffin. Can't imagine what Rimbaud would have thought of that.

One thing came out of the event though. During Blondie's stay in town Jimmy paid us a visit. Full of guilt, he swore he'd make it up to me. He would, he said, write the Gary Valentine story.

I told him not to bother.

▶▶

Although it mostly catered to signed acts, after the Blondie shows, the Whiskey recognized that kids would come to see local bands, provided they were new wave, and started to book them. In June 1977 Kim Fowley started a series of shows in which any band that turned up for the soundcheck could play that night. The Germs, one of LA's home-grown punk bands, got their first gig at the Whiskey this way. The club was also smart enough not to have an age requirement, which meant that fifteen- or sixteen-year-olds – even younger – who couldn't drink, still got in. If you had proof of age, your hand was stamped at the door and you were legally allowed to get sloshed.

My reputation had some advantages and Michel Meyer, who did the bookings, would let Lisa and I in gratis. With this, and the few industry people I knew inviting us to showcases and parties, we got something like a royal treatment. We were still broke, but we were becoming something like new wave celebrities. We met up with Devo again when they came to town and did a weekend with the Weirdos. We saw the Screamers, one of whom, Tomata Du Plenty (who passed away while I was writing this book) we knew from New York. The Screamers were an art rock group who had more in common with expressionist theatre than rock and roll. Like Suicide, their sound was based on keyboards and electronic dissonance. The famous illustration of Tomata by Gary Panter – who we also got to know – with his hair shooting up like a firework, smacks of *Der Sturm* or *Aktion* circa 1912. Although they never made a record, the Screamers played some unusual places, like the Camarillo State Mental Hospital, where the patients thought they were inmates too. I went to a party at their house once and all the furniture was wrapped in black bin liners. Another New York group that made the move west was the Mumps. Tired of slugging it out in Manahattan, Lance, Rob and the others tried to find a record deal in Hollywood.

We saw a lot of people at the Whiskey from the Blondie shows, but we also met some new people, like Greg Shaw from Bomp Records and Gary Stewart who would later run Rhino Records. Another new face was Steve Zepeda. Steve had seen the Blondie shows and was a big fan. He was putting together a fanzine and was also in the market to produce a record. Were Lisa and I familiar with the scene here in LA? If we liked, he could take us around.

I liked Steve and especially liked the idea that he was interested in putting out a record. He took us to Canter's, the all-night deli on Fairfax Boulevard in Hollywood's Jewish district, one of the few places where late night rockers could grab a bite, meet friends or conduct a drug deal. It had a hint of New York atmosphere, the waitresses had attitude, and during the punk years a bar attached to the restaurant, the Kibbitz Room, became a local haunt. But Canter's was unusual for LA. Most of the hangouts Steve took us to were straight out of 'I Was A Teenage Teenager'. There was a greasy burger stand on Santa Monica Boulevard known as Oki Dog, named after a concoction invented by the owner. Santa Monica Boulevard was West Hollywood's big gay strip, and the place was later closed down for being a front for the thriving Hollywood teenage prostitution racket. A less notorious burger stand was the Fatburger at La Cienega and San Vicente Boulevards.

Down the road from the Oki Dog was Melrose Avenue – of 1990s TV fame. In the eighties Melrose became a kind of poor man's Kings Road, cluttered with Dr Martens and leather jackets, but in 1977 there wasn't much there. Steve took us to Aardvark's, a second-hand clothes shop where skinny ties could be had. A few doors down was Aron's Records, a magnet for collectors. Like Zed Records in Long Beach – one of those forty-five-minute drives to the 'other side of town' LA is famous for – and Bomp in the Valley, Aron's was a central supplier of new wave. Another important record shop was Vinyl Fetish, which catered to the growing punk scene. A less specialized outlet was Rhino, in Westwood. Like Bomp, Rhino later became a major indie and reissue label.

Another important meeting place was the Capitol Records Swap Meet, in the parking lot of the Capitol Records building, a massive boot sale at Hollywood and Vine. It originally started on the first Sunday of the month, but over the years dealers set up earlier and earlier, and when Steve took us people were showing up at midnight. Collectors and vinyl anoraks would shine flashlights into boxes of old 45s, rare albums and other rock paraphernalia. Early punkers ran around hawking their wares on new independent labels like Dangerhouse and Slash. I remember the first night we went I signed a handful of *Blondie* albums and 'X-Offender' 45s that then sold for twice as much. Later, tired of the wreckage left by the punks, Capitol Records closed the swap meets down.

►►

Steve told us about a band he was thinking of taking into the
studio. One night he brought us along to a rehearsal. The
Furys were from Orange County, a part of California mainly
known for Disneyland and for being predominantly Repub-
lican. They sounded like Bruce Springsteen meets the Who,
and the lead singer, Jeff Wolfe, was a poet. Like the LA
punks but with more heart, they sang out their frustrations
with suburbia. It was clear they already had their own sound
and didn't need me, but one thing came out of that session:
one of the songs I played that night was 'The First One',
written for the second Blondie album and performed at my
last show with them at the Village Gate. It was pure pop
and Steve loved it. The lines between punk and 'power
pop' were being drawn, and Steve knew there was an underground market for a strong pop single. Immediately, he said
he wanted to finance putting 'The First One' out as a 45. All
I had to do now was find a band.

When word got round that I was looking for musicians
our telephone rang off the hook. One early candidate was
Jeffrey Lee Pierce. Jeffrey later went on to write for LA's
punk magazine *Slash* – a combination *Punk* and *New York
Rocker* – and to have his own band, the Gun Club. Like so
many from that time, he would eventually drink and drug
himself to an early death. The afternoon he came to our
room, he was shy and rather awkward. By this time Blondie
had released *Plastic Letters* and most reviewers had picked
'Presence, Dear' as the best track on the album. Blondie's
cover of the early sixties hit 'Denis', had entered the UK top
ten and they seemed on their way to stardom. Jeffrey was a
big fan – he even started the Blondie fan club – and was a bit
nervous at the prospect of auditioning for one of Blondie's
founding members. We strummed at 'Presence, Dear' and I
showed him a couple new tunes. But it didn't really gel, and
after a while I called it quits. He was disappointed but

understood. Later he wrote one of the first articles on me for *New York Rocker*.

The Mumps being in town solved the problem of finding a band to record my 45. In early 1978, Rob DuPrey, Kristian Hoffman (keyboards), Paul Rutner (drums) and I went into a basement studio in the Valley and recorded two tracks, 'The First One' and 'Tomorrow Belongs to You', a take-off of the Nazi youth hymn. I hadn't yet made the switch to guitar and played bass, and it was my first serious attempt at singing. The studio was small and minimal. 'The First One' was a straightforward love song, but 'Tomorrow' had a message. It was my anti-nihilism song, directed against the punks who were whining about no future.

Steve was calling his label Beat Records, a nod both to the beat generation and the beat groups of the sixties. He was also putting out a fanzine. *New York Rocker* would later call *L.A. Beat* 'the best American 'zine around'.* His taste was definitely and defiantly mod. By 1978, two mutually antipathetic groups had emerged in the LA underground, their version of the skinny tie and ripped T-shirt crowds that had polarized in CBGB.

It was a late seventies US West Coast take on the mods and rockers of sixties UK, with the pop crowd in the role of the mods and the punks as the rockers. In New York this had manifested in nothing more violent than a few half-comatose sneers exchanged between opposing factions. Being third best, LA had to try harder. They had also inherited three years-worth of underground music, first from New York, then from London. There's something unsubtle in the LA psyche. Maybe it's the perpetual sunshine, or maybe it's living in a bunch of suburbs looking for a city. But the New

---

* 'Fanzines au Fromage', M. Linna, *New York Rocker*, November 1978, p. 17.

York cool of Patti Smith, Television and Richard Hell didn't take. Safety pins, leather, chains and vomit – the whole UK thing – did. LA punks even developed a real hatred of New York, part of the generic East Coast–West Coast rivalry that had been going on for years. By the summer of 1977 a hard core punk scene based on the Sex Pistols and every bit as nasty had grown up in Tinseltown.

There had been an earlier local band network. In August of 1976, three LA street bands, the Pop, the Dogs and the Motels, unable to find work on the disco- and Top Forty-dominated Strip, rented a hall and got together their own concert. A local radio DJ christened the event Radio Free Hollywood. It was a success and the name stuck. A fanzine with the same title came out soon after. It had no mention of punk and in Phast Phreddie's 'Pharmaceutically 45' column the hot news is about the Flamin' Groovies and the Nerves, pop groups both.

It was this crowd that came to see Blondie. Rock and roll anoraks, into the sixties pop scene, their life's blood was cool obscure 45s dug out of some cutout bin.

Then in April 1977 with the Damned shows at the Starwood – a veteran rock club on Santa Monica Boulevard – life changed. Soon after, at a Punk Rock Invasion show at the Orpheum Theatre on Sunset Boulevard, the Dils played in front of a hammer and sickle flag, and the Germs' Bobby Pyn – later the ill-fated Darby Crash – ended their set by winning the Iggy Pop lookalike contest, covering himself in peanut butter while being whipped with licorice. At Kim Fowley's New Wave Rock 'n' Roll Weekend at the Whiskey, Darby and friends started a food fight that had them banned from the club. Darby was making a successful play to become LA's comic version of Sid Vicious and Germs' fans later identified each other by the self-inflicted cigarette burns on their arms. Other groups got the fever and followed suit.

On 4 July – Independence Day – the Weirdos burned an American flag on stage at the Starwood and were banned. The Troubador – a landmark sixties West Hollywood venue – said no to punk after a Bags show when the punters overturned tables. In July of 1977 the scene eventually produced its own version of CBGB. That summer Scots entrepreneur Brendan Mullen opened The Masque, a basement rehearsal space turned punk den of iniquity on Cherokee Boulevard in the heart of seedy Hollywood. Its house rules were 'excess, excess, excess'. Graffiti blared FAGS IS NOT COOL and KILL ALL HIPPIES. Dress code demanded swastikas. Magazines like *Slash* and *Lobotomy* kept SoCal punkers up to date with the increasingly cliquish scene. Johnny Rotten had said, 'We're not into music, we're into chaos.' LA listened, and were you a *real* punk or not became the burning question of the day.

Soon after recording 'The First One', Steve introduced me to someone I would work with for the next two and half years. Richard D'Andrea had been in the Motels, an LA group led by the moody Martha Davis. He was intelligent, serious, an excellent bass player, wrote good songs and had a sense of humor. After meeting Richard I got in touch with Joel Turrisi, a drummer I had met at the Roxy and, after trying out a second guitarist and deciding to go on as a three-piece, my own group, the Know, was born.

I came up with the name from my reading. My interest in magic and occultism had expanded, and I was devouring books on philosophy, psychology, religion and mysticism. I was especially interested in gnosticism, a mystical teaching that had grown up in the first centuries following Christ and which later influenced people like the psychologist Jung. I was spending a lot of time at LA occult haunts like Gilbert's

Bookshop on Hollywood Boulevard – which claimed people like Jimmy Page and David Bowie as customers – and the Philosophical Research Society in Los Feliz, listening to lectures by the local gnostic Stephan Hoeller. Gnosis means knowledge, and I had a raging appetite for it. Hence, the Know.

It was the first sign of a tendency that would wreck me for the music business. I was becoming too smart for rock 'n' roll.

The Know made their debut at the Whiskey, with a surprise set in between the Quick and the Mumps on 11 March 1978. Two weeks later we were back again. In April we opened for the heavy metal band Judas Priest, one of the worst shows of my life. In her *Sounds* review, Sylvie Simmons said I just about escaped alive. She was right. The heavy metallers had no idea what to do with us and the most response we got were shouts of 'terrible'. A week later we were up in San Francisco, playing with Jonathan Postal's Readymades at the Mabuhay Gardens. The San Francisco scene had really taken off, with bands like the Nuns and Crime, and had by then produced its own magazine, *Search and Destroy*. After the Mabuhay we were back at the Whiskey, then the Starwood, then the Mabuhay again. In June we opened for David Johansen's new band. The *Variety* review of our show remarked on our version of Dylan's 'I Want You', which we dedicated to 'the late great Robert Zimmerman'. After the Johansen shows I got a call from New York. Tommy Dean had heard about us and wanted us to play Max's. He'd pay the air fares and ensure decent money. In July we made our New York debut. A year after leaving Blondie I was back in town with my own band.

Our reputation preceded us, we had great press, so the shows at Max's were a success. In the same month 'The First One' had finally been released and was getting rave reviews, making its way to number eight in various new wave charts, topping Patti Smith's 'Because the Night' and Plastic Bertrand's 'Ça Plane Pour Moi'. Lisa had taken the photo for the picture sleeve: a shot of me and a copy of Nietzsche's *Beyond Good and Evil*. I was the 'pix to clique' in Greg Shaw's singles column in *Bomp. Melody Maker* loved the single. Rodney played it. So did Meg Griffin on New York's WNEW. At the same time Blondie had released 'Presence, Dear' as a single in the UK and it had already hit the top ten there. We also played the first of many shows at a new club, Hurrah, more of which later.

Reviews of the CBGB debut, sharing a bill with Wire were also good. Both *NME* and the *SoHo Weekly News* gave us raves. When we got back to LA, Lisa and I haunted the Cahuenga Newstand at Hollywood Boulevard, peering at the UK top ten list in *Billboard*, anxious to see 'Presence, Dear' stay in the charts. More gigs followed. *L.A. Beat* ran an embarrassingly long interview with me. The *Los Angeles Times* put us in its roundup of the 'hot 12' bands on the new music front, and spoke of my remarkable 'comeback' after leaving Blondie. It seemed only a matter of time before we would get signed. But not every one had as sanguine an outlook.

Although it didn't seem that way to me, around the same time as our New York success, critics like Greg Shaw were saying the punk party was over,* and not without reason. In January, after their show at the Winterland Ballroom in San Francisco, disillusioned by Malcolm McLaren's manipulations, Johnny Rotten announced the end of the Sex Pistols. Television, too, had turned itself off that August, and the year before Patti Smith had broken her neck in a fall during a show in Tampa, Florida.

---

* 'New Wave Goodbye?', *New York Rocker*, 14 September 1978.

But Shaw's main complaint was that the new music just hadn't made enough sales. The Ramones were just hanging on, and Richard Hell's debut album flopped – helped in no small part by his escalating visits to Edgar Allen Poe's living room and a seriously miscarried UK tour with the Clash. The only groups that were able to survive were acts like Blondie who, after a fling with punk, saw that that particular bandwagon was heading nowhere, and changed horses. By early 1979 they had become a disco band. 'The Disco Song', one of the tunes I first learned with Chris, sitting on my bed at Thompson Street, conquered the world as 'Heart of Glass'. By that time, Nigel Harrison, whom they were cozying up to during our Whiskey shows in 1977, had been recruited. Photos showed him in sneakers, black jeans, narrow lapels and the regimental skinny tie, looking curiously like their previous bassist.

Shaw was right, but it would take another year for the scene itself to catch up. From my perspective, in the summer of 1978, new wave, punk or whatever it was, was getting attention in Hollywood and in early October, the Know played a show at a new club in Chinatown, Madame Wong's.

Esther Wong was born in Shanghai and was the last person you'd expect to be a rock and roll impresario. She had travelled the world, and in 1949 settled in LA with her husband George. Thirty years later, in the fall of 1978, Madame Wong's, a Cantonese supper club in LA's Chinatown named after Esther herself, put aside the won tons and chop suey and made way for a large helping of new wave. Esther had opened the place in 1970 and business had been good. But by 1978, the Polynesian Review – hand-picked by Esther on her jaunts to Hawaii – just wasn't bringing in the bucks, and except for a few regulars at the bar, the place was empty. One of those regulars was entrepreneur and motorcycle fanatic Paul Greenstein. Paul, who had his hand in

Millie's, a popular coffee shop in the Silverlake District, was anxious to get involved in the local music scene. He had a chat with Esther and convinced her that giving over the place to some rock bands a few nights a week would boost sales.

Esther wasn't sure at first but Paul was persuasive. When Esther turned up for Paul's first night as a booking agent, and saw the line around the block and the room already packed to capacity, she thought that maybe he was on to something after all.

On 3 October 1978 Gary Valentine and the Know were the first band to bring rock and roll to LA's Chinatown.* On a Wednesday night, with the Furys as support, we drew 350 people in skinny ties and narrow lapels to Madame Wong's, and jammed them into a room built to hold half that number. It was the biggest LA new wave gathering to date. Most of the people who went on to have bands or to have anything to do with 'the scene' were there that night. The Sunday before the show, I went on Rodney Bingenheimer's radio show and told his audience that if they wanted to have their own scene in LA, they had better get out the following Wednesday. They did, more than we could allow in. Lisa could barely get through the crowd cramming up the stairway. I remember having to pull her up through a wall of tab collar shirts. The gig was an unqualified success. We did two great sets and so did the Furys. Afterwards we were all invited for free food to the Atomic Café, a late-night Japanese eatery in Little Tokyo that was popular with the downtown art crowd. It had recently given itself and its jukebox over to the scene. We brought a huge entourage with us and after that the place became a new wave hang out. New wave

---

* Several punk historians have written about this event. None have got it right. For the record: the Know and the Furys were the first rock and roll bands to play Madame Wong's.

or power pop seemed on the rise, and punk on the way out. To put the event in perspective: on the other side of the country, a little more than a week after our debut at Madame Wong's, Sid Vicious was arrested for the murder of Nancy Spungen, who had been found stabbed to death in their room at the Chelsea Hotel.

The food was lousy at Madame Wong's, and the drinks expensive. But LA now had its own new wave club. The Masque had closed down in February, a victim of the growing enmity between punks and the LAPD. LA cops were notoriously draconian and hadn't seen anything like the punk scene since the riots on Sunset Strip in 1967. Riots had become a regular part of the set, like the one Henry Rollins's Black Flag inaugurated at the Whiskey. LA cops were swift to close venues down. This eventually led to the Whiskey closing its doors to punk bands when, in August of 1978, Michel Meyer, who was open to groups like the Plugz, the Weirdos and the Flesheaters, lost her job and was replaced by the more conservative David Forest. The Starwood had already said no to punk. If the scene was going to go beyond the showbizzy milieu of the Hollywood clubs, it would have to produce a new venue.

It did. Richard Cromelin even made it official in his rave review of our show at Madame Wong's in the *Los Angeles Times*. Greenstein's idea worked, and Madame Wong's became the place to play in LA. At the height of their success, even the Police gave up playing at a larger and more prestigious venue to do a show there. For the next two years we were regulars, playing there something like twenty times – once even opening for ourselves as the Bookworms, in which I played drums.

But Esther would soon become disenchanted with the increasingly uncontrollable punks who were filling her club. Although bands like the Plugz would play in the early days,

Esther rapidly grew tired of the broken bottles, smashed tables and obnoxious behavior that accompanied a punk show. Esther ran a tight ship and had no time for nonsense; once she made two of the Ramones clean off the graffiti they had left on her bathroom walls. Not too long after he had paved a silk road to Chinatown for LA's punkers, Greenstein was without a job. He left Madame Wong's and got involved in other projects, one of which was another club, Blackies, which we played. Esther hired another booking agent, and innocuous 'nice' groups like 20/20, the Zippers, Code Blue, the Textones and ourselves became her usual suspects.

Seeing the success of their neighbor, in summer of the following year, the Hong Kong Café opened its doors to all who were turned away by Esther. The Hong Kong was as pro punk as Esther was anti, and the courtyard of the Chinatown village both clubs shared became the setting for frequent bang-ups between the safety pins and the skinny ties. We never played the Hong Kong and were generally despised by the punks, who blamed me for bringing the dreaded skinny tie to town, although we did make it into photographer Donna Santisi's collection of faces on the scene, *Ask the Angels*. A lot of Penelope Spheeris's ambitiously titled punk rockumentary, *The Decline of Western Civilization*, which depicts the LA punk scene at its height – or depth – was shot in the Hong Kong Café.

A week after Madame Wong's we did the Troubador. Until then it had cold-shouldered the new wave, and it would have been better if it had stayed that way. The Troubador was one of the worst places we played. After two sold-out standing-room-only sets, the owner Doug Weston told us that after expenses we had only made fifty dollars. That kind of small-town rip-off was still going on in some places in LA, but more and more clubs were realizing that starving bands out of existence wasn't a way to keep a scene alive.

A week after the Troubador we were back in New York, playing Max's. After that we did two shows with the B-Girls at the Artimis and the Hot Club in Philadelphia. Then we were at Hurrah again where we opened for the Dolls glam-clone, Japan, and then Max's again, around and around on the new wave circuit. We were becoming the house band at Hurrah, generally pulling in around three thousand dollars for a weekend and usually sharing the bill with a local group, the Student Teachers, that Jimmy Destri had taken under his wing. By this time the old Blondie wounds were forgotten and Jimmy and I had become friends again. There was even talk of him producing an album with us. He got us into the studio for a demo for Chrysalis, but nothing came of it. I wasn't too disappointed. We were getting lots of good press and other labels like Warner Brothers and A&M were showing interest. It seemed like it was only a matter of time.

On one trip to New York I met the LSD guru Timothy Leary. My interest in altered states of consciousness had grown and I was reading everything I could about them as well as conducting some personal experiments. Leary, who had spent the last few years in jail, was making a comeback, doing a form of psychedelic stand-up comedy. I had seen his lecture at the Masonic Hall in LA and a mutual acquaintance told Tim of my interests. Leary was eager to attract a younger audience, and the idea of doing a show with a new wave rock band was appealing.

We met at a coffee shop in Greenwich Village to talk about splitting a bill at Madame Wong's. Leary was lively, animated and chatty, nothing like the burnt-out acid head I was told to expect. He was extremely intelligent and the only sign that he may have overdone it with drugs was a strange sparkle in his eyes. Throughout the meeting he flashed that manic grin I had seen in dozens of photographs from the sixties. I told him about the mystical literature I was reading and my experiences with psychedelics. He gave me one of his books and told me about his ideas on life extension and space migration, the new message he had for the seventies. Then he asked if I knew that Debbie Harry had been one of the people at Castalia, his acid community in upstate New York in the sixties. I didn't. Oh yes, he said, with a smile. Unfortunately, by the time we were both in LA, Leary had either forgotten about our idea or was too busy, and the show never happened.

In the meantime we were becoming as much a New York group as an LA one. For the next two years, we took the red-eye back and forth across the country becoming possibly the only bi-coastal band on the scene. Air fares back then were incredibly cheap, and it was easy to get from LA to New York for a hundred dollars – anyway, most clubs would pay our fare. Just on the eve of one our New York jaunts Joel, our drummer, proved unreliable, leaving the group to join rival band 20/20. I was tempted to cancel the shows, then had an idea. I called Clem Burke in New York and asked if he'd like to do the gigs. Clem said yes, so did Jimmy, and with Rob DuPrey we did a weekend at Hurrah, packing the place with a kind of mini-Blondie reunion.

On one trip I had a brainstorm and decided that instead of flying back to LA, I'd take the Greyhound. I wore my black suit and climbed on board with a suitcase, my guitar and an amplifier. It was probably the most gruesome experience of my life, even worse than the angel dust I had smoked with Debbie. It was a three day non-stop run and I found it impossible to sleep. The driver stopped at the worst places for food and I saw the bus stations of practically every major city across the nation. By the third day I was hallucinating. In New Mexico the cacti were waving at me. When I got back home it was Christmas Eve and a party was going on at the house, but I was too dazed to do anything but crash out. I had been in New York for the last two months, and the first cracks in my relationship with Lisa were beginning to show. I was increasingly attracting and responding to the attentions of other women and, like all girlfriends, she could tell. Whether I liked it or not, she was still in touch with my presence.

By 1979 the band was averaging at least one performance a week. We also met some people. At a party in Hollywood, I met Tom Waits, who was then living in an old Buick in the parking lot of the Tropicana Hotel. At a show at the Whiskey, Stiv Bators from the Dead Boys jumped on stage, pulled out a harmonica, and we went through an unplanned version of the old Dolls' cover, 'Pills'. The Dead Boys were on their way to extinction, having failed to crack the charts, and would soon be dropped by Sire. Stiv was in town looking for his next meal ticket. Sadly, in 1990, he would die in a car accident in France. A producer we were working with on a demo for Warner Brothers knew how much I liked the first Modern Lovers album and brought me to a studio where Jonathan Richman was recording. He tried to introduce us but Jonathan was in his own world and didn't have time for a fan.

February saw us back in New York, where the big news was the death of Sid Vicious. In March we did one of our weirdest shows; our booking agent got us a date in Salt Lake City, headquarters of the Mormons. Utah is a dry state. Bars sell only wine and beer and the crowd that weekend at the Abbey Road had no idea what to make of us. Not a skinny tie in the place. We were billed as one of the hottest new LA bands. At least when we played with Judas Priest the head-bangers booed. Here they did nothing. I tried a Donny and Marie Osmond joke – both are Mormons – but that had no effect. We went through our set, picked up our thousand dollars, and went home.

Soon after, at Madame Wong's, Peter Leeds showed up. Although he hadn't lifted a finger to help my career he was, in theory at least, still my manager. 'Presence, Dear' had sold some ridiculous number of copies. Leeds knew there was industry interest and wanted to secure his grip. By this time Debbie and Chris were kicking themselves for signing that contract. Leeds had made a lot of money from them and they wanted to pry him loose. Leeds stood against the oriental backdrop, beamed an unctuous smile and handed me an envelope and a package. A gold record for 'Presence, Dear' was in the package. The envelope held a check for five thousand dollars. Then he put on the charm. 'You know, Gary,' he said, 'you're really not a performer; you're a poet.' I don't remember what I said.

▶▶

By early 1979 the punk scene in LA had started to implode. The Canterbury Arms, an old Hollywood apartment building a bottle's throw from the Masque, had become a kind of punk flophouse, with groups like the later cutesy Go-Go's learning the ropes in the basement. As in Haight-Ashbury after the summer of love, the rock pioneers brought in the low life homesteaders, and what had been party central became the scene of rapes, violence and even worse drugs than the punks were already taking. In March at the Elks Lodge near MacArthur Park – locale for Jimmy Webb's sixties psychedelic ditty – a riot broke out during a show featuring the Plugz and the Alleycats. The LAPD arrived, and two sources of SoCal belligerence and psychosis met head-on. For the rest of its existence, confrontational violence would characterize the LA scene. We had played the Elks Lodge earlier in the year with the Readymades, and even at our relatively harmless show, the police were in evidence, looking for any reason to shut us down.

In April, the *LA Weekly*, a new freebie paper that was bidding to become a West Coast *Village Voice*, ran a long piece entitled 'Yes, There Are Punks In LA', trying to rally the dwindling forces. In the same issue Lisa had an editorial, 'At Punks' End'. The piece included extracts from a local scenester's 'punk diary': 'By the time we went to the party at the Tropicana, everyone was really drunk. KK drank a whole glass of straight rum and then champagne and pretty soon he passed out on the grass and he stayed there all night ... We went CRAZY. This is Hollywood. The police came ...' Lisa's editorial bemoaned the 'deadly serious nihilistic approach' of the *nouveau* punks, faddists who had 'illegitimately appropriated' the 'razor blades, safety pins and vomit' of the British scene and turned these into a sick fashion. 'The Dervishes,' she wrote, 'are dancing madly to somebody else's tastes ...'

Lisa had been one of the originals, reading her poetry at CBGB before I had even heard of the place, and now she saw what four years of punk had wrought. Worse was to come. As mass interest in punk faded, a new hard core contingent threw themselves – and others – into a last blaze of glory. An extremely violent, fascistic skinhead crowd from the suburbs and beach towns started to invade the Hollywood clubs. Where the Hollywood punks had some inkling of the symbolic value of violence, these guys just liked to bang heads – anyone's that was different from theirs. Pogoing had been *de rigueur* for years and one agile young fan known as Spaz Stick had made a name for himself by going head over heels in somersaults on the dance floors. But now slamdancing had arrived, and thick-headed, shorn-scalped Neanderthals from Huntington Beach and points west lurched dangerously at anyone they cared to. It wasn't long before most clubs were seeing their own mini-versions of the demonic Rolling Stones concert at Altamont Speedway, ten years earlier. It was mob violence to a 4/4 beat. Gangs of skinheads would slam into anyone next to them, throwing them onto the floor, into tables or against the wall. People were hurt. Fights broke out and there were stabbings. Lisa and I just stopped going to clubs. It was too easy to attract attention. We were so obviously unpunk that we were easy targets. Even at our own gigs, skinhead surfers got off on smashing faces. As far as the punks were concerned, by this time Rimbaud was on his way to becoming Rambo.

In September we played at the M-80 New Wave Festival in Minneapolis. The bill included Devo who played as Dove, Richard Lloyd's new band, the Specials, ourselves and a dozen other groups. It drew close to five thousand people. We got two encores. Then we were in New York at Hurrah again with the B-Girls. On New Year's Eve we played Madame Wong's.

By the end of 1979, not only punk was at an end. My relationship with Lisa was winding down. Two things precipitated the final split: one was my obsession with magic, the other was sex.

▶▶

One day I saw an advertisement for an Aleister Crowley magic group at Gilbert's Bookshop. Not expecting much to come of it, I answered it. Two days later, we got a knock at the door. It was my first encounter with someone we later took to calling 'He who is not to be named'. The reason for this will become apparent.

Over the next few months I got deep into Crowley's magick, performing rituals, wearing robes, developing my astral vision, practising tarot and engaging in various other occult activities. I was initiated into two of Crowley's magical societies, the A.A. and the O.T.O., dedicated to his religion of 'Thelema', which was centered around discovering your 'true will'. The ceremony took place in a tent in a room in some LA suburb.

After that, along with other occult disciplines, four times a day – at dawn, noon, sunset and midnight – I had to perform an adoration to the sun. Getting up at dawn was my own affair, but my assiduous practise often embarrassed Lisa. She never really took to my suddenly standing up in some Hollywood coffee shop and, facing south at noon, intoning 'Hail unto thee Ahathoor in thy triumphing, even unto thee who art Ahathoor in thy beauty . . .' while making the necessary occult signs. The chants of 'Hail Isis, mighty mother' coming from the second room we had finally taken, as I practised the Greater Ritual of the Hexagram, got on her nerves. But it was my mystic mentor that really pissed her off.

'He' turned out to be an occult freeloader, who used my fascination with strange powers to his own advantage. He borrowed money and took to having his meals at our house. He managed to get one of the girls who lived with us under his spell and moved in with her, even getting her to sew magical robes for the two of us. They practiced sex magic together, and my mentor apprised me of its benefits. I tried it with Lisa, but she said nothing doing, and our erotic life shrank after that. Every time I wanted to make love, she thought I was just using her to contact the higher planes. He had some peculiar personal habits, one of which was wearing a concoction of civet and sandalwood, which was apparently a favorite of Crowley's. His car had a leaky fuel pump and reeked of petrol, and the combination of scents gave me a headache. He also turned out to be a part-time junkie. Things would go missing around the house, and after a while we figured it out.

Like Freemasons, members of the O.T.O. were supposed to help each other, providing jobs for brothers who were down at heel. He was broke most of the time and eventually suggested we use him as a roadie. He was horrible at it. He had no idea what to do with an amplifier, and couldn't fit a drum kit together to save his life. We wound up doing all the work ourselves and eventually the other guys threatened to quit if I didn't fire him. Luckily, after a few gigs my mentor decided that hauling equipment in his smelly car was too lowly a position for an exalted magus and quit.

The magic group turned out to be little more than an Aleister Crowley fan club. We got together, smoked grass and thought how great it would be if, like Crowley, we could climb a Himalaya or live in a house near Loch Ness. Some of the guys were into Crowley's gay sex magic, and mentioned it to me. I wasn't impressed. Others practiced his mystical masturbation techniques while travelling on the astral planes. They took a lot of acid and make frequent trips to the desert, hunted for magic mushrooms and practiced weird rituals. They dressed up like Crowley, smoked meerschaum pipes, and said 'Do what thou wilt' every chance they got.

Lisa knew from the start that he was a creep and tried to get me to see reason. He had Lisa pegged as the enemy and tried to turn me against her. I knew she was right, but my desire to penetrate the mystic darkness was too great. I had also read so much about wild sex and drug orgies happening around these groups that I was loath to drop out before I had experienced one. I was also very serious about my magical exercises, which occasionally produced strange results. It is also possible they were having an adverse effect.

Around the same time I had a strange series of anxiety attacks that convinced me I was about to have a cardiac arrest. My heart would thump and a queer vibration would start in my chest and arms. Lisa suggested I get checked out. On the application form at the clinic I entered 'Thelema' as my religion. What the doctor thought of that I don't know. After hooking me up for an ECG, he told me there was nothing wrong with my heart and suggested I try psychotherapy.

Toward the end I finally had my shot at the mystic orgy. I was invited to attend a performance of Crowley's Gnostic Mass. Part of the ritual included eating a communion wafer spiked with menstrual blood. When I mentioned this to Lisa she looked at me as if I was insane. I went, duly appointed in my mystic robes and hood, ate the wafer and waited. Other people in robes and hoods stood around an altar. Incense burned. The priestess entered. I thought perhaps she would be deflowered on the altar, but no such luck. After some intoning and a few passes of a mystic cup, the party was over. People pulled back their hoods and somebody opened some beers. I lost interest in Crowley after that.*

Sex, however, was another matter.

In LA, Lisa came to every show, and more times than not, chased any groupies out of the dressing room. One time at the Whiskey, it was clear to both of us that some new wave hopeful sitting across from me had come out without her underwear. She inched her skirt up every few minutes and did ballet splits in a sitting position, hoping to catch my

---

* My interest in magic continued for a while. During my New York period, in preparation for a ritual celebrating the autumnal equinox, I took a twenty-four-hour vow of silence. I spent the day as I usually did, and ran into a lot of people. When I declined to speak to them they all thought I had lost it.

eye. I was mildly curious, but Lisa fumed. Finally she produced one of her classic lines: 'Why don't you fold up your
legs and go home?' But when I was in New York I was on
my own. Practically every night I saw dozens of girls I was
curious about and it was only a matter of time before I found
out about them.

The first time I did was at CBGB. I'm not sure how we met,
but I wound up with some punketta at the pinball machine.
She was attractive, and as I showed her how to manipulate
the flippers, she leant her bottom into me and left it there,
swaying invitingly. We played a lot of pinball that night. One
thing led to another and after a few drinks we went back to
her apartment. We started making out and then she said she
had a surprise. She opened a closet, pulled out a mink coat,
laid it on the floor and undressed. I can still feel the electric
sensation of her naked body against the mink. I saw her a few
times after that, and there were a few others. It was incredibly
easy to pick up girls. But these were all brief incidents and
nothing much came of them. And then I met Lulu.

Lulu was a model and had sex written all over her. She
had raven black wavy hair, bright red lips, white inviting
breasts and an eagerness to try anything. The six months we
were together were one long erotic encounter. After months
of a relationship with a stalled sex life, I was voracious. I was
twenty-three and until my recent infidelities had slept with
only three women, the first time with disastrous consequences. Lulu had seen one of our shows at Hurrah and
wanted to meet me. A mutual friend obliged. At our first
encounter both of us knew that sooner or later we'd wind up
in bed, and sooner rather than later. The mutual friend got
the vibe as well and was pissed. He had staked Lulu out as
his own property and had to settle for her girlfriend. After
Lulu and I broke up, eager to make up for my slow start, I
bedded the girlfriend as well.

On our first date Lulu suggested we really get to know each other. Sitting at a café on the Upper East Side, she pulled out an unusual ice-breaker: a bag of *psilocybin mexicana*, magic mushrooms. Lisa was drug-free; an early bad experience eating hash brownies had turned her off getting stoned for life, and she hardly ever drank. Lulu had no such inhibitions. I was impressed. She popped a few 'shrooms in her mouth and gulped. I knocked mine back with an espresso. Then we looked at each other.

'Well,' I said. 'What do you want to do?'

She had an idea: she wanted to go to the planetarium. It was late afternoon and if we rushed we could just about make it. We ran out of the café and grabbed a cab. Near the Museum of Natural History the cab stopped and we hopped out. Just as we got to the door, the planetarium closed.

'Shit!' she said.

'What now?' I asked.

Then we looked at each other. A tingling had started in my stomach and I had the strongest urge to laugh. The mushrooms were coming on. Lulu must have felt it too because she had a ridiculous smile on her face. All I wanted to do was lie on the ground and roll around, but it was rush hour and the street was crowded with people. Lulu flagged down another cab, grabbed my hand and said, 'Come on!'

We hopped in. She blared out some direction; I couldn't tell where because I was too busy giggling. Then she pulled a joint out of her bag and lit it. I wasn't surprised. I had smoked joints in cabs before, but the mushrooms seemed very potent and I was already flying. But Lulu liked getting stoned. She took a drag, handed it to me, then took it back and knocked on the window to get the driver's attention.

'Hey! You want some of this!'

'Wow,' the driver said. 'Shit, no I can't, not while I'm driving.'

'Oh, too bad.'

Then she opened the bag and pulled out another one.

'Here,' she said. 'Take this for later.'

'Wow. Thanks.'

I had no idea where we were going and was rapidly losing any worries about it. In the course of that taxi ride Lulu changed her mind half a dozen times, turning down side streets and up avenues in a crazed pattern. We had finished the joint and were somewhere in mid-town. The mushrooms were gurgling through our bloodstreams and the rush hour traffic seemed like friezes on an ancient temple. Lulu looked out the window and seemed sunk in thought. Then she must have decided that there was really only one place she wanted to go. She leant against me and grabbed my hand.

'Listen,' she said, looking into my dilated eyes. 'Do you want to go to my place?'

'Sure,' I said.

Then she told the driver to turn around.

Lulu's place was the Gramercy Park Hotel. At the time I was living on my friend John's couch in his tiny apartment on Perry Street in the West Village.* I was making money but not living too lavishly. For Lulu to afford the Gramercy Park meant that she was making money too.

By the time we got to her room all my inhibitions were obliterated and the only thing I wanted was to get her clothes off. She was ready to oblige. But first she wanted me to know

---

* One of my favorite New York memories is of that apartment. One morning, after a long night out, I woke up to pee. Standing over the toilet, I looked out the window at the roof of the neighboring building. At first I didn't believe it, and chalked it up to the hangover, but no; I was right. A naked woman was dancing on the roof. She was beautiful, and I stood watching her prance across the tar without a stitch. I woke up John. He couldn't believe it either. Then we saw the guy with the camera and realized she was being photographed.

something. She said she didn't want this to be a one-night stand. She was falling in love with me and didn't want to get hurt. If I wasn't serious about her then we should just stop now. She knew I had a girlfriend but the minute she saw me on stage she knew she wanted me. If I didn't want her then I should just go.

All right, I said, and kissed her. Then we got undressed.

When I got back to LA, Lisa knew something had happened.

Not long after that the band moved to New York.

►►

In the beginning of 1980 we recorded a track, 'I Like Girls', a parody of the boy-loves-girl standard, for a Planet Records new wave sampler called *Sharp Cuts*. It got good reviews, but by this time most record companies weren't taking many chances and the whole procedure just felt like going through the motions. Then, in late March, we played our last show at Madame Wong's.

It was an apt farewell. We got a part in a TV film, *A Cry For Love*, with Susan Blakely and Powers Boothe. They played a speed-freak, alcoholic couple in a drug-filled romance, an early entry in the recovery genre that would hit big later in the decade. Craving a fix, Blakely needs to score. Boothe knows just the place and takes her to Madame Wong's.

If they really wanted punk, the art director picked the wrong band. We didn't care; the money was good and we'd be on prime time. But the fifty or so punks who always turned up whenever Hollywood needed extras weren't happy. We lip-synced to our song. Through the whole shooting, they shouted 'These guys suck!' 'Get 'em off!' 'Fuck them!' It took a lot to keep cool, but at the end I picked up the check and went home. The best thing about it was that I called my parents and told them I'd be on TV again.

Four days later we were playing the Town Hall in New York's Theatre District, on a bill with the MC5, the Dead Boys and the Troggs, the sixties legends that had given the world 'Wild Thing'. We had also picked up a very good new drummer, John McGarvey. We had auditioned a few, got along with John and liked working with him the best. It was unfortunate, though, that he'd be with us only a short time. It was the start of the last days of the Know, which for the rest of its life was a New York band.

When I first got to New York I stayed with Lulu at the Gramercy Park Hotel. After living in a house with four other people for two years it was heavenly. Lulu worked for the best magazines. She did fashion shows, and frequently went off to Tokyo and Paris. I was collecting royalties and making two or three thousand dollars a weekend at the clubs. We had money. Room service woke us with coffee at noon, picked up our laundry and brought it back the next day. We'd amble down to a favorite restaurant on Third Avenue for lunch. If we felt like exercise we'd make the hike to the East Village and the Kiev, the Russian coffee shop that had opened a couple years back and featured punk rock waitresses. Lulu had a key to Gramercy Park itself, which is private, and after lunch we'd shut ourselves off from the New York crunch and stroll among the flowers. At some point we'd head back to the room and make love. Then dinner somewhere with wine, drinks after, maybe with some friends, and back to the room for more sex. A vial of coke would appear and we'd get inspired. Then we'd have more sex. Finally, somewhere around midnight, we'd get ready to hit the clubs.

By 1980 both CBGB and Max's had passed their prime

18 NEW YORK ROCKER

and the new spots were Hurrah, the Ritz, Irving Plaza and
the Mudd Club.* There were a handful of other places. All
of them I played and in all them of I spent more time than
I care to remember.

Hilly Kristal had tried to expand CBGB, gambling on the
notoriety of a scene that was already four years in the past.
His venture into the music industry with the *Live At CBGB*
album had been none too successful and you'd think he
might have learned a lesson. But as early as 1977 he had
taken over the building next to CBGB and transformed it
into the CBGB Theatre. It was a flop, and the fire marshal
closed the place after a week. Other additions were a pizza
parlor and a record shop. Although it continues to draw
crowds of weekend tourists, eager to see the birthplace of
punk, and out-of-town bands who want to say they have
played there, by 1977, CBGB had lost the magic of its early
days. Hardly anyone who made the place what it was spent
a lot of time there. Today it has the same appeal as the
Cavern Club in Liverpool. Bands play, people come, and on
a good night you might see the ghost of Richard Hell.

Max's too had lost its cachet. We still played there and
drew big crowds, but the energy of a couple years back had
dissipated. The audience degenerated into johnny-come-late-

---

* The Ritz was a massive hall on 12th Street between Third Avenue and
Broadway; Irving Plaza was another huge venue, named after the street it
was on, neatly tucked away between Gramercy Park and 14th Street. By
1980 there was a proliferation of small, truly underground clubs, many of
them occupying basements. Club 57 on St Mark's Place gained a reputation
as an early retro psychedelic spot, offering classic 'bad' films and an arty
Day-Glo interior. At another club whose name I no longer remember, I
caught an early, sizzling performance by a reconstituted Richard Lloyd
and his new band. The place was in the basement of some office building
and the ceiling was so low that if you were over six feet tall it was truly
uncomfortable.

lies who were just getting hip to punk as it was going through its death throes, and who had come to town looking for safety pins. I have a recording of one of our last performances there, doing a version of Lou Reed's 'Heroin' ten years after the Velvets did it at Max's for a live recording of one of their own last performances. Not long after Max's closed down for good. By the early eighties, it was gone. The last time I walked past, a deli was there.

Mickey Ruskin, the original brains behind Max's, had kept his hand in the club scene. After Max's passed to Tommy Dean, he opened the Manhattan Ocean Club, in Tribeca, a stretch of downtown Manhattan on the West Side near the Hudson, which is fabulously fashionable today but which back in 1975 was off the beaten track. I saw John Cale and Lou Reed there, and caught Patti Smith and the Talking Heads. Ruskin's Ocean Club didn't last very long although a later venture was going strong when I returned to New York in 1980. Lulu and I spent a lot of time at One University Place, a restaurant hangout on the edge of Washington Square Park. Bands didn't play, but for a while it was the place to be seen. It had the same 'back room chic' as Max's, and it took some clout to enter the inner sanctum. Once you did you were with the gods. My two close encounters happened in the toilet. On two separate occasions a muscular bodyguard came into the men's room and asked everyone to leave. One time it was for Mick Jagger. The other was Bob Dylan. Superstardom comes at a price. Evidently neither could piss if someone else was in the room. Assuming, of course, they came in there to piss.

After staying with Lulu for a few weeks we decided it was better if I got my own place. I wound up in a tiny two-bedroom ground-floor apartment on Thompson Street, near Bleecker, just a few blocks from Debbie's old apartment. The rent was high. For the first few months I didn't have a kitchen floor, and the shower was primitive at best. But it was New York and it was mine. At first Richard, my bass player, split it with me. Later John, my novelist friend, moved in. It was in the heart of Greenwich Village. On weekends you could barely get out of the place because the streets were jam-packed with tourists.

To rehearse we shared a room on Grand Street with Lydia Lunch and a band called the Swinging Madisons. I didn't get to know Lydia very well, but I don't remember her being that cheerful. And I'm pretty sure the Swinging Madisons ripped us off for an amp.

Punk had died and so had new wave. 'No wave' was the current shibboleth. Acts like the Bush Tetras, Klaus Naomi, Arto Lindsay, Teenage Jesus and the Jerks, the Contortions and others threw out the 'fuck art, let's rock' mentality of 1977–8 and decided to screw dancing and make art. It was a reaction to the co-opting of new wave by the industry, a determination to make 'music' as uneuphonious and hence as unmarketable, as possible. They were successful. None of these bands would have anything like the effect of the first wave from 1975. The magic formula for intelligent rock had been found six years earlier, when Patti, Tom and Richard wed the rocking sounds of the *fin de siècle* to the three chords any decent punker knew. If the Dead Boys had brought a new, numbing imbecility to the scene, the no wavers dried it out with a dessicating cerebral austerity that only dedicated New York art junkies could appreciate. Noise became the going thing, the roots of eighties performance art growing in the faded gardens of street rock.

The other contenders were the 'new romantics' from England. The glittzy style of Bow Wow Wow, Adam and the Ants, and Duran Duran had replaced the Sex Pistols' anarchy. Nobody cared very much. It was just another fad. I saw Adam and the Ants one night at the Ritz and wasn't impressed. Bow Wow Wow too. I didn't get it. But I probably wasn't a very good judge of pop music at that time. On one of her modeling jaunts to Japan, Lulu had picked up a new toy. It was called a Walkman. No one had seen one and I'm pretty sure I was one of the first people in New York walking around with earphones. (I remember the look of surprise on people's faces when they saw me.) This was another big nail in my rock and roll coffin. By that time I had stopped listening to rock and had discovered the classics, and would stroll through the Village with Mahler or Prokofiev as a soundtrack. After that, it was difficult to get back into the Ramones. It was also around this time that I started wondering whether I should look for another line of work. By that time playing and hanging out at clubs wasn't a profession; it had become a habit, facilitated by a ridiculously expensive white powder called cocaine.

Cocaine was a big thing in 1980 NYC, and for a while it was impossible to go anywhere and not find it. The two clubs where I indulged in it the most were the Mudd Club and Hurrah.*

Hurrah was a massive room on the third floor of a

---

* Cocaine really was the lingua franca of the scene at this time, and if you didn't have it or couldn't get it, most people didn't want to know you. Practically everyone I knew made an appearance at least one night a week at one dealer's loft space in Chelsea. It was large enough to accommodate a lot of people and often we saved ourselves the trouble of going out and coming back for supplies by hanging out there for a night. The dealer didn't mind. With credit and easy access, people threw restraint to the wind and greedily sucked the stuff up. By the end of the night, the loft was filled with a dozen coke heads, grinding teeth and nattering away. The dealer, however, was less than reliable. One friend made the mistake of using the space to house his stereo equipment while he was in between apartments. When he went to collect it, it had disappeared, hocked by his host to cover some dope debt.

building on Broadway and 62nd Street, a coke spoon's throw from Lincoln Center. We did our first show there in the summer of 1978. It had only recently decided to go new wave. Before that it had been a disco – still was in fact for our first couple shows – but it had been losing customers steadily with the rise of Steve Rubell's Studio 54. Those were the years of the Bee Gees, 'Disco Duck' and Rollerena, a 54 regular who got a name for hitting the dance floor in roller skates.

New Yorkers had discovered clubbing in the mid-seventies, with places like Larry Levenson's Plato's Retreat offering a moving Roman orgy to the well-heeled and libidinously intemperate. Anonymous heterosex and a lot of it was offered at Levenson's roving gang bang, while Studio 54 became synonymous with cocaine, disco, celebrities and bisexual one-nighters.* It was as if Weimar before the Nazis had hit mid-town Manhattan; all the same sex and all the same drugs that had tickled Sally Bowles were turning up. Other hot spots were Danceteria, another disco in mid-town, and the Peppermint Lounge. Hurrah, which had originally opened as Harrah's until some hate mail from the Reno casino of the same name changed the owner's mind, had been disco central until 54 put up its velvet rope. For a while it hoped to bring in the gay money by running Divine's stage act, 'Neon Woman'. When this failed to fill its coffers, Hurrah's owners needed to find a new angle.

Robert Boykin, who owned the place, brought in Jim Fouratt to manage things. Fouratt had been a sixties radical and he made drastic changes. For one thing, he chucked out Donna Summer and brought in Grace Jones. 'Warm Leatherette' replaced 'Staying Alive'. Hurrah was still a disco, but

---

* I went to Studio 54 once for, I think, a Grace Jones party. I hated it.

now it was a new wave one. Soon after this, Fouratt brought in live bands. The place got punk cachet one night when Sid Vicious slashed Patti Smith's brother Todd in the face with a broken glass. Later, Hurrah was the last date on an ill-fated Joy Division tour, which was cancelled because their singer, Ian Curtis, hanged himself. Lester Bangs, who died in 1982 from an overdose of cough medicine – his current recreational drug – interviewed me in the dressing room for his Blondie book. From the summer of 1978 to the winter of 1980, I played Hurrah at least twenty times, my last performance in December, a tribute to John Lennon, a week after he was murdered.*

Cocaine was was rife around Hurrah. Often bands would get paid in merchandise instead of cash. The toilets were full of it, the stalls standing room only with co-ed sniffers. You'd close the door to share a line then cop a brisk feel through

---

* I was in LA when I heard the news of Lennon's death and was heading back to New York the next day. I arrived in a city nearly silent. With thousands of other people, I went to Central Park – not far from the scene of Lennon's murder – for the memorial service. A week or so later, Jimmy Destri, my drummer John McGarvey, a few other musicians and I played a tribute at Hurrah to raise funds for one of Lennon's charities. I sang 'Instant Karma' and 'Cold Turkey'. Strangely, the other rock death that week was Darby Crash, lead singer of the Germs. The day before Lennon's murder, Crash had offed himself with a massive shot of high quality heroin, as part of a suicide pact. His girlfriend survived. He was twenty-two.

Ironically, one of my earliest exposures to the LA punk scene was at a party at the infamous Tropicana Hotel. Some punks had a Beatles video on, 'All You Need Is Love' and were throwing everything they could get their hands on at it, cursing the Beatles all the time. It was the standard slagging of the previous generation. But even in death, the old school won out. Crash's stupid end earned a column in the *Los Angeles Times*, but by the next day he was eclipsed. Lennon's pointless murder was mourned around the world.

the fishnet and leather.* Likewise the hallways and stairwells. People congregated at any semi-private spot where you could get away a quick blow and the first gropes of that night's fuck. Your social standing depended on whether you had it, or whether you were cool enough for other people to offer it to you. People developed a relationship with it unlike any other drug.

Boykin had a large apartment near 72nd Street and a crowd of teenagers, gay and straight, would congregate there. For a while my friend John lived there, while he was writing *Death of a Punk*, and I visited often. John was also acting as a booking agent; he told me Robert had us play so much because he thought I was cute. Toward the end Hurrah was planning to start an independent label, with us as the first release. But the high living scrapped that idea and after recording a couple tracks the plan was dropped. Sometime in the eighties, Robert died, a victim of Aids, which was just then beginning to throw a new darkness over the underground.

Like Madame Wong's, Hurrah became our regular gig. Lulu and I loved it. Our shows were always crowded. This was the time of Fiorucci, when Hell's ripped shirts had become the hot fashion statement and were fetching high prices at uptown boutiques. Having money helped. Some-times we'd hire a limousine and in between sets drive around town or head to the Oyster Bar at Grand Central Station. Sometimes we settled for a taxi. Once, right before a show, the dressing room emptied and Lulu and I were left. She locked the door and grabbed my hand. She had taken off her panties and wanted to show me. We didn't answer the door and the show was delayed by ten minutes.

---

* Toilets were handy for another reason. Most of the cocaine then was cut with baby laxative.

The Mudd Clubb wasn't the same as Hurrah. It was darker, more decadent, and we didn't play there often, gracing its stage only once in fact, doing a show in the summer just before I broke up the band. But I hung out there often enough. It was like being on a permanent set for *Night of the Living Dead*. I saw Marianne Faithfull's show the night Anita Pallenberg famously urged her on, standing behind stage, waving a syringe. The dominant ambience was the nihilism of CBGB taken to a necromantic extreme, a pre-Goth obsession with pallid skin, anorexic limbs and subcutaneous injections.

Steve Maas, who owned the Mudd, wanted to create a kind of anti-Studio 54. Mudd's location was enough of a guarantee for that. White Street was two blocks south of Canal, deeper into Manhattan's bowels than most 54ers would ever want to venture. There was nothing nearby except for Dave's Luncheonette, an old soda fountain on the corner of Canal and Broadway, where the night flock would fill up either before or after stepping in the Mudd. Maas filled the place with ratty old furniture found at second-hand shops and hired a DJ to play the strangest music possible. He also threw in as many 'uncool' people as he could find, grabbing ill-dressed individuals off the street, giving the place an air of Felliniesque weirdness. It was also famous for its two-seater co-ed toilet. Lacking a screen, this facilitated some instant intimacy and who knows how many dark romances. The idea of Mudd was that it was a kind of negative zone, a hole in New York's night world. It opened on Halloween 1978. I don't remember whether I went to the party or not. But I was in town, so I probably did.

Like all in-crowd scenes, the Mudd made people wait. Queues stretched down the steps and on to the narrow cobblestoned street, while the doorman decided whether you were 'hip' enough to let in. Sometimes the street was lined with limousines Maas had hired, to give the impression that some beautiful people were inside. If they were, they were usually upstairs in the VIP room, admission to which was gained once you passed the heavy iron chain that kept out undesirables. The usual crowd were the standard downtown set, black-clad late punkers with enough rings under their eyes to be mistaken for sequoias. Bands like the Cramps were regulars, but an older crowd of dark stars also made the scene, people like Jagger, Iggy and David Bowie.

I had already had a close encounter with Bowie before the night I ran into him in Steve Maas's VIP room. I was invited to attend a session at David's court, which he was then holding in his mid-town loft, somewhere on the West Side. I was accompanying a friend who was making a delivery. When we arrived, David seemed delighted.

Once he had availed himself of our delivery, David grew inspired, and walked around the place, rambling on about a number of topics. A crowd of hangers-on, ourselves included, followed like a flock of gnats, eager for a dropped pearl or numbed nostril. Somehow, the conversation – monologue really – got on to the occult. David had been interested in this for some time, being a big fan of occult Nazi books like *The Morning of the Magicians* by Louis Pauwels and Jacques Bergier and Trevor Ravenscroft's *The Spear of Destiny*. My friend, eager to make some contribution beyond the pharmaceutical, interjected that I knew all about this stuff, having read Colin Wilson.

'Colin Wilson!' Bowie exclaimed, all excited. 'He runs a coven of witches in Cornwall, and traces pentagrams on the doors of people who have crossed his path.'

I didn't meet Wilson until 1983 but I knew enough about his work to know this was untrue. I ventured this opinion to David.

'I don't think that's true, David.'

'Oh yes!' Bowie said, after an enormous sniff. 'He invokes the spirits of ectoplasmic Nazis and calls down their astral forms to do his bidding.'

'David, I don't think so.'

'Wilson, I tell you, is a witch, and practices black magic.'

'I think you're wrong David.'

The conversation went back and forth this way for a few more volleys, while the coke spoon made the rounds. Bowie was a skinny man, very pale and shaky, and I got the impression he didn't care to be contradicted. His two female bodyguards felt that way too. After a few more exhanges during which I basically informed David he didn't know what he was talking about, they approached me and pulled me aside. They were large girls, like the centerfold assassins from one of the Roger Moore James Bond flicks.

They quietly got me away from the Thin White Duke, and in pleasant but firm voices informed me that, as far as I was concerned, the party was over.

'David's tired,' they said. 'Maybe you'd better leave.'

I concurred and did.

Not long after this I bumped into Ziggy Stardust again, this time at the Mudd. Lulu was with me and we had been invited upstairs. Maas liked to collect an assortment of celebs – big names and the sub-famous, like myself – and mix them up to see what happened. I had the impression he was the kind of person who needed to be around people – a psychological profile of practically everyone in the place – and he would keep the party going as long as possible. I don't remember who else was there that night, but Bowie was one of the contestants. It was something like 4 a.m. and someone remembered that on the Iggy/Blondie tour way back, David and I had shared a stage. A conversation started up.

That night Bowie was waxing philosophical and we somehow got on the topic of World War Three. He seemed to think the possibility of another global conflict was strong, was, in fact, inevitable. I opined that it had already been going on for the last thirty years, under the code name Cold War. He seemed impressed by my acumen but, as I soon twigged, was really giving Lulu the once over. He then gave her the twice-over. Lulu had a sexual instinct as infallible as a Geiger counter and could detect excited testosterone blind-folded, but you'd have had to be an idiot not to have seen that Aladdin Sane had the late-night hots for my girlfriend.

At that point our relationship was open and we had both played around. In that sexual swamp it was inevitable. People would get together the morning after and compare notes, the women too, discussing who gave the best head. Basically every-one was fucking everyone else, and I'm surprised I walked away with little more than the occasional urinary infection.

Bowie was in the middle of giving Lulu the thrice-over while giving me his take on Orwell when I saw she was responding to his gaze. Why not? Lulu wasn't a groupie, but to have a roll in the hay with at least one rock star would look good on her CV. And maybe Bowie remembered my recent visit and wanted to show me who called the shots. Lulu was known for penetrating conversation, but not of the intellectual kind. However, at this point she made a few contributions that David found particularly brilliant. Whether it was the blow, his ego or Lulu's evident interest, Bowie then let us know where the matter stood. He'd love to carry on their conversation if Lulu would like to come back to his place. Alone.

I feigned cool and took it in my stride. Lulu thought about it. But then she surprised me. She turned him down. Come to think of it, she surprised David too.

Nevertheless, our affair was reaching its end. It's high point was a trip to Paris that summer. Lulu was going ahead for work, and I would meet her in a couple weeks. Before she left, she gave me the keys to her room at the Gramercy Park. I went twice. Once because I missed her and grabbed a pair of her panties to keep by my bed. Another time when I missed her even more and brought back the cute girl who ran the door at the Ritz to assuage my loneliness.

The three weeks we spent in Paris were the most intensely erotic time of my life. I remember making love with Lulu in the afternoon in the bathroom of our hotel. She was holding on to the taps, and I gazed out of the window at the Parisian rooftops, amazed to be there. We made love in some unusual places.* Parisian taxis are not as accommodating as New York's, but we adapted. On a trip to Strasbourg we missed our return flight and had to take the train. Our compartment didn't lock but we did it anyway, for most of the long ride back, not caring if anyone found us. The whole trip was like a dream. In Montmartre we went to La Coupole one afternoon for lunch. When we went back a few days later, the windows had been smashed during a student riot. At the Georges Pompidou, Lulu cruised a young punkess, trying to entice her to our hotel. But the big surprise came one afternoon in a trendy new wave clothes shop in Les Halles. We walked in and browsed through the racks, and after a few minutes 'The First One' came over the PA.

But by the time we got back to NYC, we had peaked. We carried on for a while, out of habit and for the good sex, but it was over.

I couldn't write songs. Lulu just wasn't inspiring me. It wasn't her fault; I had just lost interest. Richard, my bass player, could tell. He was sick of living in New York and thought I wasn't paying enough attention to the band. He was probably right. After he got mugged on Thanksgiving

---

* Once we even tried it in the dead of night in Washington Square Park. But it was winter, there was snow on the ground, and it was just too cold.

on his way back from watching the Christmas tree light up in Rockefeller Center, it was only a matter of time before the southern California sunshine called him back.

For a while a few possibilites kept us going. A rookie woman film director who would later become very successful had approached us about working with her on a project. She had seen our shows, loved 'The First One', and wanted me to be in her next movie. She took us to an overpriced restaurant in SoHo to discuss the film. By this time SoHo had been taken over by trendy shops and unaffordable watering holes, very different from when I had lived there with Chris and Debbie. Halfway through lunch I felt something soft touch my leg, then make its way up the inside of my thigh. It found its target and settled there, pressing softly. I swallowed and looked down; a black-nyloned foot was resting on my crotch, toeing it gently as if slightly revving the motor. I looked across the table at the director. She smiled and gave the engine some gas. I surprised myself by being able to carry on an intelligent conversation while having a size six massage my privates. By the time the espressos came I thought I was going to burst.

I told the others the director and I had some other things to discuss and we went to her hotel. It was my first and last time on the casting couch, and at the time I thought I passed the audition. We made love and then I went back to my apartment. Later I heard I didn't get the part. The money ran out and the project was scrapped.

After two cities, three demos, two years, one single, 115 performances and no deals, Richard was tired. We had come close several times and he felt we had missed our chance. The thought of facing a New York winter oppressed him. He had had it and was going home. Our last show together was at Max's. John and I carried on a bit longer, but effectively that was the end of the Know. We did a few more gigs, using some musicians from the scene, but my heart wasn't in it. Our last night was at the Ritz. I was sad, but told him I had to stop. For the next couple of months I read a lot and picked up girls at the clubs, finding my way to after-hours places like the Nursery, on Third Avenue and 13th Street, where night owls who refused to have the party end would wind up at 6, 7 or 8 a.m.. Practically every night attractive and uninhibited women would offer themselves and I remember one particularly liberated encounter on someone's twelfth-floor balcony. There was sex and there were drugs. But there wasn't as much rock 'n' roll.

10. THE IG AND I

I had been out of music for seven months when Rob DuPrey called and asked if I wanted to go on tour. At the time I was living in an apartment on 10th Street and Second Avenue, two blocks north of my old storefront. Legend had it that Hubert Selby Jr had lived in the apartment next to mine and had written some of *Last Exit to Brooklyn* there. It was August 1981. For the last year Rob had been working with a singer. They had just played three nights at the Ritz and were about to hit the road for two months. Ivan Kral, the second guitarist, had jumped ship and they needed a replacement badly. The pay was good, the material easy – I probably knew half of the songs already – and it would be fun.

Rob said they were heading to Providence, Rhode Island for the next show and I asked when were they leaving.

'Tomorrow.'

I said okay and learned the songs on the bus.

The singer's name, by the way, was Iggy Pop.

►►

By 1981, Iggy had been through a few incarnations. When I last saw him, in 1977, he was riding high on his resurrection via the hands of David Bowie. He had even cleaned up his act enough to appear with David on the *Dinah Shore Show*, when the godfather of punk met Miss Wholesome Americana in front of a live televised audience. In the years before that he had followed a downward spiral. After the break-up of the Stooges in 1974, Iggy plunged into a dark pool of drugs and self-destruction, culminating in his committing himself to the UCLA Neuropsychiatric Institute in 1975. He told his doctors: 'I've been addicted for a long time to very heavy drugs . . . I'm a fool who uses pills and slobbers a lot. Would you help me? Would you lock me up here so none of my so-called friends can get at me?'

His path to the UCLA NPI was strewn with enough weirdness and self-mutilation to provide thesis topics for a whole class of budding headshrinkers. I first saw Iggy on television in August of 1970, when NBC broadcast *Midsummer Rock*, the first televised rock festival. I was fourteen. Filmed in June at Cincinnati's Crosley Field, the other names on the bill were Traffic, Mountain, Grand Funk Railroad and Alice Cooper. Big names all. But the next day, it was only Iggy that my friends and I talked about. We had never seen anything like him. He was bottom of the bill but his performance that night made rock and roll history. Iggy tore off his shirt and leered at the crowd, flicking his tongue like a demented lizard – aptly, as he got the tag Iggy from his first band, the Iguanas. He pointed his gold-laméd finger at the cheering thousands like a perverse schoolmarm. It was part revival meeting, part Nuremberg rally. The music was manic, unlike anything we had ever heard. 'TV Eye' and '1970' weren't songs, they were sonic jackhammers, bashing into our brains. Iggy threw himself into the crowd and the surging teenagers carried him aloft. Like Jesus on the water, Iggy walked across their hands and shoulders, the spotlights on his glistening back, sweat pouring off him. This wasn't Crosby, Stills, Nash and Young and it wasn't Woodstock. This was dark, demonic and dangerous. It was also fucking exciting. Later in the show he pulled out the peanut butter, smeared it on his chest and poked at it with a pair of drumsticks.

Over the next five years Iggy became famous for various acts of self-mutilation and for a seemingly inexhaustible appetite for drugs. He realized that the sight of blood excited an audience and he sought to please. Things started out small, a sharp fingernail slicing through a little flesh. Then he worked up. In 1973, during a show at Max's, he tore his chest with the stem of a margarita glass. Blood flowed onto the stage. He was taken to an emergency ward after the show; the next two performances had to be cancelled so that his stitches could set. The same week, at a Mott the Hoople and Dolls concert at Madison Square Garden's Felt Forum, influenced by a medley of intoxicants, Iggy walked straight into a door and had to receive treatment again. That same year he took to performing clad in only a jockstrap. In LA in 1974, at Rodney's English Disco, Iggy performed the 'Murder of the Virgin'. During this he cut up his chest with a knife. Again he needed emergency treatment. His press agent spoke of 'Iggy's most totally commited artistic statement ever'. Meanwhile Iggy made a banquet of quaaludes, barbiturates and alcohol. After the meal, he took that room at the UCLA NPI.

One of Iggy's visitors at UCLA was Bowie, who at that point was himself fairly saturated with various substances, as well as obsessed with black magic and fascism. David had played guardian angel to Iggy a few times before and now the dynamic duo packed their bags and headed for Berlin. Iggy cleaned out his system. They made some music. In March 1977 *The Idiot* was released, and Blondie opened for Iggy on our first North American tour. *The Idiot* presented a new, mature, self-disciplined and professional Iggy Pop and it was probably his most successful effort since the early days of the Stooges.

Between then and 1981, Iggy enjoyed declining success with three albums and various bands. He was adopted by the rising punk generation and worked with people like Ivan Kral from Patti Smith, Brian James from the Damned and ex-Sex Pistol Glen Matlock, famously kicked out of the Pistols because he admitted to liking the Beatles. But the albums that followed *The Idiot* didn't sell, Bowie had his own affairs to take care of, and Iggy found himself in a familiar position: a legend among rock connoisseurs but barely able to pay his bills. Like all legends, he didn't let it get him down.

►►

By the time I hooked up with him Iggy had released his third album on Arista Records, *Party*. As the title suggests, he had reverted to the excesses of his earlier persona. One of the reasons Ivan Kral gave for leaving the band at such short notice – he wound up working with another singer, John Hyatt – was that he couldn't handle the endless partying any more. The band had been on tour almost constantly since early 1980. Iggy kept his nose to the grindstone – as well as to other kinds of rocks – and was fond of the bottle, and Ivan saw others getting pulled into the whirlpool. He had also had a troubling insight into Iggy's personality. Iggy, he said, could be cruel. He told the story of an older woman coming backstage once, and Iggy taking one look at her and shouting 'You're old! Look at you. Just look at you.' The woman cried. Iggy didn't care. Like most of the 'stars' I came across in my rock and roll years, he could be ruthless and mean and then seemingly forget all about it. As I would find out on the two long tours I did with Iggy, Ivan wasn't far off the mark. From the beginning of August to the end of December 1981, I had ample experience of the complex personality that was Iggy Pop. If I thought I had got away from sex, drugs and rock 'n' roll, here was my very rude awakening.

Rob had been playing with Iggy since 1980. The Mumps

had broken up and Iggy had come across Rob at one of the clubs in town. Rob told me to come down to their rehearsal studio for a quick audition. It was a mere formality. I dusted off my Fender Stratocaster and showed up. Iggy was friendly, and through the haze of years and assorted inebriants, remembered me. He told me to call him Jim, his real name. I did. This was the first sign of the individual I'd be working with. When I met him that afternoon, 'Jim' wore glasses, thick wonky ones that made him seem like a chartered accountant with a side taste for the sleazy and indelicate. Like Clark Kent and Superman, it was only when he pulled off his specs that his true identity was revealed. Again, like most stars, Jim/Iggy was a dual personality. He could be charming and warm one minute, and the next throw you out of a moving car if he didn't like your looks.

That day I also met the other guys in the band. Michael Page had played bass for the Dolls in one of their several reunions and had toured with one of rock and roll's legends, Chuck Berry. Dougy Bowne, the drummer, had worked with John Cale. Richard Sohl, had been Patti Smith's keyboardist. Later, Iggy would fire Sohl and Bowne would leave. Clem Burke and Carlos Alomar, David Bowie's guitarist, would be brought in. Like Ivan, Dougy wearied of the endless partying and wanted to move on to 'serious' music. Iggy fired Sohl because he didn't have the rock and roll persona he wanted in his group – taking lots of drugs and fucking lots of girls. Richard wasn't a stranger to drugs, but the fact that he was gay prevented him from meeting the second requirement.

I don't remember what we played, but we jammed for a while and Iggy was happy. Rob mentioned that one of my songs had been a top ten hit and Iggy seemed interested. Although he was the godfather of punk, Iggy wanted commercial success and thought that he and I could work together and write some tunes.

I must have disappointed him. Writing songs was the last thing on my mind. I liked the idea of being a hired gun, and for the first time in my career actually looked forward to being a backup musician. I decided that this tour I would just be one of the boys. The only thing I brought to read was a book about extraterrestrial civilizations. Iggy noticed it and asked what it was. I told him. 'All right,' he said. 'From now on you're our expert on extraterrestrials.' It made sense. Working with him was like being out of this world.

I got my first taste of what playing with Iggy would be like when I saw the tour bus. It was massive, much larger than the Winnebago we used back in 1977, and it stuck out like a submarine in mid-town Manhattan, parked in front of the Algonquin Hotel, where Iggy and the boys were staying. Iggy had hired it from a firm out of Nashville and its last occupants must have been a disco band, because the interior certainly looked like one. Tiny blinking lights, like Christmas decorations, lined the walls. There were plush seats done up in a sparkling almost fluorescent upholstery, a giant video screen loomed overhead, and the fridge was chock-a-block with beers. It was like something out of *This is Spinal Tap*. The whole thing reeked tackily of rock band. But the pièce de résistance was the back room. This we came to call Iggy's hideaway: a small round cave at the back of the bus with blue-mirrored walls, blue lights, even plusher seats and a mirrored table. Whether the table was purpose-built or there just by chance, it was perfect for the lengthy lines of coke we frequently chopped out. Iggy used that room a lot, and it took on a seamy sordid ambience. If we hit a town and were leaving that night, Iggy would retire to his den with some girl – the raunchier the better – and close the door. The next day he'd emerge and the girl would wake up to find herself in a different city, hundreds of miles away. Sometimes he'd keep her around for another day or so, but most times he'd be bored, and kick her off the bus. Then she'd be left to make her way back home under her own steam.

Iggy's itinerary wasn't the same as 1977. He was mostly booked into very small venues – really *too* small, given his notoriety. Aside from a few larger clubs seating a thousand or fifteen hundred and a legendary slot opening for the Rolling Stones – more on this later – we were playing a lot of dives. Iggy didn't have a lot of money, Arista weren't forthcoming with tour support, and to most promoters he just didn't have the kind of draw to fill a larger hall. Iggy had been taken up by the punk generation, but in most towns the punks didn't number more than a few hundred. Iggy had been punching it out in small venues in Europe and the States for the last couple years and the strain was beginning to show. *Party* needed to be a hit; Arista had pretty much told him that if it wasn't, he'd have to look for another label.* There was a sense of desperation, a feeling of last chance hovering around the tour. Rolling into places in that funky tour bus – the Paramount Theatre in Staten Island, the Left Bank in Mt Vernon, Toad's Place in New Haven, the Spit in Long Island – it seemed I had hitched a ride with a rock and roll Wild Bunch. At one godforsaken place in Rochester, New York – really just a sleazy roadside bar – we didn't even have a dressing room. A door behind the stage just opened onto the parking lot. We got off the bus, did the show, then got back on.

Twenty years on, most of these shows are just a blur – even on the road they tend to blend into one another – but I do remember a few things. Early on we ran into trouble. On our second show, right after Providence, we got stuck on Storrow Drive in Boston, notorious for its low overpasses.

---

* It wasn't and he did.

Our driver – who Iggy took to calling Farfel* – hadn't kept an eye on the road signs and didn't realize the bus was too tall. At the last minute he hit the brakes, but it was too late; the bus slammed to a halt, wedged under an overpass. Traffic backed up for miles. We were on our way to a club called the Metro. Commonwealth Avenue was nearby and I remember running down the street, waving people down, offering them money to take us to the gig. When they got a look at us, they sped away. Eventually the bus got free but had to back up a mile or so to get off the road. Later that night at the club, we met Rick Okasec and some of the other guys from the Cars, and I remember some local hipster hanging around, trying to get Iggy's attention, waving a little white packet like a flag. Iggy finally deigned to give the guy a few minutes of his time. The guy opened the packet, scratched out a line, and offered Iggy a rolled-up bill. Iggy grabbed the bill, put it to his nose and snorted the whole packet. The guy's eyes fell out of his head. Then Iggy handed back the bill, said 'Thanks' and carried on his conversation.

Iggy's intake on those tours was phenomenal. Jim could put more stimulants into his system than any of us, although a couple of the guys ran close seconds. I invariably ended up in last place. Most of the stories have the same punchline, with Iggy taking a massive handful of something and either smoking, swallowing or snorting it. Drugs and getting them was one of the themes of the tour. (The other was screwing groupies, which I'll get to soon.) Playing music really became the pretext for our rolling party, and since pushing the *Party* album was the central idea, Iggy thought it best to act the part. Generally, we didn't have much trouble. At practically every gig, someone would be there putting something into your hand. Some of the guys had hit these towns so often

_____
* The name of a dog in an old Nestlé's chocolate TV commercial.

they knew the local dealers and would call ahead with their orders. We'd pull into town and the man would meet us at our hotel with the merchandise. Later, one of the guys, distrusting the kind of stuff we were getting on the road, set up a kind of mail order service with his dealer in New York. We'd be in, say, Richmond, Virginia, and discover we were running low. We'd get our order together and make a phone call. Two days later an express mail package would be waiting at our hotel in Raleigh, North Carolina. The bus was full of smoke most of the time, especially just before we had to cross the border into Canada. Miles before the checkpoint Henry, our long-suffering tour manager, would tell us to either smoke what we had or throw it away. Immediately everyone would light up and we passed into places like Kitchener, Ottawa and Montreal with enough THC in our systems to keep us stoned for days.

Once, in San Francisco, we were taken to some dealer's house for a Thanksgiving Day meal. After the turkey and stuffing, he mentioned that he had some digestifs. He took us to a room upstairs and opened the door. There were several bushels of different kinds of grass, all with little flags sticking out of them, indicating the brand and the price. Another time, in San Diego, the dealer turned out to have been a police sergeant for years who after a bust had got curious and sampled some of the evidence. It changed his life. He quit the force and set himself up as the biggest dealer in town. He knew his crop and did a good deal, letting us have some of his best stuff at real bargain prices.

Sometimes our various scams didn't work, and we had to make do with whatever was available. I remember, somewhere in the South, a long drive out to what looked like a shanty town. We waited in the car for an hour while Jim haggled over the price of some really rotten stuff. It turned out to be pretty bad and they ripped us off, but it wasn't a buyers' market.

When all else failed, Iggy fell back on his other stimulant of choice, alcohol. Part of the rider for the tour – the list of things absolutely necessary for the show to go on – was that each night he would have a bottle of Jack Daniels waiting for him in the dressing room. Invariably, Iggy would turn up shortly before going on and ask: 'Is Mr Daniels here?' or: 'Has anyone seen Mr Daniels?' If Mr Daniels wasn't there, Iggy wouldn't go on until the owner got a bottle and brought it to him. Then, ceremoniously, he'd open it and take a hefty swig, sometimes with a glass, sometimes without, let out a satisfied 'Ahhh!' and say 'It's showtime.' After this, like a football team, we'd huddle around him and he'd throw his arms over our shoulders and get us worked up for the show, whether it was some rinky-dink joint in Fort Lauderdale or one of the larger clubs like the Agora Ballroom in Cleveland, where I had opened for him four years ago, on that first tour with Blondie. More times than not, by the end of the night, Mr Daniels had left the building.

Iggy had some peculiar personal habits. A few of his idiosyncracies were impossible not to notice. For one thing, the only places he would have the bus stop for food were McDonalds. He seemed to think that if you were on the road, you had to order a 'BFC': burger, fries and coke. It was mandatory and he would look at you in consternation if you essayed a variation. After a while, realizing I couldn't get a McSalad anywhere, I gave in. As with his intake of recreational substances, Iggy had a tremendous appetite, and could get through a few Big Macs without batting an eye. He did vary his diet though. One time, playing a place called Bogart's in

Cincinnati, he expressed a desire for barbecued ribs. He had heard somewhere that the absolute best barbecued ribs in the world could be found in Cincinnati. He mentioned this to one of the local scenesters who, after the gig, took the whole band down to a tiny rib joint in a black neighborhood. We filed in wearing various late punk/new wave outfits, raising eyebrows, and walked out with piles of steaming ribs smothered in barbecue sauce. On another occasion, we were again somewhere in the South and had a couple days off. Jim wanted a 'real sit-down dinner' at a fancy place, and had Henry track one down. We wound up in a colonial-style house, sitting around a giant oak table in our rock and roll best, while the other diners gawked at us. Jim put on the airs of a Southern gentleman, courteous throughout, delicately sniffing his after-dinner brandy. On another occasion, some- where in the Midwest, he ordered a snifter of the most expensive cognac at the hotel bar, and asked for it to be put on his bill. There was some problem and the bartender couldn't do that, and asked Jim to pay. He didn't have a cent on him, and had to telephone Henry to take fifty dollars out of petty cash to pay for his drink.

Usually at lunch Jim would eat enough for three, then sleep it off in the hotel until the gig. On the few occasions I was asked to wake him, I got a look at his room. More times than not it seemed a hurricane had hit, with bottles and assorted articles of clothing, male and female, hanging from lamps and strewn over chairs. And sometimes his guest would still be there.

Iggy's taste in women always surprised me. Although really attractive sexy babes would fall at his feet – and other body parts – he seemed to have a thing for fat raunchy chicks, the kind the rest of us wouldn't look twice at. I think he had an appetite for the unusual in sex and found these hefty babes compliant. On the long bus rides, Iggy whiled away the hours watching videos; I've already mentioned that one of his favorites was *Pink Flamingos*. Two of the stars of that epic of bad taste, Divine and 'Eddy the Egg Lady', weren't what you'd call slim. Iggy watched that film over and over, at least once a day for weeks at a stretch, and maybe seeing Divine's massive frame whetted his appetite. When I told him I knew Divine, who had assured me the dog shit he eats at the end of the film *really* is shit, Iggy's next question was, 'Did he tell you what it tasted like?' His other favorite flick was *Debbie Does Dallas*, a seventies porno effort in which a reasonably svelte blonde provides services for a football team. He watched this almost as much as he did *Pink Flamingos*, with *The Elephant Man* running a close third.

Iggy certainly did attract uninhibited types. Once in Washington, DC, when we were playing the Bayou, a club the Know had done a couple years back on a bill with 999, he met up with a blowsy blonde he knew from an earlier tour. Maybe they had got together earlier in the day or maybe she was just fondly recalling a past intimacy, but in the dressing room, packed with people including an assortment of babes waiting for the band to make their choice, she produced a memorable one-liner. I didn't hear much of their conversation – I was too busy making my intentions clear to a groupie – but I did hear this: 'Iggy,' she said, in a clear Southern accent. 'You know your cock always tastes so much better after it's been in my cunt.'

The girl on my lap was impressed. 'Wow!' she said. 'I've never heard anyone talk like that before.' The next morning the bus had to wait while my own Southern belle and I conducted some last minute maneuvers.

Along with drugs, sex was incredibly easy to get on those tours; Iggy wasn't the only beneficiary. There was no question of seduction and barely any sense of a hunt, other than

cruising the club and picking out likely candidates. At some
places it was like a bordello, with a six pack of chicks vying
for your attention. If it turned out that the one you wanted
hooked up with someone else, that was no problem. You just
took another. Or maybe you could barter. On some occasions
the girls themselves would want the same guy and took turns.

The first time I realized how easy it was was in Chicago.
A girl who had dated Ivan the last time the band were in
town was disappointed he had left. After a few moments'
frustration she looked at me. 'Well,' she said, 'you're not
Ivan. But you're cute anyway.' After the show she came back
to my hotel room. From there on in it was plain sailing.

Sometimes you didn't even have to say anything or go
back to the hotel. At some party in Minneapolis, I sat on a
couch next to a reasonably attractive girl. The room was full
of people: other girls, the band, the local scenesters. The girl
had on a very low-cut loose top and was bra-less. Her sleeves
were so wide that when she raised her hand I could easily see
her nipple. After a while, purely out of curiosity, I reached in
and touched it. 'Oooh,' she said, and turned to me. I didn't
know if she was offended and muttered, 'Sorry.' 'Don't be
sorry,' she said. 'That's what they're there for.' Then she looked
around the room, grabbed my hand and said, 'C'mon.' She
took me outside to the yard, planted me on a bench, upzip-
ped my flies and knelt down. Fifteen minutes later we were
back at the party. Other liaisons were less abrupt.

Some were very strange. Memphis, Tennessee, for
example, was a very weird place. Not only did Graceland,
Elvis Presley's estate, turn out to be the world's first rock
and roll mausoleum – complete with decorative plots for the
King and his doctor and a fast food joint across the road
where one could get a 'Hound Dog' – but the people were,
I'm convinced, totally inbred. They all seemed to look the

same. And the girl I brought back to our motel – situated on a strip lined with at least a dozen live sex joints – was a real case. When proceedings hotted up, she started hitting me in the head, then biting and scratching me, sinking teeth and digging three-inch-long fingernails into my flesh, shouting 'Harder! Harder! I want to feel it!' I was scared she had drawn blood and wanted to get a tetanus shot. Earlier in the evening, I met a boyfriend of hers who tried to talk her into going back with him. He had his arm in a cast. The next night some scenesters took us to the local punk dump and there he was, bashing away at a guitar on stage. How he managed it with the cast I don't know.

Some adventures were funny. In Florida a really wild redhead came back to the motel. Halfway through, I got a knock at the door. We had an early call the next morning and Henry, our vigilant road manager, wanted everyone to get their luggage ready to be picked up. I was absurdly conscientious for a rock and roller and was responsible enough to comply. I told my partner this would only take a minute, threw my trousers on and packed my bag at top speed. Then I carried it down to the motel office, where the roadies would get it in the morning. I raced back to the room. The whole procedure couldn't have taken more than five minutes. The door was locked and I had forgotten to take the key. I knocked. No reply. I knocked again. Still nothing. I knocked once more, harder this time, and said, 'It's me, let me in.' Silence. I kicked, knocked, rattled the handle and banged on the window for the next half-hour. Either she had crashed, left, or was pissed at me for leaving and wasn't letting me in. I found somebody with an extra bed and slept there, cursing my stupidity. I never found out what happened. When I got the hotel manager – who was nowhere to be seen at 2 a.m. – to let me in the next morning, she wasn't there. No one else had bothered with their bags, we were late taking off, and for the rest of the tour Iggy and the others wouldn't let me live it down.

Some encounters were pathetic. In Toronto we played at an outdoor festival on a bill including the Police and a half-dozen other bands. I met a girl and afterwards she wanted to drive me back to our hotel. When we got to her car we saw that the back window had been smashed in. It was her brother's car and she was pretty upset. She was also very high on percadan. We drove to town, the wind ripping through the car. When we got to the room I said, 'You seem a bit upset. Are you sure you want to do this?' 'Yeah,' she said, 'otherwise the night would be a total waste.' Others were sweet. In Montreal we did a show in what must have been an Austrian cultural center. The walls were hung with flags depicting the double-headed eagle of the Habsburgs and Jim got off on this, breaking into a German accent and tossing off Hitleresque one-liners. I met a French-Canadian girl with beautiful long blonde hair and startling blue eyes. Her English was shaky and I had less French, but we managed a conversation and later discovered we actually liked each other. Months later she came to New York and spent a week. When she left she said, 'Maybe you'll write a song for me now too?' We wrote letters for a while but eventually lost touch and I still wonder what might have happened if we had got together.

Others visited me as well. Everyone said they wanted to come to New York and being nice, I gave them my address and said look me up. They did. One time I took pity on one of the girls Iggy kicked out of the bus. He had picked her up in one state – both geographical and psychic – and three days later cast her off in another. I felt sorry for her and told her that if she ever came to New York to give me a call. Eventually she turned up in Manhattan, but by that time I had moved on. The friend I had sublet my apartment from, however, made out. When the tall blonde turned up looking for me, she was disappointed but decided to stay anyway. It was the easist lay of his life, he said, delivered right to his door.

In San Francisco we did two nights at the Old Waldorf and one at the Market Theatre. One night Allen Ginsberg came to our dressing room and he, Iggy, Clem and I shared a joint. I told Allen how much I liked *Howl*, and he smiled, giving me the once-over. (Later Clem wondered if he and Jim would get it on.). Then a very attractive diminutive girl asked if I wanted company. I knew her vaguely from CBGB and was surprised to see her on the West Coast. She's since acquired some notoriety as one of the top groupies of the time. I didn't know this then; I just thought she was pretty and liked the way she spoke.

When we got back to my room we undressed and lay on the bed. She ran her hands over me. 'Hmm. You're a pretty boy. You know, I don't go with many pretty boys. You have a great body, like Nijinsky.'

Around the same time, Iggy had given me the manuscript of his book, *I Need More*, which he was writing with the journalist Anne Wehr. He knew I was a reader and wanted my opinion. The next morning I thought I would take a look at it over coffee. I couldn't find it and thought my guest had made off with it, knowing that Iggy's original manuscript would make a nice addition to some anorak's collection. I was worried for a day but then it turned up in my bag. After Florida, I had made a habit of packing well in advance and forgot I had stashed it in there.

Iggy had a voyeuristic streak, and when the boys piled onto the bus for the next long drive, he'd ask about last night's adventures. 'Who got the redhead? Did she smell? Did she want anything dirty? Did you do it doggy style?'

Then he would make us go through everything in detail. Not all the stories were pleasant. Once some poor stoned-out girl climbed in a car with us on our way to a gig. She was on acid or something and was really out of it. I don't know how it started but someone grabbed her, probably just as a joke, but it got out of hand and soon the rest of us had our hands on her in some kind of feeling frenzy. Understandably she freaked. Later I heard that she had had an accident and hurt herself pretty bad and I felt very stupid after that.

►►

This account might give the impression that all I did on these tours was have sex and get stoned. We actually did play – fifty-three performances in forty-five cities. Most of the set came from the *Party* album, but we did a lot of other material: '1969', 'Lust for Life', 'I'm Bored', 'Nightclubbing', 'Sister Midnight', for example. We weren't the best rock and roll band in the world, but we were good. Most of the time my contribution was simple rhythm guitar, adding a strong background to Rob's, and later Carlos Alomar's leads – both of them much better guitarists than me. Occasionally, Iggy would give me the nod and I would take a lead. I wound up doing it a lot on 'I'm Bored', and a couple other tunes, and one time – I can't remember where – both Carlos and Rob forgot their parts and I jumped in. I was chuffed later when Iggy patted me on the back and said I had saved the show. He also got off on my jumping around and often we would get into some manic stage moves together. Although the crowd would call out for it, Jim had mostly cast off his self-destructive persona, but he would still throw himself from one side of the stage to the other, or leap from the drum kit to grab the mic, folding himself in half like a switchblade, then standing stock-still like a statue, his gaze commanding the audience to attention. He was always generous with his praise, as he was with his displeasure. With Clem and Carlos in the band, Iggy took to calling us his 'super group', a tag late sixties bands like Blind Faith and Crosby, Stills, Nash and Young had picked up. But at one show – again I forget where – we gave a rotten performance and he let us know, telling us that his 'super group' – he said it with disdain – had let him down. He was pissed at us for days and didn't keep it to himself.

Some funny things happened. At the soundcheck for some show in Canada, a journalist wanted to talk to Clem and me about working together again. Blondie's success had peaked and Debbie had started her solo efforts. We talked with the journalist for a few minutes, then Clem stopped. 'Hey,' he said. 'Aren't you the guy who wrote that shitty review of our show back in . . .' The guy gulped. 'You're a real fuck,' Clem said, and lunged at him. The guy freaked, and Clem chased him down the street for a few blocks. I've never seen a rock reporter run so fast.

To ease the boredom of touring, Carlos Alomar brought along a bow, arrow and bullseye, and at some hotel in Texas set it up on the roof. I went with him and watched. He let off some shots and then we heard a siren. We thought nothing of it. A few minutes later, a handful of police came charging through the door, pistols in hand. Someone in a neighboring hotel had seen us and told the police there was a sniper on the roof. In New York the roadies used the equipment truck to go to some club and left it parked outside. When they came out it had been broken into and the stuff stolen, the Fender Stratocaster I had used in the Know gone for good. In New Orleans we played on the Riverboat President, a paddle wheel steamer that travelled up and down the Mississippi for four hours packed with ourselves and the local punk establishment. Earlier in the day, Iggy, Rob and I toured the Latin Quarter, eating po' boys and crayfish, checking out the scene. Iggy was particularly interested in the dozens of transvestite shops that lined Bourbon Street.

At one show, Iggy surprised us with an addition to the act. Ages ago he had smashed a front tooth on a mic and had it capped. Somewhere on the tour the cap came loose, and at particularly intimate moments, he'd reach up, grab it and pull it off, revealing a dark gap. Later he lost the cap and until he could get a replacement he would flash his toothless grin at the audience.

▶▶

The most memorable shows, of course, were the nights we opened for the Rolling Stones. For two nights running 80,000 people packed the Silverdome in Pontiac, Michigan. They were not there to see Iggy Pop.

Iggy got the shows through Keith Richards. Keith was a fan, and thought that since the Stones would be playing so close to Detroit, Iggy, a local boy, should open. The second support act was Santana.

The Silverdome is a massive indoor football stadium. I don't think Iggy had played a place that size before. I certainly hadn't. You could say it was like playing in front of the Grand Canyon, but it was more like playing in front of the night sky. All you saw was a wall of black with Bic lighters flicking on and off like stars.

I remember meeting Carlos Santana backstage, and watching Bill Wyman and Charlie Watts play table tennis. I met them and saw Jagger, Richards and Ron Wood. I didn't meet them, but Iggy hung out with them.

It was a prestigious event, and the guys invited family and friends. I asked Lisa to come. One of the guys flew his mother out, and, swear to God, after the show I saw them chopping out lines together.

Off and on during that tour, Iggy had worn women's

clothes. He said he did it for comfort. One night it was a skirt, the next a dress. Sometimes stockings, other times panties. It had a definite effect on the audience and with the missing tooth he often looked very strange. The first night we played the Dome, Iggy wore men's clothes. We were booed; the audience obviously wanted to see the Stones, and we did a short set.

Iggy was pissed. The second night he had a change of clothes. He wore a white blouse, a brown leather miniskirt and a pair of coffee-colored stockings. He neglected to put on any underwear.

When we got on stage I felt incredibly small. But once we started playing it seemed all right. It was just difficult to know what kind of response we were getting. The Stones had allocated a limited area of the stage to us, and we were far from the front. Iggy had more leeway, but even he wasn't used to having the audience so distant. It was literally like playing in the dark, with photographers' flashbulbs lighting up as they followed Iggy in his stockings across the stage.

We got through one number, then another, and it wasn't until the first few missiles hit that I realized something was happening. And then it started.

In his memoirs, promoter Bill Graham said of this event that, 'Never in the history of rock and roll have more material objects been thrown at *any* artist. Hair brushes, combs, lot of Bic lighters, shoes, sandals, bras, sweaters, hats. *Tons* of shit. I had never seen anything like it. I thought the Sex Pistols had set the record at Winterland. But now we were in the *Silverdome*. Eighty thousand people throwing shit.'

It came out of nowhere. For the next half-hour I played guitar, staring straight into the blackness, hoping I'd catch a glimpse of the beer can or wine bottle a second before it hit me. Objects appeared, hurtling at you out of thin air. It didn't stop. For the whole set. No applause, no cheers, just a constant shower of projectiles. Bill Graham covered most of the items but not all. An open penknife fell at my feet. I was hit by a bullet, which I later kept.

Throughout, Iggy was as provocative as he could be, lifting the skirt, spreading his legs, fondling his crotch, leaving nothing to the imagination.

After our set, Bill Graham had someone collect all the stuff and itemize it. He came into our dressing room. 'Ig, I gotta tell you. You broke every fucking record in existence.' Then he had an idea. He told Iggy to go back on stage and instead of doing an encore, to read off the list. Item by item.

Iggy did. He and Graham went back, and with Graham holding the box, Iggy went through the list. 'I want to thank you all for being so generous tonight.' And then he started. Twenty Bic lighters. Six sneakers. Ten combs. Five pairs of underwear. The audience didn't get it at first but then they twigged. Six pairs of sandals. Roar. A dozen bic pens. Yaaah.

Afterwards, Graham gave the box to Iggy as his tribute. Iggy brought it back to the dressing room and asked us each to take something as a memento. I took the bullet. Iggy kept a few things and chucked the rest. But what Graham didn't mention was the money. I don't know how many quarters hit the stage. Iggy asked for a couple bags, put them in and took them back to the hotel.*

▶▶

---

* The rest of the night was equally weird. I went out for the Stones set. Even with privileged access, it was like being in a sea of writhing mindless flesh. The strangest thing was that I could barely hear the music, only a constant roar. I looked up at the stage. Every so often Keith Richards or Ron Wood would clap their hands over their heads, playing to the crowd. The rhythm didn't miss a beat and I thought that was strange.

After the Silverdome there were just a few gigs more. It was getting near Christmas and Iggy and I had taken to singing a little song, 'Iggy, the Red-Nosed Rock Star'. We'd make up lyrics sitting in airports waiting for a flight. I don't remember how it went but at the time we thought it was hilarious. He wanted to finish it, get it down on tape and maybe record it. But that never happened, which is just as well.

Toward the end of the tour Iggy asked if I'd like to do it again. He said he liked playing with me and mentioned Europe. I was tempted and thought about it. Europe, I thought, would be fun. But in the end I said no.* Four months of non-stop sex, drugs and rock and roll were enough. My experiment at being one of the boys was over. At the end of 1981 I packed away my guitar and for the next fifteen years didn't touch it. For the time being, my life in the Blank Generation was over.

---

* It was just as well that I declined Iggy's request. His next tours in 1982–3 were called 'The Breaking Point'. After them he committed himself to a detox centre and didn't hit the stage again until 1986. He didn't go to Europe. The last time I saw him was at his show in LA in 1983, which I reviewed for the *LA Weekly*. Backstage I said hello and jokingly asked Jim if Pop was spelled with two 'o's. He said dryly 'No, Gary. That would make it Iggy Poop.'

Epilogue

BLONDIE RECIDIVUS

Fast forward fifteen years.

In late August of 1996 I returned to my room in Hampstead, north London, after a grueling month-long tour of Eastern Europe, playing guitar in a gypsy band and covering an arts festival in Bosnia for the *Guardian*. I had been living in London since the beginning of the year, having relocated from California. After a brief academic career – and the collapse of my first marriage – I decided that at age forty I would try to do what I had always wanted to do: write. I came to London not knowing what to expect and was, more or less, ready for anything. Except maybe one of the messages on my answering machine.

I clicked it to playback and heard an eerily familiar voice. When the penny dropped and I figured out who it was, it sent me back about twenty years.

It was Chris Stein.

That was strange enough, but the message he left was even weirder. He wanted, he said, to put 'the band' back together and was desperate that I get in touch with him.

To say I was surprised would be an understatement. Since I had retired from music after the Iggy tours I had given it little thought and occupied myself in other ways. I studied philosophy, earned a university degree, taught English literature and even managed a new age bookstore.* But strangely, ever since I had landed on England's shores, odd reminders of my rock and roll past had been turning up. For one thing, I had been interviewed for *Q* magazine. Admittedly, I had asked them if they were interested in a story about my Blondie years. Like any other freelance writer, I was looking for a market. *Q*, unfortunately, decided they'd rather have an interview than a story. I figured something was better than nothing and agreed. In the end it turned out to be a good idea, because Chris, who had been looking for me for months, saw the interview and tracked me down.

Then I had a run-in with Patti Smith. That summer, through Ruth, my partner, I got involved with the Poetry Olympics Weekend at the Royal Albert Hall, a thirty-year encore of the famous Wholly Communion Poetry Festival held in 1965. Along with Patti, a lot of other people were involved like Michael Horovitz, Nick Cage, Damon Albarn, John Cooper Clarke and Ray Davies. I hadn't seen Patti in ages and was certain she wouldn't remember me. But curiosity and nostalgia won out, and after a minute's hesitation I walked up after her reading, told her who I was and said hello. She grunted a brief acknowledgement and pushed through the crowd. Same old Patti.

When I finally called Chris, he was ecstatic to hear from me. It's difficult to convey how happy he was. He kept saying how glad he was that I had taken the trouble to call, and went on and on about how great it was to hear my voice. He even said he had had seen some of my writing and was impressed. I was touched. Even with all the trouble we had,

---

* Strangely, during my time managing the bookstore I had a brief encounter with Tom Verlaine. I spotted him checking out the used section, walked up and said hello. He looked at me as if I had uncovered the fact that he had three arms and walked away.

I had always liked Chris. Debbie and I had been close, as close as you can get working and living together for two years, but Chris and I had actually been friends. We had a lot in common and I thought he was intelligent. I hadn't spoken with him in years and I knew that at one point he had been very ill with a strange disease and that Debbie had put her career on hold to nurse him. I hadn't paid much attention to Blondie after I left but I knew that for a while they had been on top of the world. I also knew that they had fallen apart shortly after that. Aside from the royalty checks I still received for 'Presence, Dear', Blondie was just something I had done in the past.

Chris rambled on semi-coherently, and every so often returned to a kind of refrain. 'So, are you gonna do it? I really wancha to do it. You gotta do it. When can you come?'

'Do what, Chris?'

'The reunion!'

'What reunion?'

'The Blondie reunion! I want to put the original band back together and I want you to be part of it. You have to be. You gotta. Really. When can you get here?'

'Here' was New York. With no exaggeration he begged me to come. I wasn't eager. I was just getting my writing career going. Going back to New York to play pop music again after fifteen years wasn't the first thing on my mind. But Chris was persuasive. He said they had a record deal all lined up as well as a tour. They were rehearsing. There would be lots of money. I could play guitar; we'd record some of my songs and I would definitely be on the album. Jimmy wanted me to come, and Debbie too.

I didn't agree immediately. But after some haggling and reminiscing, we agreed terms and I said I would come in November.

Right before I left another thing happened. Before going

to New York, I spent three weeks in Berlin with Ruth, who was acting in a film. Checking my email one morning I discovered an urgent message from a friend in LA. The rookie film director who had played footsie with me in SoHo sixteen years ago was now very successful and directing a hit sitcom. She too desperately wanted to reach me. She wanted to use 'The First One' in an episode of her show. I got in touch, and sixteen years after she first made contact my song turned up in a project of hers. I was surprised and the money wasn't bad. Once again, something seemed to be drawing me back to my past.

►►

When I landed in the States that November morning, Jimmy Destri met me at JFK. At first I didn't recognize him. I hadn't seen him in years, but it seemed that more than time had taken its toll. He had put on a few pounds, but that wasn't all. When I knew Jimmy he had had cute pretty-boy looks. Not any more. Twenty years had come and gone and it seemed that something hard had set into his face. There was hardly a trace of the Jimmy I used to run around Max's and CBGB with. It seemed to me that what did remain was his penchant for embellishing the truth which, if anything, had increased over the years, occasionally at the expense of his grip on reality. The drive into town in his jeep had, for me at least, the feeling of a dream.

When we got to Chris's loft the dream-like quality increased. It even got close to becoming a nightmare.

Chris lived in Tribeca, an area of downtown New York that has become highly prized in recent years. The neighborhood may have been fashionable, but not Chris's loft. Over the years his mania for collecting trash had increased and his success had given him free rein. He also carried on the Blondie tradition and was surrounded by cats; the smell alone suggested that. But the first thing that hit me when I walked in was Chris himself.

He did not seem well. From our email and telephone calls I had expected someone vital and alive, raring to get to work on a second chance that not everyone in the rock and roll business gets. When I saw him stretched out on a couch – dirty clothes, books, magazines and other piles of debris pushed aside for room – I had a sudden sinking feeling. Chris, too, had put on weight. A bare minimum income, vegetarian diet and that Eastern European tour had kept me trim, but Chris had had no such restrictions. In fact, except for Clem, all of the Blondies had filled out. Later, when people asked why I wasn't involved in their UK tour, I suggested the fact that I didn't need liposuction as one possible reason.

Chris was never the fastest guy alive. I remember those days on the Bowery when he and Debbie would stay in bed literally all day, eating junk food and watching TV. Not much had changed, except that Blondie's success had enabled Chris to indulge much more than in the past. But more than a bad diet had hit him. I didn't need to be there very long to see that he wasn't in good shape, either physically or psychologically. He seemed depressed, and shuffled around a lot. Although he was happy to see me and was glad I had come, he seemed oddly sad. I twigged that he wanted me there more than just to work with him. He wanted me there as a friend.

Living as he did probably didn't help. His place was enormous. It was also filled with a tremendous amount of trash. And the stuff that wasn't trash – books, clothes, art – was just thrown around haphazardly, as if a cyclone had been through. There were literally *walls* of clothing reaching to the ceiling. I felt I had checked into Turner's decaying mansion in Mick Jagger's cult rock film *Performance*. Stacks of porno books and videos stood near a broken television. Dishes lay unwashed in piles. Gold records, many of them, lay on the floor, covered in dust. The place had a thick air of dirty sheets and cat shit, and I later found out that Chris never emptied the litter box; Debbie would come once a week and take care of that chore, three cats' worth. I also discovered that she had been paying his rent.

His taste for the occult hadn't died and the place was filled with weirdly menacing bric-a-brac. There was a strange throne designed by the artist Geiger, famous for the sets in the film *Alien*. Chris even had a shrunken head that he claimed came from Gerald Gardner's Museum of Witchcraft on the Isle of Man. He had had some eerie experiences with it and had written about them. He showed me the story but it was impossible to make out exactly what he was trying to say. The writing was cramped and obsessive and the narrative rambling and unreadable. But it was clear the thing had deep meaning for him. Chris had an assortment of other dark items, one I found particularly unnerving. In that place it was impossible to know the time of day, and like his hero, Count Dracula, Chris often never left his bed, where he played endless video games, until sundown. But one afternoon or night, trying to impress me, he stepped into a locked closet for a minute and then stepped out with an Uzi. He thought it was a great joke, and swung the thing back and forth, pretending to spray the place with bullets.

The night I arrived, after he told me that the check he had promised would be delayed – I wouldn't see it for several weeks – he showed me to my room. It turned out to be a large closet. He had pushed aside a few mounds of clothes and thrown down a mattress. For the next month or so, that's where I lived. Every day I had to convince myself to stay. The carrot, I told myself, was worth the stick, and Chris really was in bad shape and needed a friend. In any case, we'd be working soon.

But there I was wrong. There weren't any rehearsals and, unfortunately, when we finally did get down to work, it was just like old times. Chris would erupt into his usual tantrums, shouting all of us down. Jimmy would get huffy, Clem disgusted. Debbie would pull me aside and remind me that Chris was a genius. This was the pattern of events for the next three months. During that time I heard various stories about how the reunion had got going. One had it that a couple of rich kids with a taste for rock memorabilia had run into Chris at an auction where he was selling his gold records. They were fans and introduced him to a manager friend. The manager said that if he needed money there were better ways of getting it. Putting the band back together for instance. I don't know if this story is true, but later at a dinner at the rich kids' place, full of rock mementos and kitschy Pre-Raphaelite style self-portraits, they told me that's what had happened, and when I met the manager friend, he said so too. At that stage there wasn't a record deal and there wasn't a tour.

Toward the end of the month Ruth came out and Debbie very graciously offered us a room in her apartment. It was a large swanky place in a prestigious building in Chelsea, which she shared with her dog, Chi-chi. Most of the windows looked out on neighboring apartments and Debbie told us that the mystery writer Cornel Woolrich had written his story 'Rear Window', later turned into the Hitchcock film, while living in that building. Unlike Chris, Debbie kept her place in order and I saw a lot of memorabilia from the old days. Strangely, I also came across a tall stack of French S & M magazines in a corner. When Debbie saw me looking at them she told me she never read them. A fan from Paris kept sending them to her. 'You know what fans are like,' she said.

It was strange living with them both again after so many years, even though this time it was in different places as they hadn't been a couple for a long time. And although Debbie was generous, I could tell it was a bit awkward. I got the feeling she felt she was doing me a big favor. I tried as diplomatically as possible to explain that I hdn't just happened to be in town and look her up for old times' sake. Chris had begged me to come and take part in the reunion and I was under the impression that she wanted me to be involved too. I had dropped my projects and come from London to work with them because he had asked me to and had said there'd be no problem putting me up. No reaction. Slowly it dawned on me. She wasn't as eager to work with me as Chris had said.

Around Thanksgiving we flew to Lawrence, Kansas, to perform at a tribute to William Burroughs, who had moved there after leaving his Bowery bunker. On the same bill were Laurie Anderson, Philip Glass, the poet Jon Giorno, Ed Sanders from the Fugs and Patti Smith. It was strange being in Lawrence again. The last time had been with Iggy, and I seemed to remember that he had got into a fight with one of the locals at some bar. Maybe it was there that his cap came loose. What was stranger still was being on stage with Chris and Debbie after nearly twenty years. I played guitar, as did Chris, and his girlfriend at the time, Iyla, played bass. Debbie of course sang. We did some strange numbers: a Leonard Cohen tune, one from Harry Nilsson. We also did a version of 'Heart of Glass'. Then Debbie read a passage from one of Jeanette Winterson's books, about somebody being buggered. I didn't quite get it. But I guess with all those poets there, Debbie felt she had to be literate. She always seemed intimidated by Patti Smith, which I thought was unfortunate. For my money at least, Debbie as a poet just didn't cut it.

The night before there had been a party for Burroughs. Again it was strange. I hadn't seen this kind of crowd in years but here I was, smack in hip central. I met Burroughs and told him how much I enjoyed his books, which was sort of a half-truth as I hadn't read him in years. We talked a lot with Ed Sanders and Philip Glass, and got to know Laurie Anderson.* And I saw Lenny Kaye, whom I hadn't seen since 1977 at CBGB. Michael Stipe from REM, who had been hanging out with Patti Smith, was there too. Burroughs was by this time of course an old man, and he seemed to take little interest in the proceedings. His main concern was whether his glass of vodka was topped up. Patti Smith, who hovered around Burroughs for most of the party, saw that it was.

The afternoon before the show there was a press conference. Burroughs sat at the centre of a long table, with Chris, Debbie, Laurie Anderson, Philip Glass and the others on either side. I stood in the crowd, figuring I wasn't one of the principals, but Chris waved to me and pointed to a chair. It was the only one left and it was right next to Burroughs. The conference began. After about ten minutes, the door opened and in rushed Patti Smith. She had overslept and was late. She looked for a seat but there wasn't one, so she grabbed a chair and tried to find an empty space. Finally she decided to shove her chair in between Burroughs and me. It was a tight fit. When she finally squeezed it in she gave me a look as if to say, 'Shove off, nobody!' I smiled. Same old Patti.

When we got back to New York we decided to go into

---

* Later Ruth would work with her at the 1997 Meltdown Festival in London.

the studio and record some tracks, one of which turned out
to be a song of mine from the Know, 'Amor Fati', which
means 'love of fate.' We also got involved in a project with
two of the guys from Duran Duran. I forget the exact set-up,
but the story was that if we recorded two songs of theirs, the
record company would record a few of ours. We worked on
their songs, one of which, 'Studio 54', was slated to be used
in an upcoming Studio 54 film. I didn't see the film and don't
know if it was ever made. I had never listened to Duran
Duran and didn't know their music, but the guys were
friendly enough. One of them was into bodybuilding and
'smart drugs' – vitamins and non-narcotic concoctions which
supposedly increased your intelligence. I don't know if they
worked.

By the end of the year we had rehearsed enough to record
and booked time at the Hit Factory, a studio in New York
responsible, as its name suggests, for some Top Forty record-
ings. Jimmy produced. He had a heavy hand on the board
and was excited by being back at the helm, something he
had been away from for years – I gathered that since the
break-up of Blondie he had found work in construction.

Chris couldn't pull himself away from his video games
and never made it to the studio. In the end I wound up
playing all the guitars and bass. Debbie put down a vocal
and I sang some backup. When people heard the tracks,
especially 'Amor Fati', the remarks were surprisingly similar.
If the idea was to put the *original* band back together, we
had. The song, they said, had that 'Blondie sound'.

Around this time Ruth and I moved into an unheated loft
space under the Brooklyn Bridge. It was getting awkward at
Debbie's and in any case, I wanted my own space and not
to be dependent on her goodwill. I tried to keep our relationship a professional one. It was a cold winter and we froze,
but we enjoyed exploring Brooklyn and riding our bikes in

sub-freezing temperatures back and forth over the bridge. In the evenings we huddled around the one heater and worked on songs. Since playing again, the old urge had come back, and I found myself coming up with lots of tunes.* The idea was to write material to be used on the Blondie reunion album, which we would be recording shortly.

Around Christmas we went to a party at Bob Gruen's, someone else I hadn't seen in twenty years. On the way in we ran into Legs McNeil, who nodded a brief hello as he left. Inside I saw a dozen people from my past. Bob and I reminisced and reminded ourselves of Blondie photo sessions back in the old days. Then I saw Leee Black Childers. We hadn't seen each other since that time at the Music Machine ages ago, and had a lot of catching up to do. Sadly, as we spoke, we realized that a lot of the people we knew from back then were dead. At one point we even tried to count them, but then stopped, thinking it was too morbid.

▶▶

At the end of January we returned to London. My brief was to write songs and get ready for a tour that summer. In May of 1997, I returned to New York.

Our first performance was a showcase for a selected group at a studio in mid-town. When word got out about the show, the place was packed with a couple hundred people, and the queue ran down the stairs. I invited Rob DuPrey, someone else I hadn't seen in years. It was exciting to play again, and with a full band. The crowd loved us and the next day we headed to the airport for our first real gig.

In Washington DC we played at the Robert F. Kennedy Memorial Stadium, part of a summer festival series, along

---

* Some of these have subsequently been released on our Fire Escape *First Step* CD. Available from Norfolk Square Music at norfolksquare@cs.com

with bands like Beck, Björk, Kula Shaker, the Cranberries and others. It was another Silverdome. After fifteen years of retirement, on my third gig I was playing in front of 80,000 people again. Only this time they didn't throw anything. A lot of the audience weren't even born when Blondie first recorded and probably didn't know a thing about CBGB, but surprisingly a lot of them knew the old tunes, even 'X-Offender'. We did that and a selection of Blondie hits. It was odd to play songs I didn't have any part in like 'Atomic' and 'Call Me'. But it was fun and I enjoyed playing. As usual, I jumped around. They loved us. Afterwards everyone said it was great and congratulated me. Debbie was surprised I could play so well and wasn't nervous. It was, she said, just like old times. She even asked me to sing with her on a cover of the Doors' song, 'Break on Through'.

After DC we did a show in Dallas, again to a massive crowd. Coming into the hotel lobby from my room, a group of kids ran up to me with *Blondie* albums and 'X-Offender' 45s. One even had a copy of 'The First One'. They wanted autographs. I wasn't sizing up a roomful of prospective bedmates, but that an eighteen-year-old in Texas wanted my autograph on a record I had made before he was born was touching. I signed and they asked questions. What had I been doing all these years? Had I made any other solo records? The same sort of thing happened later at another show in Connecticut, the last of our mini-tour. Then I returned to London, soon, the others said, they would bring me back to record.

In December I had to return to New York to deal with UK immigration details. While there I thought I would look up Chris. We had kept in touch via email and I was curious when we'd get going again. What he told me came as a surprise. Afterward I found the immigration board a friendlier lot.

We were talking about the reunion plans and Chris was strangely vague. Then Jimmy arrived. As soon as he walked in I could tell something had changed.

'Gary, we have to tell you something. We don't think you're right for the live shows.'

'Oh?' I said. 'I thought I played fine this summer.'

'Oh, it's not your playing.'

'Then what?'

'We just don't think you're right. But we want you to play on the album and we definitely want to use "Amor Fati".'

I left disgusted, but later thought better of it. It was fun doing those shows, but after hanging out with Debbie, Chris and Jimmy again I soon felt that touring really wasn't something I wanted to do. Later I spoke to Chris and said it was fine. And he assured me once again that I would play on the album and that 'Amor Fati' would be on it too.

►►

1998 was a cold winter. I was broke. I lived in a bedsit in Gospel Oak and to keep warm had to hunt for firewood on Hampstead Heath. I looked for work and called the editor at *MOJO* to ask if they would be interested in a story about the Blondie reunion. Honest journalist that I am, I called Chris and asked him once again if I was going to play on the album and if they were going to use 'Amor Fati'. I explained that I was writing an article and didn't want to make false claims. He assured me that absolutely, positively I would be coming out to record.

Not long after that I got a call from my editor. He had been at a music conference in the States and had heard that Blondie was back in the studio.

I called Chris and asked him what was happening.

He told me they didn't have the money to fly me out. But they were definitely recording 'Amor Fati'.

Around the same time as this I got some other news: Ruth was pregnant.

I finished the article and submitted it. Then I called Chris to ask about my song. No answer. I sent an email. No reply. This happened a few times. I tried Debbie. Ditto. Jimmy. The same. Finally I reached Clem.

He told me 'Amor Fati' wasn't on the final mix. He had tried to get them to include it, or at least to put it on the B side of the single. He even said that Craig Leon, who was producing the album, liked the track and wanted it on. But the others had said no. I called Craig and he said the same thing. Later I heard that in interviews Jimmy had said that the reason I wasn't involved in the album or tour was that I didn't want to take the time away from my writing. He was always good at inventing reality.

Of course it was a disappointment. The money alone was a big loss – especially now that I was about to have a family – but what really hurt were all those worthless promises and declarations of friendship. If they didn't want to work with me, all they had to do was pick up a telephone and tell me the truth. Evidently they are incapable of that. To this day I haven't heard from them.

In any case, it wasn't a total loss. I had the songs I wrote, I played those concerts – even if subsequent media coverage of the reunion airbrushed me out of it – and a Blondie 'greatest hits' CD released on the back of the tour included 'Presence, Dear' and 'X-Offender'. It did surprisingly well.

There is one more claim to fame. I don't know if this is true, but I think I'm the only pop star to resign from *and* be kicked out of the same band, with a twenty year hiatus in between.

Index